Modern Macroeconomic
Theory

Modern Macroeconomic Theory

Edited by
JEAN-PAUL FITOUSSI

Published in cooperation with the
European University Institute, Florence

BARNES & NOBLE BOOKS
TOTOWA, NEW JERSEY

© European University Institute 1983

First published in the USA 1983 by
Barnes & Noble Books
81 Adams Drive
Totowa, New Jersey, 07512

Library of Congress Cataloging in Publication Data

Main entry under title:

Modern macroeconomic theory

  1. Macroeconomics.   I. Fitoussi, Jean Paul.
HB172.5.M62   339   83-7139

ISBN 0-389-20411-0

Printed in Great Britain

Contents

Preface

This book aims to bring together some of the most recent developments in macroeconomic theory. It attempts to go beyond the apparent conflict between competing approaches to seek the common structure and essential points of divergence between the different theories. Thus, a wide range of issues and theories are covered – from non-Walrasian fix- and flexprice models to rational expectations full employment models – and a *positive* contribution is made to the question of the microeconomic foundation of macroeconomics.

The first chapter surveys the different theoretical frameworks, and offers a critical look at old and new approaches to macroeconomics. The eight subsequent chapters are intended to provide new contributions on topical questions within each 'school' or 'research programme'. They constitute a good sample of what is going on in macroeconomics. The contributors are among those few people who do not have a dogmatic attitude towards economics, and this gives the book a particular flavour: no definitive conclusions, no absolute statements, but a rigorous consciousness that the theoretical constructions they use are relative. Chapters 2 and 3 (which make up Part I) are the exception, because they aim to clarify the reasons for a fuzzy but general feeling of dissatisfaction with *IS–LM* analysis in the economic profession.

This book is the result of a conference held at the European University in May 1980. The papers have been revised in the light of the discussions, which were extremely lively and, for some papers, raised fundamental arguments. The process of revision has thus been a very fertile one, and the interplay of ideas has been most productive.

In editing the book, I benefited from invaluable help. Lynn Pepall went through the papers trying to single out their implicit or explicit links. She provided me with a draft paper containing a survey of the discussions and summarizing the papers. This was of great help to me, especially at a very early stage, when I was wondering about the shape of the book. However, in the end, because many of the criticisms raised during the discussions had by then been elaborated in the papers, I decided not to publish the discussions. Laura Meijer and Jessica Spataro were very efficient in helping me in the organization of the conference and in typing and re-typing some of the manuscripts.

List of Contributors

CHRISTOPHER BLISS, Nuffield Reader in International Economics, Oxford University, and Fellow of Nuffield College, Oxford

JOHN BOSCHEN, Economist, Federal Reserve Board and National Bureau of Economic Research, Cambridge, Massachusetts

JEAN-PAUL FITOUSSI, Professor of Economics at the European University, Institute, Florence, and Director of the Département des Etudes at the Observatoire Français des Conjonctures Economiques, Paris

HERSCHEL I. GROSSMAN, Stoltz Professor in the Social Sciences and Professor of Economics, Brown University and National Bureau of Economic Research, Cambridge, Massachusetts

OLIVER D. HART, Lecturer in Economics at the Faculty of Economics and Politics, Cambridge University, and Fellow of Churchill College

JOHN HICKS, Nobel Laureate in Economics and Professor Emeritus, Oxford University

PANAYOTIS KORLIRAS, Professor of Economics at the Athens School of Economics and Business Science

AXEL LEIJONHUFVUD, Professor of Economics at the University of California, Los Angeles

EDMOND MALINVAUD, Director-General of the Institut National de la Statistique et des Etudes Economiques, Paris

EZIO TARANTELLI, Professor of Economics at the Faculty of Political Sciences, University of Florence

1

Modern Macroeconomic Theory: An Overview

If I say that the world around us shows all the signs of being chaotic, this is not as despairing a conclusion as it might seem, since it is possible for a system to be chaotic at one level and regular at another: thus we may have to abandon hope of making detailed predictions of the motion of micro-scopic elements in a fluid, yet still find we can make reliable predictions of its motion on a coarser scale.

Sir Brian Pippard (1980)

Explanation of macroeconomic phenomena will be complete only when such explanations are consistent with microeconomic choice theoretic behavior and can be phrased in the language of general equilibrium theory.

A. Drazen (1980)

General equilibrium theory and Keynesian economics have always maintained an ambiguous relationship founded on a superiority complex about theory on the part of the one and a conviction of greater empirical relevance on the part of the other.[1] But the 1970s have shaken this latter conviction by verifying Friedman's (1968) and Phelps's (1970) famous 'prediction' that any rate of inflation is compatible with a given unemployment rate. This has given rise to hopes of the end of the Keynesian reign and has strengthened the

This study is the result of a long and painful struggle with the literature. I am indebted to Jean-Pascal Benassy, Herschel Grossman, Don Patinkin and Lynn Pepall for their comments on the earlier drafts of the paper; but in particular I would like to thank my friend and colleague Kumaraswamy Velupillai, without whose pertinent comments and stimulating discussion this paper would not have been written. Jacqueline Bourgonje helped me to put the first English version into shape, the original text having been written in French. Any stylistic deficiencies that may still exist are due to my persistence in sticking to my original formulation.

1

general equilibrium theorists in their assurance of superiority. Also, the reassertion of the crisis of (Keynesian) macroeconomics is paralleled by new research whose scope and diversity gives the impression of great richness.

Two axioms constitute this theoretical revival and, even when rejected *en bloc* (e.g. by Davidson, 1977), they are only exceptionally discussed *per se*.

Axiom 1 'The existence of a metalanguage': macroeconomic relations *must* have microeconomic foundations. This proposition establishes from the outset the subordination of the macro to the micro approach, and at the same time it ranks economic arguments in implicitly acknowledging that microeconomics is itself well founded. Yet it is not clear that macroeconomic relations can be derived in this fashion. If one considers a sufficiently large number of agents, the structural properties of the excess demand functions, apart from budgetary identity and continuity, vanish (Sonnensheim, 1973; Debreu, 1974). This implies that the qualitative properties of macroeconomic relations remain indeterminate. The practical significance of this result is that macroeconomic theory should set itself up as an autonomous discipline and seek also other foundations.

Axiom 2 'The existence of a metatheory': there exists a class of models that yield macroeconomic propositions while rendering explicit their microeconomic foundations: namely, general equilibrium theory, which by virtue of this axiom is given the status of a metatheory, a common structure within which all other theories must be expressed. In this framework the 'no-bridge' problem is spurious, for it is theoretically possible to represent a system at as detailed a level as one wants. The level of aggregation chosen depends on the problem one is given to analyse. In this sense general equilibrium theory is not to be identified with a particular model – that of Arrow–Debreu – but should be considered as a method that allows the choice of the states of a model where individual decisions are mutually consistent. 'The type of consistency that is assumed to exist between individual decisions is specific to each equilibrium theory' (Malinvaud, 1977, p. 7), which explains the proliferation of concepts of equilibrium.

General equilibrium, thus freed of its normative connotations, constitutes the common base of all theoretical developments. Since Keynesian macroeconomics has a traditional leaning towards explaining the short term, the reference model will be that of temporary equilibrium theory. In this framework the typical economic agent resolves an optimization problem which differs according to alternative theories by the nature and number of constraints taken into consideration rather than by the theoretical justifications of the constraint. In all models expectations are generated by functions whose specifications can be different; in particular, expectations can be rational. This latter assumption, when considered within the theoretical framework of temporary competitive equilibrium, produces radical implications for economic policy.

The existence of a common frame of reference, then, does not lead to the allaying of doctrinal quarrels. It is of little use to say that there are wide (theoretical) divergences on the very possibility of economic policy. In spite of the uniqueness of the scientific research programme, paradigms concerning the mode of co-operation between public and private agents remain radically divergent.

The new theoretical developments, their theoretical structure and the language in which they are expressed imply, therefore, that *rational behaviour* is the absolute criterion for the evaluation of macroeconomic propositions. Thus the major questions that modern macroeconomic theory seeks to answer can be formulated in the following way:

- Can rational behaviour be reconciled with the existence of involuntary unemployment?
- Can rational behaviour be reconciled with the existence of macroeconomic fluctuations?

The nature of these questions puts the debate back on to the terrain where Keynes had placed it – the theoretical plane – and marks the end of an illusion: that there is a consensus over the representative model of the economy, produced by the similarity between Friedman's theoretical framework (1970) and the neo-Keynesian analytical framework.

The first section of this essay will be a broad outline of the evolution that has led to questions of this type. In the second section I shall consider the attempt, in recent literature, to answer these questions. The final section will be devoted to an outline of the book.

Prolegomena: from equilibrium to disequilibrium, or the logic of a counter-revolution

The existence of an under-employment equilibrium represents a major challenge to what Keynes called the classical theory. Either

Keynes took as a starting point a model different from that then prevailing, or he was simply discovering states of that model that had not yet been studied. A reading of the *General Theory* gives support to both of these interpretations, thus guaranteeing the continuation of controversies on the nature of the Keynesian revolution.

However, it is clearly the second interpretation that was immediately favoured, since it made it possible to express two doctrinally opposed positions in the terms of a common language (Hicks, 1937). Here the Keynesian message appeared as specific to a situation, as dependent on restrictions imposed upon a more general proposition: price rigidity, money illusion, liquidity trap, the non-intersection of functions on a positive plane, etc. – in short, a whole series of factors implying either the introduction of arbitrary (free) parameters[2] or an *ad hoc* specification of the functions of the model (cf. Klein, 1947, 1966). The Keynesian system is then perceived as a malfunctioning Walrasian system – and the study of some pathological states of a Walrasian model is called Keynesian economics. The chapters by Hicks and Leijonhufvud in this book give important insights on these points.

The way is thus open for the re-integration of the Keynesian message into a more general system of interpretation: the neoclassical synthesis. First Pigou, then Patinkin, have claimed that the reference to an under-employment equilibrium was an abuse of language, since the real-balance effect would ensure that even a proportional fall in prices and wages would lead to the re-establishment of full employment. Even if this is an extremely painful way back to equilibrium, and even admitting its slowness, its very existence is sufficient to qualify the Keynesian situation as 'under-employment disequilibrium'.[3] Also, the differences between neoclassical theory and Keynesian economics, which previously had been strongly underlined, are not really structural differences, but *sui generis:* 'It now becomes possible, a quarter of a century having passed, to consider the General Theory as an important episode in the continuous development of the general neoclassical system' (Kuenne, 1963, p. 347). The merit of John Maynard Keynes has been to draw attention to the length and weakness of the adjustment processes generated by disequilibrium in contemporary economies; 'but in the field of static general equilibrium theory, where the existence of countervailing forces, though weak, is sufficient to produce full employment, its performance has been essentially deficient' (Kuenne, 1963, p. 361).

This re-interpretation does not seem to call into question anything substantial. The persistence of disequilibria leaves economic policy with its *raison d'être*. The spontaneous tendency towards equilibrium can be speeded up by appropriate budgetary and monetary policies, which will also allow the avoidance of the various vicissitudes associated with deflation (bankruptcies, entrapment of debtors, the self-fulfilment of pessimistic expectations, etc.). Therefore nothing essential is called into question if a dynamic adjustment relation expressing the rate of change of prices as a function of disequilibria is added to a Keynesian-type model. The model becomes sufficiently eclectic to be able to produce both Keynesian and monetarist results – monetarist in the long period and Keynesian in the short period.

The Phillips curve should then be considered more as the missing equation of a macro-system than as a theory of inflation. Its introduction permits the solution of the problem of dividing changes of nominal income into price and quantity changes. But if an adjustment relation determining the rate of inflation as a function of the deviation of the actual employment rate from its natural level – or between the production level and its full employment level – is added to an *IS–LM* model, the model then undergoes a structural mutation. Full employment becomes the stable equilibrium position (assuming that the equilibrium position is unique), and the structure of the model is altogether similar to that of a standard neoclassical model (Lipsey, 1978). The different points on the Phillips curve must also be considered as distinct moments in the same adjustment process. But

the adjustment process itself has not in general been successfully described as optimizing behaviour, the only paradigm that carries theoretical conviction in our profession. This failure, neither surprising nor discreditable in view of the intrinsic difficulties of the task, is the root of the chronic crisis in macro-economics. (Tobin, 1981, pp. 36-7)

How should the Phillips relation be interpreted? As a rule applied by the market auctioneer? But then, what is the duration of the process in real time? The study of the rule by which an auctioneer proceeds does not specify the dynamic properties of the model in the real world. It is then argued that only by taking into consideration economic agents' expectations can this task be accomplished. And there is no longer anything Keynesian in a short-period neoclassical model that explicitly considers expectations (Lucas, 1981). We are back at our starting point: either the existence of an under-employment equilibrium consistent with individual rationality can be established, or the Keynesian message will be lost in *ad hoc* specifications, not only because of the intrinsic difficulty of building a dynamic model, but because (it is argued) the persistence of disequilibria in a Walrasian model contradicts the most elementary rationality axioms. By accepting the theoretical supremacy of the competitive equilibrium model and its immediate import – that Keynesian theory is the economics of underemployment disequilibrium – Keynesians have thrown out the baby with the bath water. This is the theoretical measure of the macroeconomic crisis, if it is identified with the neoclassical synthesis.

This would not be the case if it were possible to prove that price adjustment ceases before fully accomplishing its function of eliminating disequilibria. Such a possibility can be discussed in at least three non-mutually exclusive ways. First, individual rationality would come up against the higher-order rationality of the system, which would limit the possible range of price variations. The system must have the ability to ensure its perpetuity, the permanence of its institutions, which would be eroded by an excessive price flexibility: the legal nature of the labour contract, which gives a time dimension to the wage–labour relations; the establishment of contracts in monetary terms; the protection of the production apparatus, which is sometimes linked to that of debtors; etc. It is not surprising that these considerations are to be found in different forms in the General Theory. The theory of a monetary economy with production could not neglect the institutional structure of our society. Moreover, an embryonic economic theory of social conventions exists (Ackerlof, 1979, 1980), but has not yet generated much interest, though there are some exceptions (Solow, 1979, 1980). This way of apprehending the problem gives some credibility to the study of a general equilibrium with exogenous prices in the very short period.

Second, the function of price adjustment can also be seen as a rule applied by individual agents – and not by the auctioneer – in an attempt to relax the quantity constraints that prevent the realization of their plan. Since these individual agents do not enjoy the auctioneer's ubiquity, it is perfectly possible that they will stop adjusting before a Walrasian equilibrium is established, not perceiving any incentive to go further. They also exhaust the exchange opportunities, perceived or conjectured, for lack of knowledge of real opportunities. But this implies that, at the point of under-employment equilibrium reached, the economy is not perfectly competitive (in the Walrasian sense of the term) and its structure can be approximated by, for example, that of a general equilibrium of monopolistic competition. This represents the third line of investigation to a reconciliation between the rationality of behaviour and the existence of involuntary unemployment.

Certainly the fluctuations are not and cannot be apprehended in the same way according to whether or not under-employment equilibrium is considered. The market equilibrium perspective generally leads to the uniqueness of that equilibrium being hypothesized – even if the theoretical framework used does not warrant such a result. The variations in production and employment are then analysed as supply reactions to signals that are not easy to decipher.

For non-Walrasian general equilibrium theory the task is simpler (although the fluctuation problem is not confronted): the theory effectively implies the existence of a multiplicity of equilibria whose real coordinates are different. The variations of production and employment are then perceived as the transition from one equilibrium to another.

Pure price adjustment, and pure quantity adjustment, delineate a spectrum within which all combinations are possible. The major answers to what can well be called the challenge of short-period dynamics have on the whole been placed at the extreme opposite ends of the spectrum. This way of proceeding has certain advantages: it allows the answers to be written and interpreted in the language of a theory, *viz.* general equilibrium theory, which at that time seemed to have achieved the status of a 'scientific research programme' (Arrow and Hahn, 1971), while the standard macroeconomic argument was being radically questioned (Clower, 1965; Leijonhufvud, 1968).

The common structure of (quasi-non?) Walrasian revolutions

Thus macroeconomics has been questioned at first from within the Walrasian model. A better way of understanding recent theoretical developments takes as a starting point no longer macroeconomic research as it had been identified by the very title of Keynes's book – *General Theory of Employment, Interest and Money* – but instead that of general equilibrium theory. The great achievement of this research lies more, perhaps, in the questions it asks than in the answers it gives. The reference model of microeconomics in effect has been saddled with a list of fundamental questions on its own validity. Its method of use is quite clear: the list of conditions for its use is exhaustive, or (which is the same) the situations in which the model is not applicable are made openly explicit. For example, it is clearly understood that the theory cannot be applied if a complete set of markets for future goods does not exist; or if economic agents do not treat prices parametrically (for example in small economies); or if institutions exogenous to the model, which guarantee the consistency of plans of microeconomic agents, do not exist, or if production is characterized by significantly increasing returns to scale; etc.[4]

How should the model be modified for it to apply to some of these situations? It is essentially with reference to the answers provided to this question that recent research on the foundations of macroeconomics must be evaluated.[5] Frequently these answers have a Keynesian flavour with some relevance to the problems of our time. They elaborate concepts of equilibrium qualified as 'quasi' or 'non-Walrasian' according to whether or not they are consistent with the under-employment of men or of production capacity. What diversifies concepts of equilibrium has nothing to do with the problem of 'co-ordination' – the whole set of models being founded on the existence of a *tâtonnement* process – but depends on the kinds of constraints that appear in the individual optimization problems.

Microeconomic foundations

Rationality simply means that economic agents take the best action open to them under perceived constraints. To demonstrate better the common links between theoretical approaches, first all constraints will be described, then later they will be taken singly in order to reach a taxonomy of equilibrium concepts.[6]

Maximize $u_i(\mathbf{x}_i, m_i, \sigma_i)$ subject to (s.t.) the following constraints:

$$\left.\begin{aligned} \mathbf{x}_i &= \omega_i + \mathbf{z}_i \\ m_i &= \bar{m}_i - \mathbf{p}\mathbf{z}_i \end{aligned}\right\} \tag{1}$$

$$\underline{z_{ih}} \leqslant z_{ih} \leqslant \overline{z_{ih}} \tag{2}$$

$$\underline{z_{ik}} \leqslant z_{ik} \leqslant \overline{z_{ik}}, \quad k \neq h \tag{2'}$$

$$\left.\begin{aligned} p_h &= \bar{p}_h, \quad \underline{z_{ih}} \leqslant z_{ih} \leqslant \overline{z_{ih}}, \quad h \notin h_i \\ \underline{z_{ih}}[\mathbf{p}_i, \theta_i(\sigma_i)] &\leqslant z_{ih} \leqslant \overline{z_{ih}}[\mathbf{p}_i, \theta_i(\sigma_i)] \end{aligned}\right\} \tag{3}$$

where the r goods are indexed by h, the m agents indexed by i, and $\mathbf{x}$ is the vector of consumption, ω that of endowments, $\mathbf{z}$ that of net demands, and $\mathbf{p}$ a vector of prices, $\bar{m}$ and m are monetary balances at the beginning and end of the period, and σ a vector of current information from which expectations are derived. (The barred variables will be defined at appropriate places.) Constraints (1) obviously must always be satisfied. Their consideration alone, or alternatively with the other three, allows at least four concepts of temporary equilibrium to be defined.

Temporary competitive equilibrium

The absence of a complete set of future markets has many implications, the most significant of which is to give money something to do.[7] Such absence implies effectively that exchanges take place at all dates – and no longer at the beginning of time as in the Arrow–Debreu model. The sequential nature of the economy then becomes an essential characteristic of a monetary economy (Radner, 1968, 1972), in the sense that it is a necessary condition[8] for the existence of an equilibrium where the value of money is positive.[9] A further consequence is the introduction of a form of uncertainty in the problem of decision-making by individual economic agents. This uncertainty is relative not only to the plurality of states of nature, but also to the vector of prices that will clear markets in each of those states. Economic agents must also make forecasts, and their expectation function will be one of the important ingredients of the programme that they try to resolve. This function makes expectations depend on present and past information that the individual has on the structure of the economy and that, within the temporary competitive equilibrium framework, is limited to the series of current and past prices and the rules of economic policy parameters used by the 'government'.

The function u_i must therefore be understood as an intertemporal index of utility which can be obtained as a solution of a dynamic programming problem: future-period consumption levels are derived from the information vector by the mediation of an expectation function. Evidently only constraints (1) are relevant for this type of model; they imply that the individual is sure to realize his current plan even if he has only faint confidence in his future plans. A temporary competitive equilibrium, therefore, is an equilibrium where present choices of agents are pre-reconciled while their future plans are not co-ordinated. But the existence of an equilibrium is subject to severe restrictions and implies a series of conditions on the structure of expectations.

The reasons for this can be easily understood. An elasticity of expectation that is 'too' strong produces an intertemporal substitution effect between goods whose direction can be opposite to that of the real-balance effect. And even a unit elasticity of substitution can be 'too' strong if the ratio between expected and current prices is greater than the marginal substitution rate at the point of initial endowments (Grandmont, 1983, ch. 1). For the same reason it is possible that monetary policy alone will be unable to control the interest rate or the nominal supply of money.[10]

For a temporary equilibrium to exist where money has a positive value, the expectations of some or all agents, relatively to prices or interest rates, must be largely insensitive to current prices and interest rates (Grandmont, 1983). These conditions are unlikely to be fulfilled in an inflationary environment. Thus, beyond the introduction of an element of 'disequilibrium' into a Walrasian model (the non-coordination of agents' future plans), the theory of temporary equilibrium reopens the controversy on the effectiveness of regulation mechanisms in a competitive economy and, notably, on the real-balance effect: price flexibility is not a sufficient condition for the re-establishment of equilibrium, and an excess supply in particular can exist at all positive prices. Keynes was 'intuitively' right. But the spirit of the model is more Austrian than Keynesian (Hicks, 1979), and the difficulties of establishing a Walrasian equilibrium do not imply in any case the existence of an under-employment equilibrium.

What, according to Hicks, represents a problem in competitive temporary equilibrium theory is the mutual interdependence of equilibrium prices and expectations in the short period (a week). Current prices are effectively determined taking expectations into account and expectations, taking equilibrium prices into account. This simultaneous and mutual determination transforms a theory conceived as dynamic into a 'quasi-static' model.[11]

Starting from this proposition, two lines of investigation are opened; the first seeks to substantiate Hicks's suggestion of introducing a lag into the model. Current prices partially determine expectations which in turn determine future prices. Obviously, the simplest method of eliminating any feedback between prices and expectations in the current period is by assuming that prices are fixed at the beginning of the period (general equilibrium with rationing) or that expectations are exogenous. A second line of investigation considers, on the contrary, that temporary competitive equilibrium theory contains 'too' many potential disequilibria. It should be possible to introduce greater co-ordination into exchange agents' future plans (Walrasian equilibrium of rational expectations).

'Non-Walrasian' equilibria with fixed prices

If prices do not change instantaneously to clear markets, a convenient hypothesis is to consider them rigid in the short term. The fixprice method (Hicks, 1965, ch. VII) represents, therefore, the methodological justification of general equilibrium theory with rationing.[12] This implies not that prices are invariant but that they are determined outside the model, and, more precisely, outside the temporary equilibrium period. During the period only quantities are free to change while prices are subject to inter-period adjustment. The existence of disequilibria (in the Walrasian sense) implies, then, that in the determination of his plans the individual takes into account not only price signals but also the quantity signals he gets from the market.

Suppose that these signals are objectively determined; the economic agent thus resolves the optimization problem defined by the utility function u_i – where σ_i must now be interpreted as also containing information relative to present and past quantity constraints – and constraints (1) and (2). $\underline{z}_{ih}$ and $\bar{z}_{ih}$ represent the maximum quantities of good h that can be sold or bought. Taking into account these signals, an optimum transactions vector can be determined. The simplest way of describing the process leading to equilibrium is to use a *tâtonnement* procedure. Drèze (1975) chose this method. Agents receive a vector of signals, which establishes the upper and lower limits to their exchange opportunities. They then determine their constrained demands and supplies on all markets and transmit this information to the auctioneer. The auctioneer revises quantity signals until an equilibrium in transactions is reached. A Drèze equilibrium is a fixed point of this *tâtonnement* process in the space of quantity constraints. Three hypotheses are needed to reach this result: balanced exchanges; voluntary exchanges (i.e., no individual can be forced to exchange beyond his intentions); and rationed agents all belong to the same side of the market.

As Grandmont (1977) has noted, in the Drèze model there is no exchange of information relative to the intensity of rationing experienced by individuals, for individuals are limited in the messages they send to the market. Exchanges take place only when quantity constraints form a coherent whole; that is, in equilibrium. It is in the nature of the method used that it cannot generate information on the divergence between intention and realization: in a general equilibrium model individual agents' plans are realized at the equilibrium point. Hence the difficulty in giving a measurable content to the notion of involuntary decisions.[13] A possible solution would be to seek a measure of disequilibrium by comparing the solution vectors of (two) different optimization programmes by norming the relevant vector space. Call x the solution vector associated with the programme s. And consider the programme s', which differs from s only in the existence of a supplementary constraint. The comparison between x and x' – the solution of the second programme – provides an indication of the intensity of frustration of economic agents as a result of the introduction of an additional constraint. This, after all, is the method underlying Clower's dual decision hypothesis. In Clower's model, however, s is the programme associated with competitive general equilibrium theory, and its solution x has only a notional character in that it is not communicated to the market.

The hypothesis that an economic agent does not take into account the constraint he perceives in the market where he expresses *his effective demand* permits a generalization of the dual decision theory. By definition, his effective demand for good h is the solution of the optimization problem defined by constraints (1) and (2'); z_{ih} is therefore obtained by considering the set of constraints except that concerning good h (Benassy, 1975). The set of effective demands z_{ih} is obtained by the solution of n different optimization problems, n being the number of markets. However, the transactions are a solution of the programme s', which simultaneously considers all the constraints, like in the Drèze model. The comparison between effective demand and transactions gives a measure of the intensity of the rationing confronting the individual. Therefore markets are not balanced in the space of effective demands. A system of rationing schemes associates agents' transactions in a market with the set of effective demands expressed in that market. It represents a mechanism for allocating goods between incompatible demands, but is not necessarily known to individuals. Therefore it has to be supplemented by a perceived rationing scheme 'which depicts the way agent i views the relation between his actions and their consequences' (Benassy, 1977, p. 149). The perceived rationing scheme has the same properties as the objective rationing scheme and encompasses the latter at the point of effective exchange.[14] The two relations represent data of the problem. An equilibrium in Benassy's sense or K-equilibrium is a fixed point of the *tâtonnement* process in the space of effective demands.[15, 16]

For a given system of prices the equilibrium allocations in the Drèze and Benassy models are identical. However, the problem of utilizable information in the dynamic study of the sequence of short-term equilibria remains unresolved. Benassy's model certainly produces some information – the set of effective demands – but it is not quite satisfactory because of the somewhat artificial character of the process that determines it. An agent's effective demand vector remains potential because it does not necessarily satisfy his budget constraint. The disequilibrium measures thus obtained cannot therefore provide the foundation for price dynamics. Certainly they always have the 'right' sign (Benassy, 1983), but their quantitative importance should be treated with caution.

Because of the distinction established between effective demands and transactions, Benassy's framework is generally used in the macroeconomic applications of general equilibrium theory with rationing (cf. in particular Barro and Grossman, 1971; Benassy, 1977; Malinvaud, 1977, 1980a, b; Muellbauer and Portes, 1978). In general three goods are considered, but there are only two markets (a good and labour), while money is considered as representing one side of all transactions. It is then possible to proceed towards a typology of disequilibria according to the value of exogenous variables. Malinvaud (1977), by using an asymmetric treatment of firms and households – because the good is not storable, the expectations of enterprises were not taken into account – distinguished three types of 'disequilibrium': classical unemployment (excess demand in the market for goods, excess supply in the labour market); Keynesian unemployment (excess supply on both markets); repressed inflation (excess demand on both markets). The reconciliation within the same theoretical framework of the classical (Pigou) and neo-Keynesian approaches to unemployment represented a fundamental contribution of general equilibrium theory with rationing, even though the probability of classical unemployment was considered low by virtue of a possible asymmetry of price adaptations.[17] It became possible to establish a one-to-one correspondence between the type of disequilibrium and the constellation of exogenous variables (price and quantity of money), and to found a typology of economic policy rules adapted to each situation.[18] It is important to note that the correspondence established between the type of disequilibrium and the structure of prices presupposes a relationship between the sale of output and the current demand for input in the very short period of temporary equilibrium. It is difficult to find a foundation for such a relation because it implies a very particular structure of expectations. If stocks and expectations of enterprises are explicitly introduced into the model, the map of disequilibria becomes infinitely more complex. First of all, a fourth type of situation must be distinguished where enterprises are rationed on both markets (excess supply of product, excess demand for labour), qualified as 'under-consumption' (Muellbauer and Portes, 1978) or as 'over-capitalization' (Fitoussi and Georgescu-Roegen, 1980). Second, the constellation of prices, wages and monetary balances is no longer sufficient to characterize disequilibria from the viewpoint of economic policy. This characterization will depend also on the profile of constraints expected in future periods. Here, the number of possible cases becomes very large, to the point where it would be particularly difficult for economic policy to decipher the current period. For example, a situation that would be characterized as Keynesian unemployment with regard to current period demands could very well correspond to classical unemployment if demand expectations by enterprises were sufficiently optimistic (Neary and Stiglitz, 1983; Benassy, 1980, 1983). When expectations are given by stochastic functions the map of current-period disequilibria is not modified but the conclusions of economic policy can be inverted: for instance, a fall (and not a rise) in wages would permit an increase in the employment level under Keynesian unemployment, when production by enterprises is not limited by pessimistic expectations of future demand.

This explains, perhaps, the exploratory nature of the dynamic analysis of sequences of temporary equilibria with rationing (e.g. Böhm, 1978, 1981), and the need to base those analyses on simple and specific models with relation to the matter under study. This strategy has proven enlightening, notably in the study of the medium-term evolution of distribution variables and of the persistent or transitory character of different types of unemployment (Malinvaud, 1980a).

Thus, general equilibrium theory with rationing allows the establishment of a typology of equilibria and bases its analysis on rational behaviour in the sense of choice theory. Nevertheless, a necessary condition for the existence of an under-employment equilibrium remains the rigidity of one or several prices.[19] On this point even Pigou would not have objected. Also, in fixprice models the novelty is not in the initial hypothesis but in the detailed and explicit discussion of its consequences. Therefore, the basis of the hypothesis of exogenous prices is a major question. It is true that a converging series of reasons that seem to militate in favour of this hypothesis exist – and some of them have been noted in the first section of this chapter – but they are not integrated into a coherent theoretical analysis,[20] and they are vulnerable when questioned from an individual rationality viewpoint. Why do economic agents not exhaust their exchange opportunities? This recurring question establishes the failure of this type of approach (Barro, 1979; Kantor, 1979; Lucas, 1980a; etc.). But the criticism is not as well founded as it seems, in that it confuses the rationality of an external observer endowed with powerful analytical instruments with that of an economic agent who deciphers only part of his own economic environment. There is no *decentralized* theory of price formation, and the assumption of the instantaneous adaptation of prices cannot be deduced from principles of individual behaviour. The theory of price determination outside equilibrium still has a long way to go (Fisher, 1981). So the two schools of thought confront the same issue, but are solving it by diametrically opposite assumptions. Hence the impossibility, contrary to what has been expressed by Lucas in recent writings (1980a), of eliminating 'free' parameters from theoretical structures: an impossibility that underlines the unavoidable ideological content of economics.

The theory of 'disequilibria' had been presented at the beginning as the theory of imperfectly co-ordinated systems,[21] but the models that have been discussed are all founded on *tâtonnement* processes, which ensure a perfect co-ordination through quantities. Hence the allocation of goods in equilibrium depends on the rationing scheme, which cannot itself be deduced from agents' behaviour. In some sense, therefore, fixprice models do not really present a theory of quantity determination: the above critical remarks concerning the assumption of the instantaneous adaptation of prices applies, *pari passu*, to the case of instantaneous adaptation of quantities.

Non-Walrasian equilibria with endogenous prices

If price determination were the object of individual decisions, the beginnings of a solution to the preceding problem could be offered. Price rigidity would no longer be a cause but a consequence of under-employment equilibrium. The most general solution consists of supposing that an economic agent adapts his prices to explore the more or less constraining character of the quantity signals he receives from the market. Out of Walrasian equilibrium, as Arrow had noted (1959), agents are no longer confronted with infinitely elastic demand curves. Imperfect competition, more than perfect competition, would then constitute the reference model of macroeconomics. In such a structure individual agents determine their prices on the basis of conjectured supply and demand functions. The existence of a general equilibrium of monopolistic competition has been established by Negishi (1961), but until recently had not been linked to the problem of the microeconomic foundations of macroeconomics.

Benassy's model (1976, 1983) accomplished this. Consider the optimization programme defined by constraints (1) and (3). Goods are distinguished by the markets in which they are exchanged and by the individuals who control their prices. For example, individual i controls the subset of goods h_i, while the prices of other goods are viewed as rigid ($p_h = \bar{p}_h$, $h \neq h_i$). The conjectured functions of demand and supply are represented respectively by z_{ih} [$\mathbf{p}_i$, $\theta_i(\sigma_i)$] and $\bar{z}_{ih}$ [$\mathbf{p}_i$, $\theta_i(\sigma_i)$]; where θ_i are the parameters estimated from the information set (σ_i). The conjectured curves obviously pass through the observed point. The solution of this programme gives a price vector $\mathbf{P}_i^*$ considered as optimal taking into account the agents' conjectures. The formulation adopted here is rather general in that it allows the simultaneous consideration of fixprice and flexprice markets. A non-Walrasian equilibrium with endogenous prices is a K-equilibrium where economic agents do not perceive any incentive to modify their prices; that is to say, a K-equilibrium at the optimal price vector $\mathbf{P}^*$.[22, 23] If one considers a macroeconomic model, classical unemployment disappears as a category of the analysis in so far as it is always optimal for an entrepreneur who determines his price to satisfy demand at the current price. But it would seem that Keynesian unemployment would also disappear unless wage rigidity is assumed or a special concept of under-employment is used: an equilibrium $E(\mathbf{Z}, \mathbf{P})$ of the model would be characterized as an under-employment equilibrium if another equilibrium $E'(\mathbf{Z}', \mathbf{P}')$ existed such that the employment level would be higher. This is the concept used by Hart (1979) in a model where agents have monopoly power but know their true exchange possibilities. 'Unemployment' is then the result of monopolistic behaviour by trade unions.[24] The spontaneous equilibrium of the model can therefore be characterized by a low level of employment and activity. Fiscal policy by virtue of a process analogous to that of the multiplier would allow a higher level of employment. This definition of a state of under-employment does not seem convincing in so far as it could also be applied to a Walrasian model. In such a model, if equilibrium is not unique, and if an equilibrium where the level of employment is maximum existed, then any other state of the model could be characterized by under-employment equilibrium. Furthermore, it is possible to show that in the Walrasian model the level of employment and output depends in equilibrium on the importance of the (balanced) budget of the state (Tobin and Buiter, 1976).

A possible way out is to assume that the existence of monopoly powers is not intrinsic to the model but simply reflects the existence of disequilibria (Hahn, 1978). The full-employment Walrasian equilibrium always represents one of the solutions of the model. The structure of the economy is thus competitive, but price determination is decentralized and is the subject of individual decisions. To reconcile these two contradictory characteristics, Hahn assumes that agents' monopoly powers are not exogenous to the model. An agent who does not meet any quantity constraint could accept the market price. If no agent receives quantity signals, Walrasian equilibrium is reached. On the contrary, if an agent is constrained in some way, he conjectures that altering prices would allow him to relax the quantity constraints confronting him. A conjecture function retraces the relation established by the agent between the price he announces and the quantity he thinks he can exchange in excess of his constraint. This formulation assumes that the conjectured supply and demand functions are kinked at the current price.[25] For the rest, the model is formally similar to that of Benassy.[26] A conjectural equilibrium is a Drèze equilibrium where agents' conjectures are confirmed, in other words a state of the economy where agents do not perceive any incentive to modify their responses to the market signals they receive. Hahn has proved the existence of a conjectural equilibrium where only one side of the market is rationed, in the sense that the conjecture functions of agents who are on the long side of the market are not infinitely elastic. This characteristic implies a particular structure of information; non-rationed agents do not attempt to take advantage of the 'rationings' of other agents. It would be interesting to know whether, under the opposite assumptions, only a Walrasian equilibrium could be achieved.

A conjectural equilibrium can be qualified as an under-employment equilibrium for the reasons stated previously, namely because a state of the model exists where the employment level is higher (Walrasian equilibrium).

The assumption that conjectures are exogenous is considered by some (McCallum, 1980b) as an *ad hoc* assumption which would establish the vulnerability of this type of model. If perfect rationality is imposed on to agents' conjectures the Walrasian equilibrium would become the only solution of the model.[27] It has already been stressed that this criticism rests on a confusion between the concepts of rationality and centralization. Strictly speaking, in a centralized economy an entity external to the market can make experiments (assuming that the cost of those experiments is either zero or independent of their number) to discover the 'true' parameters of excess demand functions. But to stipulate that in a decentralized economy every agent who specializes in information on his immediate environment proceeds in the same way is a requirement that need not have anything to do with rationality.

The study of non-Walrasian models could lead the *naïf* to ask certain questions. For example, it has been proved unimpeachably that price rigidity leads to unemployment and that an economy with monopolistic structures generally functions at too low a level of activity; but these results give a strong impression of *déjà-vu*, and thus one is led to wonder whether improved solutions to macroeconomic problems have been found. But it is not, it seems, on this question that the evolution of recent theory must be judged.[28] The reconciliation of macroeconomics and rationality is a precondition for progress in the Keynesian approach, and this concern is the subject of the new developments in macroeconomic theory.

Perhaps it is useful at this stage to reconstruct the story of this reconciliation, as I see it.

The General Theory could be interpreted as containing two definitions of effective demand, which are generally confused because of the Keynesian assumption that short-period expectations are always realized. The first concept defines total demand as primarily a function of income (for a given state of long-term expectations). A second definition considers effective demand as that value of total demand expected by entrepreneurs, which corresponds to their current decisions on prices, employment and production.[29] It seems that the concept of conjecture applies particularly well to this definition and that by assumption entrepreneurs in the Keynesian theory are in conjectural equilibrium. Now if households in their capacity as consumers and suppliers of labour are considered as 'price-takers', they will adapt their behaviour to the price vector announced by entrepreneurs according to a process analogous to that defined by the fixprice models: their effective demand according to the first definition is the constrained demand that they communicate to the market. If the value of the constrained demand is equal to that of expected demand, entrepreneurs will not have any incentive to modify their decisions on price, employment and production since their conjectures are confirmed by the market. In this 're-reading' of the General Theory there is no reason for entrepreneurs to modify wages, since, once their employment decision is taken, the real wage is the profit-maximizing one at the employment level chosen: 'The volume of employment is uniquely related to a given level of real wages – not the other way round' (Keynes, 1936, p. 30).

Walrasian equilibrium of rational expectations

A careful distinction must be made between the problem of knowledge and that of rationality: to assert that a greedy agent makes the best use of his perceived environment tells us nothing of the difference between what is perceived and what is 'true', or about the conditions of their identity.

The confusion of these two problems results in the disappearance of learning processes – that is to say, the adaptation delays or, as some people prefer to call them, the 'free' parameters. But in fact this procedure amounts to selecting a particular value of these parameters: a zero adaptation lag or an infinite speed of adjustment. It is difficult to understand the reasons why such restrictions should confer a greater generality to a theory. Certainly the argument is not of a theoretical nature, and the empirical considerations that would justify it do not seem to be conclusive (Lucas, 1980a, pp. 711–12);[30] unless it is demanded that the economy should be simultaneously in a state of temporary equilibrium (market clearing) and of stationary equilibrium (rational expectations) i.e. that one considers *only* situations where the learning process has ceased (Hahn, 1982).

The concept of a competitive temporary equilibrium is a powerful analytical instrument, in that it allows a dynamic evolution to be accounted for without otherwise stipulating the existence of a disequilibrium. But it contains 'too many' potential disequilibria; the absence of co-ordination of future plans makes the present configuration of the economy too dependent on the past and not dependent enough on the future. The problem arises because the expectation function is specified in an *ad hoc* manner. By construction the model implies that agents are rational, know how to solve their optimization problem and are able to exhaust their exchange opportunities. Why not apply the same rationality principle to their expectation behaviour? The expectation function in fact describes 'the theory' of the agent as to the generation of future variables relevant to his current optimization problem. If this theory shows itself to be false in that it leads to systematic forecast errors, the agent will have to revise it. Expectations are rational when they lead to forecasts that, in comparison with realizations, do not induce the agent to modify his 'theory'. This assumption implies that forecasting errors are not correlated with any of the information available to the agent when he forms his forecasts and that they are, therefore, serially independent and distributed around a zero mean. This amounts to a steady-state equilibrium condition: expectations are rational when they lead to agents taking actions whose results do not contradict their expectations. To consider the rational expectation of a variable as the 'true' mathematical expectation of that variable conditional on the information set available to agents[31] is a particular form of the hypothesis, although generally used (Lucas, 1972b; Sargent, 1973; Sargent and Wallace, 1975; Barro, 1976).

Consider the optimization programme defined by the utility function u_i and constraints (1). Suppose, on the other hand, that the information set σ_i contains everything agent i needs to know to have complete information. Finally, suppose function u is quadratic so that excess demand functions are linear or log-linear. The perfect foresight equilibrium is, then, the certainty equivalent of the rational expectations equilibrium.[32] The model has the same properties as the Arrow–Debreu model, the assumption of perfect forecasts being a substitute for that of the existence of a complete set of contingent markets. Of course this type of model tries to explain not unemployment, since markets are always in equilibrium, but fluctuations. So far, the introduction of uncertainty leads only to random deviations around the path of perfect foresight. This can hardly be considered a theory of business cycles. Something else is needed for cycles to be generated.

Expectations are calculated by applying present and past data available to economic agents to the representative model of the economy. However, the use of the relevant model with incomplete information can lead to some fluctuations. The reason is simple: in a sequential equilibrium model where technology and preferences are given, changes in production and employment from one period to the next can result only from a change in the state of nature. Incomplete information can lead to perceiving what is actually a purely nominal perturbation as a change in the state of nature. The intertemporal substitution induced by a variation in current prices (wages) relatively to expected prices (wages) is supposed to be strong enough to generate sizeable supply changes (Barro, 1976; Lucas, 1977). Lucas (1972b) has shown, within the framework of an intergenerational model, that monetary shocks can generate real effects by confusing signals, thus aggravating the difficulty of distinguishing between absolute and relative price changes.

The possibility of cycles therefore rests entirely on a particular specification of the information set. As Tobin (1980, 1981) has noted, this possibility presupposes an asymmetry of information between sellers and buyers that really has no theoretical foundation. More generally, the set of models that try to explain fluctuations as equilibrium phenomena presupposes that monetary aggregates are not observable in the current period. Now in most countries current monetary data are available (cf. Grossman's chapter in this volume). Therefore the assumption of incomplete information is as vulnerable from the viewpoint of rationality as is the assumption of price rigidity (Barro, 1981). Thus equilibrium theory does not really provide a convincing explanation of economic fluctuations. The problem seems to be of the same nature as that of the rationality of conjectures: how should the optimum information set be determined? Which are the conditions necessary for this optimum set not to cover the complete set? In other words, what are the conditions for fluctuations to exist? Works on this question are much less numerous than those on log-linear macroeconomic models that assume the problem to have been solved. The question is important, though: on the one hand, the information behaviour of the individual agent must be rational for expectations to be rational;[33] on the other hand, the incompleteness of information presupposes a certain irrationality or implies an *ad hoc* assumption on the comparative costs of the acquisition of information and of macroeconomic fluctuations.

This type of analysis gives particular importance to unperceived monetary shocks as a primary cause of economic fluctuations. Therefore a Phillips curve can exist in the short period, but it does not offer any opportunity for intervention to economic policy. This is the well-known proposition about the ineffectiveness of economic policy that is derived from a set of equilibrium rational expectations models. In general, this ineffectiveness rests on a particular macroeconomic specification of the theory whose fundamental equation describes the behaviour of suppliers on the labour market or on the product market: total supply is the sum of a constant and of a term representing the expectation error about the general price level. If this term is zero, and its mean is zero from the assumption of rational expectation, systematic policies of aggregate demand regulation have no effect on the level of employment and production. This equation is known as the Lucas supply function (Lucas and Rapping, 1970), and the inter-generational model presented by Lucas (1972b) is considered as its microeconomic foundation. But, in fact, the reduced form that it is possible to derive from the latter model is a relation between the equilibrium level of production, the equilibrium level of prices and the probability distribution of the price level (Azariadis, 1981). Moreover, the only policy-neutrality proposition that can be derived starting from Lucas's model is highly restrictive. This point deserves further analysis.

In a temporary competitive equilibrium model, the excess demand functions are not generally homogeneous with respect to current prices and money balances. The reason is simple: the absence of money illusion that characterizes these models implies that an equiproportional variation of the set of prices (current *and* expected) and of the quantity of money leaves the excess demand functions unchanged. For this property to apply in the short period a unit elasticity of expectation would be necessary (Grandmont, 1977). This restriction – expected prices always being proportional to current prices – is an *ad hoc* assumption in that it cannot be deduced from fundamental principles of rational behaviour. However, it is possible to show that a particular category of monetary policy is neutral *on condition that agents believe in its neutrality* (Grandmont, 1983). Suppose that the government announces it will increase the quantity of money in the current period by means of transfers proportional to monetary balances held by each agent, with a proportionality coefficient equal to λ. This kind of monetary policy is chosen to avoid distribution effects which, of course, have real consequences. If agents believe in the neutrality assumption, their price expectations will be homogeneous of first degree with respect to current prices and the λ parameter. Therefore, this type of policy measure will be neutral. If monetary policy consists of announcing a vector of λ parameters applicable to current and future periods, the neutrality proposition is maintained.[34] But if the monetary authorities give advance notice of a modification in the time profile of λ parameters, monetary policy – it goes without saying, perfectly anticipated – will have real consequences. This is due to the liquidity constraints to which agents are exposed in different periods.[35]

If we consider a model with internal money, the neutrality proposition becomes even more specific: an equiproportional variation of initial monetary balances and of bank money is neutral if agents believe in its neutrality (Grandmont, 1982, ch. II). Once again, this proposition reaffirms the neutrality of a reform of the monetary unit: such a reform is neutral not just because it applies to monetary balances held but because it modifies in the same proportion the total liabilities and assets expressed in monetary units (Tobin, 1980, ch. II). Contrary to Lucas's suggestion (1981), the analysis of this kind of policy measure does not exhaust the study of the consequences of monetary policy. Therefore the non-neutrality of monetary shocks is the general case even when they are completely expected.[36] What is clear, on the contrary, is that the proposition of ineffectiveness of monetary policy has been demonstrated within the framework of a very special model and for a type of policy measure that is also very special: a change in the scale of monetary unit. Certainly this is an interesting result, but it could not constitute the basis for a general recommendation of economic policy in view of the extremely specific nature of the theoretical structure that generates it. Nevertheless, this result has, without caution, been incorporated into a series of macroeconomic models (Lucas, 1973; Sargent, 1973; Sargent and Wallace, 1975, 1976; Barro, 1976; McCallum, 1978; etc.), which have become frames of reference for economic policy debates (McCallum, 1979, 1980a; Lucas, 1980b; Grossman, 1980). Now, it is worth repeating that in the general case it can be shown that a systematic monetary policy will always have an effect on the equilibrium level of production and employment because it influences the terms of trade between present and future. This proof has been produced within the framework of the very model that is the foundation of the general equilibrium theory of rational expectations: Samuelson's inter-generational model (Azariades, 1981; Hahn, 1982; Grandmont, 1983).

At this stage in the analysis an important point deserves particular emphasis. Even if previous criticisms are rejected, the neutrality proposition of systematic monetary policy rests, necessarily, on the assumption of the uniqueness of the equilibrium. But, in general, the equilibrium of an Arrow–Debreu model is not unique. For example, this can be true when production is characterized by constant returns to scale. An increase in the quantity of money, then, can lead to an equiproportional increase of production and employment or can be divided between price change and quantity change or, finally, can generate only a price increase without any modification of the real magnitudes in the economy. Any of these consequences can be rationally expected and therefore be self-fulfilling (Hahn, 1980a, b; 1982). It goes without saying that several equilibrium paths of rational expectations exist under this assumption and that in the majority of them agents must *also* form quantity expectations. Therefore the real coordinates of the economy would not be invariant with respect to monetary policy.

Even if the assumption of uniqueness is accepted, the stability and convergence problems are not resolved in the least. If the system is globally stable, an infinity of paths that converge towards equilibrium exists. Each of these paths represents a rational expectation. The dynamic evolution of the system therefore remains indeterminate. If the system is globally unstable all the paths will be divergent. Only under the assumption that equilibrium is a saddle point is there a solution which allows the calculation of the unique rational expectation path (Burmeister, 1980; Begg, 1982, ch. III).[37] The general case, therefore, seems to be that of the indeterminacy of the dynamics of the system. Expectations rationally formed will be divergent and no mechanism will ensure their return to a convergent path, since the stochastic behaviour of variables remains indeterminate (Burmeister, 1980).

For all these reasons and more, the proposition of ineffectiveness of monetary policy in particular and of stabilization policy in general remains extremely limited.[38] Of course, it is always possible to modify some relations of an elementary macroeconomic model, adding a variable here and a lag there, considering deviations rather than levels, so as to re-establish this proposition (McCallum, 1980a). But the lack of foundations, both for the model and for the modifications introduced, damages the credibility of this undertaking. Nevertheless, it would seem that this proposition has been taken seriously and even been interpreted as representing the basis of the policy of monetary discipline recommended by Milton Friedman. But this is only one of the doctrinal contradictions generated by the new classical school. In the singularly limited domain to which it is applicable, the 'theorem' of ineffectiveness of economic policy states that *any* systematic monetary rule, whatever its nature, has no real effect. No reason is given as to whether an 'open loop' rule should be preferred to a 'feedback' rule.[39] This result should generate consensus within the profession since the supporters of the neoclassical synthesis (e.g. Modigliani, 1977; Tobin, 1980) can be interpreted as advocating the adoption of a systematic rule of aggregate demand regulation.

Nevertheless, it is true that there is a general sense in which the ineffectiveness proposition is well founded. In this case I prefer to re-christen it the 'uselessness of economic policy axiom'. If an Arrow–Debreu equilibrium is the certainty equivalent of a competitive equilibrium with rational expectations, any economic policy without distribution effects will be much more than ineffective: it will be useless. It would be particularly difficult to discover the need for it.

It is hardly a new proposition in economic theory that there is no trade-off between inflation and employment at full employment.

This axiom derives not from the rational expectations assumption alone, but from its incorporation into a competitive temporary equilibrium model. It has already been seen that if the equilibrium is not unique, the rationality of expectations would not necessarily contradict the effects of monetary policy. *A fortiori*, this is true if the framework of the Walrasian model is abandoned for the more general non-Walrasian models previously analysed. There, monetary policy will be especially more effective if it is rationally expected since it will modify the quantity constraints confronting economic agents.[40]

More generally, the rationality of expectations is a useful working hypothesis, and one of the merits of the new classical school is the stress on its consequences in the important field of economic policy evaluation. The argument is extremely simple (Lucas, 1972a, 1976; Lucas and Sargent, 1979). The simulation of the effects of different economic policy measures implies the identification of the structural form of econometric models. This identification implies a series of assumptions and *a priori* restrictions: restrictions as to the matrices of endogenous and exogenous variables; as to the matrix of random errors; the *a priori* classification of variables between exogenous and endogenous, etc. The identification problem is precisely that of never being sure of having correctly detected the structural form of the model. In particular, macroeconometric 'Keynesian' models use *a priori* restrictions which are not generally consistent with the rational expectations assumption. If agents' forecasts are calculated starting from the whole model and all of present and past data, restrictions concerning the matrix of errors will be generally contradicted, in the same way as is the classification of variables into two categories (Lucas and Sargent, 1979). For in the majority of 'Keynesian' models, the expected value of a variable depends only on past values of the same variable. The difficulty comes from structural parameters so identified not being invariant to those actions of economic policy whose effects are to be measured. If the estimate of these parameters depends on the economic policy rule previously chosen, the evaluation of other economic policies will be generally mistaken. The right strategy should be to make economic policy explicit through a relation in the model and to establish a series of cross-equations restrictions, since a modification of economic policy rules will have a feedback on the parameters of other equations of the model. This critique, therefore, leads not to a general condemnation of econometric models but to proposing statistical, econometric and theoretical strategies able to resolve the problem of economic policy evaluation.[41]

This criticism is regarded as fatal for Keynesian economics, however. It is in the nature of the General Theory that it leads to *a priori* restrictions starting from arbitrary rules of thumb instead of considering the intertemporal optimization problem of economic agents as a whole. This leads to an arbitrary distribution of zeros in the Jacobian of the model. For example, this is the case with the consumption function or with the liquidity preference function. The structural form of a Keynesian model will therefore never be capable of being identified (Lucas and Sargent, 1979). What was only a specific and *well founded* critique of the current use of large-scale econometric models in the majority of Western countries becomes the death certificate of a theoretical approach. And, as always, the excessiveness of a critique draws attention to its own weakness. At first it goes without saying that the generation of non-Walrasian models is also based on problems of intertemporal optimization. There is no reason why the 'right' estimation strategy should not be applied to these models and why a feedback rule describing the behaviour of public bodies should not be explicitly introduced among the equations. Then the rational expectations assumption cannot be tested independently of the theoretical structure in which it is embedded (Shiller, 1978). By itself, this property establishes no hierarchy of alternative approaches. Finally, and above all, the general affirmation that it is impossible to discover the 'true' structural form should be applied not only to a particular class of models. The identification problem can be solved only relatively. The reality approximated by our estimation methods is *always* of a greater dimension than that of the models that we use. Any system of a lower dimension than that of the phenomenon it tries to represent is always vulnerable from the point of view of the identification problem. This is particularly true of a macroeconomic model that restricts the space of phenomena to a very reduced dimension. (And macroeconometric models built by the new classical school are generally much smaller than the traditional Keynesian model; cf., e.g., Sargent, 1976.) But this is also true of any economic model.

The very concise and partial account of the 'rational expectations revolution' (Begg, 1982) given here can be seen as over-critical, but the reader can also interpret it as underlining certain problems that deserve to figure in the research agenda of the new classical school.

The equilibrium assumption, even when formalized within a dynamic model, does not yet seem to be able to produce a convincing explanation of macroeconomic fluctuations.

Conclusion

Of the two possible interpretations of the General Theory, 'modern macroeconomic theory' has essentially retained that which has a familiar look. This has led to a Walrasian reading of macroeconomics. The theories presented here all have a common filiation and the same limits as the original model: the coherence of the system as a whole is presupposed instead of being explained. The auctioneer is still alive and well, the theory of price determination is evanescent, and the theory of quantity allocation is exogenous to the model. But perhaps it is not fair to quarrel with this. Since the study of equilibrium is given a special status, the reasoning is cast within the framework of perfectly co-ordinated systems. And one of the major contributions of recent developments is to have shown that, within such a framework, rationality does not necessarily lead to full employment equilibrium or to the stationarity of that equilibrium. Another positive aspect of recent research is that it is expressed in a common language, thus allowing a dialogue and a cross-fertilization of different approaches.

But at the same time, this establishes the partial characters of the new developments. The theoretical structure chosen singularly limits the range of relevant questions, namely the domain of macroeconomics. Perhaps the problem is not uniquely that of knowing whether Keynesian results can be deduced from a microeconomic analysis of general equilibrium or whether Walrasian conclusions can be obtained starting from the *IS–LM* model. It would still be necessary to build theoretical structures able to generate new questions and/or to pose other questions to existing structures. If a macro-system as a whole has coherence, perhaps it would be useful to study directly the reasons that determine its coherence. This probably is the course underlined by Keynes when he stressed his intention of studying 'the system as a whole'. If a macroeconomic logic partially independent of that which determines individual behaviour exists – an under-employment equilibrium is surely an equilibrium relative to the system and not to the individuals composing it – perhaps that logic deserves to be analysed in itself. That it has only rarely been analysed does not represent an impossibility theorem. My conviction is that macroeconomics has its own dimension which must be considered and not just alluded to. J. R. Oppenheimer wrote: 'common sense is only wrong if it requires that what is familiar to us should necessarily reappear in what is not and if it leads us to hope that every country visited should resemble the previous one.' Whether it has been wrong to visit the General Theory with a Walrasian guide remains an open question.

Outline

The certainty surrounding the policy debate probably gives a misleading image of what is going on in macroeconomics. Here all is at the level of tentative conclusions, prototype models, non-robust outcomes, as is normal when dealing with such complex phenomena as unemployment and inflation, in particular after the experiences of the 1970s.

The essays collected in this book are, without exception, cautious and arrive at modest conclusions. There is no sign of a straightforward policy recommendation of a quantitative kind, no monetary growth rule. This is because they are evolving at the frontier of macroeconomic theory, and thus are asking fundamental questions, and because models or even theories are far too simple for dealing, in an unambiguous way, with such complex entities as the social system. How exact a science economics is depends on the extent to which a social system is operating as a mechanical analogue. That this extent is small is still as much in dispute between economists today as ever.

The arrangement of the book follows that of the introduction, starting with a reconsideration of the *IS–LM* framework and, via a study of non-Walrasian approaches to macroeconomics, offering a critical appraisal of the market-clearing rational expectations model.

'What is wrong with IS–LM?'

The *IS–LM* framework is no longer the reference model of macroeconomics, but it is still used in many textbooks and in the papers of some rational expectations theorists. As has been shown, it is a very innocuous framework if a price equation is added to it. For reasons now obvious (see the first part of this chapter), it is rejected more by Keynesians than by monetarists. But to answer the question, 'What is wrong with *IS–LM*?', a deeper insight into its own foundations is needed. This is accomplished in the chapters by Sir John Hicks and Axel Leijonhufvud.

In his paper '*IS–LM*: An Explanation', Hicks clearly states that '*IS–LM* was in fact a translation of Keynes's non-flex-price model into my terms'. The problem he addresses, then, is not that of the Keynesian nature of the framework but, as a separate question, the problem of its own consistency. *IS–LM* is built from a Walrasian analogy and could be analysed as a temporary equilibrium model with two prices fixed. With great economy of means, Hicks shows how this 'disequilibrium' interpretation can be worked out on Walrasian lines with the quantity exchanged on fixprice markets appearing as arguments in the excess demand functions. But there is a problem here. There is, at the same time, the demand for output being a function of actual employment and the demand for input being a function of actual sales. But in the temporary equilibrium period (the week), the latter relation has no foundations, the output decision being mainly predetermined by the past. The only way of closing the model is to introduce a rule linking current output to current input which will substitute for an explanation as to why agents perceive a disequilibrium in the product market as permanent.

Whereas the 'disequilibrium' interpretation fails because of its very specific structure of expectations, the equilibrium interpretation solves the problem only if the liquidity preference function is interpreted in a very peculiar way. If a longer period (a year) is considered, there is no harm in assuming the product market to be in equilibrium during that year. The economy is treated as if it were in equilibrium over the period. But this raises a tricky question. *IS* is a flow relation and refers to a period, whereas *LM* is a stock relation and refers to a moment in time. A stock equilibrium implies, then, that the economy is in equilibrium at each moment in time throughout the period. How can this be reconciled with liquidity preference, the theory underlying the construction of the *LM* curve? Hicks proposes a solution, but, apparently, his faith in it is not very strong. These far-reaching conclusions suggest that Keynesian theory is not founded on Walras. In the disequilibrium approach, the Walrasian analogy suggests static expectations, because of the missing link between current input and sold output. In the equilibrium interpretation there is no room for liquidity because of the stock-flow equilibrium nature of *IS–LM*.

Leijonhufvud, in his paper, 'What was the Matter with *IS–LM*?', rejects the *IS–LM* approach to macroeconomics precisely because of the problem of expectations. In his terms, '*IS–LM* has served us ill in three long-lasting controversies': in the Keynes and the classics debate, in the loanable fund versus liquidity preference controversy, and in the monetarist debate. The reason for this back-tracking is that '*IS–LM*, as it is most frequently utilized, is neither static nor dynamic. It is a short-run model.' As such, it leads to wrong conclusions when attempts are made to use it in comparative static analyses. What is important is the implicit sequence of decisions subsumed in the *IS–LM* apparatus. This is shown to be the consequence of a particular specification of the information set of the agents. To identify this information failure built into the model, Leijonhufvud constructs a reference model, that is a benchmark by which *IS–LM* propositions could be evaluated: a full-information macroeconomics (FIM) model 'where agents have learnt all that can be (profitably) learnt about their environment and about each others' behaviour'.

Whatever the qualifications, the FIM model can be interpreted as a market-clearing–steady-state equilibrium model. Whether a full-information state will be reached or not depends on the completeness of information and not on the time horizon considered. It can then be seen that the monetarist controversy springs from an implicit specification of the information set rather than fundamental assumptions on the true structure of the economy.

IS–LM analysis, suggesting that real and monetary factors are *always* linked, is contradicted by FIM results where the neutrality of money proposition applies.[42] The emphasis put on the elasticity of *IS* and *LM* curves is also misplaced, as Leijonhufvud's conclusion that the rational adaptation to 'monetary' or 'real' shock will induce a move in *both* curves shows. Two kinds of information failure are seen to lead to transitory *IS–LM* results: a failure of intertemporal prices to respond appropriately to a change in perceived intertemporary opportunities and/or a temporary information asymmetry between employers and employees. Thus the source of the trouble lies in the information problem, and it is therefore misleading to treat the *IS–LM* solutions as if they were static. Adjustments have to be completed to reach full co-ordination.

The divergence in the conclusions of these two reconsiderations of a framework that has dominated the scene for more than 30 years is striking. Hicks rejects *IS–LM* because Keynes should not be read through Walrasian glasses. For Leijonhufvud, on the contrary, it is better not to use *IS–LM* as generally it does not lead to FIM results.

The fixprice approach to macroeconomics

The approach underlined by Leijonhufvud aimed at constructing models able to explain both 'co-ordination successes and failures'.

This is not easy and so far relies too much on an answer to a question that, perhaps, cannot be answered: 'Who knows what when?' Another approach Leijonhufvud suggests is to consider co-ordination problems that arise when agents are prevented from carrying out their preferred decisions, the so-called 'general equilibrium with a spanner in the works'. Fixprice models obviously pertain to that approach. Two papers, by Malinvaud and Korliras, try to extend this type of analysis by taking into account investment decisions in the broad sense.

In 'Notes on Growth Theory with Imperfectly Flexible Prices', Malinvaud reconsiders economic growth theory after recent results in fixprice temporary equilibria. The study of the dynamics of fixprice equilibria is still in its infancy for reasons given in the preceding sections. The paper claims no more than to raise interesting questions and to delineate important issues, but, not surprisingly, does more than that. Malinvaud states clearly why he chose this approach: 'Some disequilibria may be sustained over a rather long period and the existence of these disequilibria reacts significantly on the growth process.' That the theory of rational behaviour has not yet explained the reasons for such persistent disequilibria does not mean that their sheer existence should not be considered. In particular, excess supply or demand may persist, but Malinvaud's innovative approach faces the issue of price disequilibria as well (see also Malinvaud, 1980a). He introduces two disequilibrium concepts: excess capacity and profitability (the latter concerning prices). Malinvaud's analysis is distinctive in its full consideration of investment behaviour, making the investment decision depend on these two types of disequilibrium, apart from relative prices. The main question then is whether there is a Schumpeterian cumulative process in economic growth and whether such a process, under different initial conditions, could explain the varied historical experiences of different economies. This is very topical. Is there a causation chain running from profitability to profitability, passing through investment, productivity and competitiveness? How could such a virtuous circle be entered? Would a low interest rate policy stimulate or sustain such a process?

A dynamic model representing this causation chain would be too complex, and an heuristic discussion analyses the result of a sudden decrease in the real interest rate on investment via profitability, assuming an initial Keynesian stationary state. For this a simple dynamic system is built and analysed in an appendix. The answer depends on the magnitude of the various parameters of the model and is generally not as positive as might have been expected: a 'too' low real interest rate could just as well lead to an output level smaller than it was initially – that is, before the decrease in the interest rate.

The model can be criticized on several grounds: the wage rate and the level of autonomous demand are assumed to be constant; there is no money, or financial assets. This leaves the determination of the interest rate – and hence of profitability – problematic. But Malinvaud considers these shortcomings as producing questions for further research rather than a defect of the approach itself.

In the review of fixprice 'non-Walrasian' models, the consideration of expectations leads to a more complex picture of disequilibria states because the relation between current variables is mediated by the quantity expectations formed by agents. For example, a decrease in the sale of labour does not necessarily imply a decrease in the effective demand for goods. Saving and inventories will act as buffer stocks provided that the present disequilibrium is considered as transitory. Korliras's paper: 'Conjectural Stock and Flow Responses to Market Rationing', starts here. The paper sets up a typology of agents' responses to market rationing and studies their effect on output and employment multipliers. Three kinds of responses are distinguished: a flow reaction; a stock reaction, which implies a change in the level of liquid wealth or inventories; and a price reaction. The adjective conjecture qualifies these reactions probably because of the analogy that Korliras sees between his analysis of stock responses and the conjecture function studied by Hahn.

However, it is worth remembering that the latter concerns the relation between an agent's price and the quantity he conjectures that he can exchange in excess of his constraint. The stock response, the reaction whose consequences are analysed in the paper, depicts the agent's behaviour in a market, consequential of his experiment of a binding constraint in another market. Thus, an unemployed agent could either restrict his demand on the product market or dissave, or both. This is why his quantity expectations are so important in explaining his decisions. Similarly, inventories play, for the firm, a role analogous to that of liquid wealth or money balances for the household. A simple Clower-type model with three goods, two agents, two periods and two markets is used. Agents' decision-making is based upon the logic of the dual decision hypothesis. The central part of Korliras's paper comprises an analysis of the effects of pure or mixed stock responses on the magnitude of the relevant multiplier, that is on the degree to which the spillover effects are 'deviation-amplifying'. The model suggests that the stock reaction dampens the size of inter-market spillover effects and hence leads to a smaller contraction of employment.

Flexprice approaches to macroeconomics

The flexprice approach covers a wide range of models. Two criteria distinguish them: the definition of the information set, which does or does not allow for perfect present co-ordination, and the hypothesis on the structure of the economy. Hence, for example, the competitive temporary equilibrium model implies a complete pre-conciliation of choice on the markets open during the period and a competitive structure of the economy. If the economy is seen as not perfectly competitive, while agents have a perfect knowledge of their demand curve, one obtains the pure monopolistic competition model. In between these two extreme cases we find the conjectural equilibrium approach.

The two chapters of Part III try to prove, in a certain sense, that the problem of information is not intrinsic to the story.

The paper by Christopher Bliss could be seen as a criticism of the temporary equilibrium model and of what the author considers its main assumption: 'the expected prices adjust slowly even in the face of evidence of disequilibrium, while present prices respond rapidly to equate supplies and demands.' The problem is to try to impose consistency of future plans even when agents hold dissimilar expectations. This is a step towards full intertemporal equilibrium, but the set of 'consistent temporary equilibria', the new concept elaborated by Bliss, does not quite look like the Arrow–Debreu equilibrium, since, for instance, the saving decisions of households are determined by their dissimilar price expectations.

The consistency of agents' future plans is achieved by a filtering process within the capital market. This market thus imposes quantity constraints on the agents' optimization problem even if all prices are flexible and present markets perfectly efficient. The ordinary temporary equilibrium approach considers that claims on the future (borrowing) are perfect substitutes one for another. But this is not a proper assumption if agents are allowed to value future goods differently. A rule of financial prudency should be imposed by the market, constraining agents to solvency through the application of a set of reference prices to their supply of future money (i.e. borrowing). The plans of the borrowing agents are assumed to be known to everybody. A proof of existence of a consistent temporary equilibrium follows, provided that the capital market only knows the borrowers' intentions and the aggregate amount of lending. The co-ordination of future plans is thus achieved in spite of the arbitrary and heterogeneous expectations assumed in the model. This result is not surprising because future plans are evaluated not in terms of those expectations but through the application of a set of reference prices. The weakness of the model lies precisely here: there is no convincing story for the determination of these prices. The consistent temporary equilibrium is not Keynesian, although it could provide a link between investment and labour market equilibrium. But this is only a suggestion, not an explanation.

Monopolistic competition models may themselves exhibit Keynesian features even though, as has been seen, they use a some-what far-fetched concept of unemployment. In the model considered by Hart, the labour market is imperfectly competitive but firms and unions set prices optimally. The type of imperfect competition assumed is rather special: no syndicate is significant relative to the economy as a whole, but workers have a monopoly power in the segment of the labour market in which they are operating. The framework is provided by an overlapping generation model with rational expectations. In order to allow for fluctuations, a stochastic component is introduced into demand functions by distinguishing between two classes of young workers: those who have a regular utility function, and those who derive utility from consumption only when they are old. The proportion λ of the first group is a random variable, but its realization is public knowledge. When the labour market is perfectly competitive it is shown that full employment is always achieved because of the real balance effect. However, there is no guarantee that competitive equilibrium will be unique.

When workers have monopoly power the result no longer stands. Assuming the state of nature is a slump (λ small), the maximization of the syndicate's objective function may lead to unemployment in a particular sense – *voluntary* rationing of labour time, not of labour power – because the objective function of the union is to maximize its total wage receipts. And the union may *choose* unemployment if it is of the opinion that wage reduction needed to guarantee full employment is too large to be consistent with its objective function.

A balanced budget fiscal policy would be effective for increasing employment because it can be analysed as an increase in λ. On the other hand, a monetary policy would be ineffective for two reasons: the rationality of expectations and the homogeneity property of the objective function. Hence the Keynesian flavour of the results. But the model is rather specific and is considered so by its author. It was intended principally to reconcile (voluntary) rationing and endogenous price determination.

Rational expectations and macroeconomic fluctuations

The rationality of expectations is generally considered as a useful assumption by the profession because it endogenizes the forecasting behaviour of agents and because no credible alternative way of modelling expectations exists. It is *not* a theory of learning but a (useful) 'as if' assumption, and focuses attention on those states in which the learning process has ceased. Market-clearing as an 'as if' assumption is also a non-falsifiable hypothesis. This is Sargent's 'observational equivalence proposition'. What can be falsified, however, are their joint implications. It is then a matter of taste as to which particular assumptions have been rejected by the test. But, typically, the authors prefer not to quarrel about expectations, but rather to argue about the structure of economies.

The paper by John Boschen and Herschel Grossman – 'Monetary Information and Macroeconomic Fluctuation' – tries to deduce the proper test of the equilibrium approach to modelling macroeconomic fluctuations from a theoretical model.

In the second section of this overview it was seen that the information set has to be short of some relevant data for non-random macroeconomic fluctuations to exist, though it would not be consistent with the rational expectations hypothesis to suppose that agents do not use readily available information efficiently. In particular, equilibrium models should not abstract both from the existence of contemporaneous preliminary monetary data and from the process of the gradual accumulation of revised monetary data. That perceived contemporaneous money shocks should not have real effects, whether expected or not, is a straightforward implication. The paper by John Boschen and Herschel Grossman is a precise proof of this statement. Taking a typical macroeconomic model (from the rational expectations literature), including both a Lucas-supply function and a generalized policy equation (which consists of three parts: a constant, a feedback rule and a random factor), they prove that current aggregate output is independent of the contemporaneous measure of money growth. They carefully specify the information set whereby expectations are conditional and take explicit account of the gradual process of accumulation of revised monetary data. They end up with what seems to be an inescapable implication of the market-clearing–rational-expectations model: current aggregate output and currently available estimates of contemporaneous money growth are uncorrelated. This testable implication seems to be rejected by empirical evidence, so the authors conclude that the equilibrium approach to modelling macroeconomic fluctuations should also be rejected.

The paper by Tarantelli could be seen as a reconsideration of the theory of the Phillips curve under both the rational expectations and disequilibrium approaches to macroeconomics. Accepting that expectations are rational does not exclude, as has been shown in the second section, the possibility of involuntary unemployment. The method is that of partial equilibrium, Tarantelli's main focus being on the labour market and the framework is provided by a revised version of Holt's description of the stock-flow equilibrium of the labour market. The framework is expanded along three lines. First, unlike the conventional model of the Phillips curve, the wage behaviour of both the unemployed and the employed are explained. Second, the policy rule of a Keynesian state aiming at dampening fluctuations is fully described and the regressive expectations based on it are rational. As is normal when dealing with 'disequilibrium' states, quantity expectations have to be taken into account, so the unemployment rate is also rationally expected. Third, in disequilibrium, the probability of finding a job and the time spent while unemployed are no longer reciprocal. Consequently, the central variable of the model is the expected probability of finding a job defined as the ratio between the flow of hiring and the expected unemployment rate. This broader framework allows Tarantelli to reach interesting results. The Phillips curve he constructs is more stable than the usual one and exhibits anti-clockwise loops. He provides an explanation for the downward rigidity of wages in terms of the rational expectations of a Keynesian-type policy. However, the problem of defining the process of generating rational expectations in a partial equilibrium framework remains unresolved.

Notes

1 An ironic illustration of such a view will be found for example in Hahn (1977a).
2 Modigliani (1944), for instance, seems to support such an interpretation: 'The ability of the model set out in the General Theory to explain the persistence of unemployment could be traced primarily to the assumption of wage rigidity.'
3 For a complete discussion of the real balance effect see Tobin (1980, ch. 1). But Tobin himself, and in spite of the lack of empirical relevance that he assigns to the real-balance effect – by virtue of a probable asymmetry

between the propensities to spend of debtors and creditors – seems to fall in with this interpretation of Keynesian economics.

4 As Hahn notes (1980c, p. 127), 'Indeed, if it is the case that today General Equilibrium Theory is in some disarray, this is largely due to the work of General Equilibrium Theorists and not to any successful assault from outside'. cf. also Arrow (1978, 1980) for a similar view.

5 The viewpoint defended by Weintraub (1979) is that, when considered in this way, the 'Walrasian research programme' appears as a progressive one.

6 For reasons that will become clear later, the formulation used will be Benassy (1983).

7 The majority of concepts to be used here have a Hicksian link and a Swedish connection (see n. 11 below). The concept of temporary competitive equilibrium in particular represented one of the major contributions of *Value and Capital* (1939), and Hicks later devoted an important chapter to it (ch. VI) in *Capital and Growth* (1965). The modern development of this concept is due to Grandmont, who has shown in a series of articles that the idea of temporary equilibrium could lead to a monetary theory and how it allowed some of the results of the neoclassical synthesis to be called into question: such as properties of homogeneity, the role of monetary policy, etc. (Grandmont, 1973, 1977, 1983; Grandmont and Laroque, 1973, 1975).

8 It is not, however, a sufficient condition, as will be seen in the discussion of a Walrasian equilibrium with rational expectations.

9 The difficulty of proving the existence of such an equilibrium within Patinkin's model (1965) had been stressed by Hahn (1965) and 'solved' by Grandmont: 'The price of money is positive in equilibrium because people believe it will be positive with some probability in the future' (1977, p. 551).

10 Hicks (1965, pp. 71–2) had already stressed the limits of monetary policy. Although he referred to the existence of a 'spectrum of interest rates', the reasoning was qualitatively the same: the possibility of affecting the spectrum of interest rates, controlling some of them, depends on the behaviour of agents' expectations.

11 Lindahl's method (cf. Hicks, 1965, pp. 73–4; 1977, pp. vi–viii), on which the Hicksian approach is directly based, implies that the length of the period of temporary equilibrium is chosen so as to be equal to the expectation lag. The chain of periods is then naturally derived: each period leaves to that following a capital stock and a determined value of expected variables. When the expectation lag is reduced, the length of the period is also reduced. In the short-run Walrasian equilibrium model the simultaneous determination of prices and expectations implies an arbitrary choice of period length.

12 The fertile matrix of this class of models is the fundamental article by Clower (1965) on the Keynesian counter-revolution, in that it gave a theoretical content – in terms of the general equilibrium model – to the concept of effective demand. This concept is obtained by considering an additional constraint generated by imperfect wage flexibility in individual economic agents' optimization problems. Thus, emphasis was put not on the rigidity of one price but on the non-instantaneity of its adaptation. This course was very similar to that of Patinkin (1956, 1965, ch. 13), which dealt in a symmetric fashion with optimization by a firm. It remained for Barro and Grossman (1971, 1976) to synthesize the two contributions into a general disequilibrium model, while the existence of an equilibrium where only wages are rigid had been established by Glustoff (1968). Thus, originally,

emphasis was put on all these circumstances where prices were prevented from changing 'freely'. The information problem evidently appeared *en exergue*, and the very absence of an auctioneer in a general equilibrium model seemed sufficient to produce Keynesian results. Hence the apparent similarity between the path taken by Leijonhufvud and that of the new microeconomics of employment and inflation (Phelps *et al.*, 1970), as shown by the numerous references to Alchian (1970) in Leijonhufvud (1968). But obviously the similarity is only apparent, for the methodological approaches are radically different. While a spillover effect across markets underlies the effective demand concept *à la* Clower that cannot be understood outside a general equilibrium model framework, the new microeconomics couched its argument in terms of a partial equilibrium analysis – essentially of the labour market – and could not conceive of unemployment other than as a transitory stage in an adjustment process (Phelps, 1970) or as an entirely voluntary phenomenon generated by a misperception of exchange opportunities (Lucas and Rapping, 1970; Mortensen, 1970).

13 Refer in particular to the article by T. Haavelmo (1950), who presents an extremely interesting discussion of the notion of involuntary economic decisions.

14 These properties include to some extent the hypotheses formulated by Drèze – equilibrium of transactions and voluntary exchange. The third hypothesis – rationing on one side of the market only – is not a necessary hypothesis in a Benassy-type model, since markets can be characterized by the existence of frictions (Benassy, 1977, 1983).

15 A K-equilibrium is a Nash equilibrium, where every agent considers the actions of other agents as given. Therefore it is possible to interpret general equilibria at fixed prices in terms of non-cooperative game theory. In particular the non-cooperative equilibrium of Malinvaud and Younes (1977) includes the notion of K-equilibrium when prices are fixed. The non-cooperative behaviour is the source of the inefficiency found in fixed-price equilibria models; cf. also Böhm and Levine (1979); Heller and Starr (1979).

16 It is true that Benassy (1975) also elaborated a concept of equilibrium in terms of a *non-tâtonnement* process, but the concept pertains more to the category of stationary equilibria than to that of temporary equilibria (cf. in particular Dehez, 1982).

17 Models in which demand is never rationed, thus abandoning the possibility of classical unemployment, have since been elaborated, and rely more on the assumption of the rigidity of relative prices than on that of nominal prices (e.g. Kurtz, 1982; Dehez and Drèze, 1982).

18 This correspondence has been questioned by Hildenbrand and Hildenbrand (1978). Fitoussi and Georgescu-Roegen (1980) have shown that there may not exist rationing rules to achieve a classical equilibrium and that the conclusions of economic policy derived from the Malinvaud model depended on the particular specification chosen for the utility function. In the general case a rule of economic policy directed at reducing Keynesian unemployment cannot be deduced from the model.

19 Therefore it should not be surprising that the real-balance effect plays an important role in these models. When the real wage corresponds to its Walrasian level, under-employment is generally the result of a 'too low' level of the quantity of money.

20 The theory of implicit contracts does not justify the existence of market disequilibria, contrary to what Solow has said (1979, 1980). On the one hand, this implies the real wage rigidity (and not money wage rigidity) and on the other, it is a theory of full employment. The existence of long-term nominal contracts (Fischer, 1977, 1980) and of transaction costs (Howitt, 1979) is another justification. Keynes's invocation of the rigidity of relative wages is probably one of the most convincing explanations.

21 cf. Leijonhufvud (1968, 1981). The co-ordination problem cannot generally be treated in models favouring microeconomic foundations because it is, in essence, macroeconomic.

22 A problem stressed by Benassy (1983, p. 140), similar to that found in the study of competitive temporary equilibrium, is that the determination of p_i and θ_i is simultaneous, while θ_i is also a function of p_i via σ_i. Another concept of equilibrium with endogenous prices has been defined by Grandmont and Laroque (1977). There prices are fixed by entrepreneurs at the beginning of the period and are not subject to revision within the period.

23 The proof of the existence of a K-equilibrium with flexible prices requires, however, beyond all the usual assumptions, a certain number of supplementary assumptions (Benassy, 1983).

24 'The trade union' determines the wage rate in an optimal fashion. But it is possible economic agents may wish to work more at the wage so determined.

25 A class of similar models, which begin from the very outset with the assumption that functions are kinked, has been presented by Negishi (1977, 1979).

26 The strong distinction established by Drazen (1980) between Benassy's and Hahn's model is very artificial. The processes of price and quantity determination are simultaneous in Hahn as they are in Benassy. It is thus not on this point, contrary to Drazen's analysis, that the models differ.

27 Hahn (1977b, c) has shown that, for conjectures that are 'locally' rational (the first derivatives of the conjecture functions are correct), an underemployment conjectural equilibrium would exist. For a discussion of the rationality of conjectures see Drazen (1980). But for reasons to be illustrated in the text, this question does not seem pertinent.

28 Even if a positive answer could be given, cf. notably Malinvaud (1977, 1980a, b).

29 This interpretation corresponds almost literally to Keynes's definition: 'The value of D [the proceeds which entrepreneurs expect to receive] at the point of the aggregate demand function, where it is intersected by the aggregate supply function, will be called *the effective demand*' (Keynes, 1936, p. 25).

30 The following could be a justification: *all* the parameters of the model would have to be derived from a programme of optimization by microeconomic agents. The consideration of the adaptation lag or the adjustment speed is external to that programme. This is true, but it does not allow the justification of any particular choice. Perhaps it may be necessary to recall that in a competitive model price determination proceeds not from 'individual experiment' but from 'market experiment', and that this is the work not of individual economic agents but of a totally disinterested institution, the auctioneer (Patinkin, 1956).

31 Adding a random variable not correlated to the information set to the conditional mathematical expectation gives a more general version (Sargent and Wallace, 1976), but this is rarely used in the literature.

32 Because functions are linear, solutions do not differ other than by a serially independent random term with zero mean.

33 This requirement of the model has itself been the subject of controversies (Taylor, 1975; Blanchard, 1976; B. Friedman, 1979; Arrow, 1978, 1980).

34 Even if the government does not announce its monetary policy, its effect will be neutral if all agents have a positive monetary balance. In fact, it is sufficient for agents to look at their own balances to discover parameter λ. For a scalar change of the quantity of external money to have real effects, it is, on the contrary, necessary that some agents should not have monetary balances. Since in Lucas's model the new generations do not have an initial monetary balance, this second condition is satisfied. This would seem the only source of non-neutrality in this type of model (see Grandmont, 1983, ch. 1).

35 For a proof of this result cf. Grandmont (1983, ch. 1). A similar line of reasoning is followed by Tobin (1980, ch. 3).

36 There are a number of reasons why changes in the quantity of money should not be neutral. They are both theoretical and institutional (cf. Fischer, 1980); generally they imply either that a change of monetary aggregates has distribution effects, or that it generates a change in the capital stock through its effect on the interest rate (Fischer, 1979; Fair, 1978).

37 By definition, an equilibrium is a saddle point if only one convergent path exists, all the other paths being divergent.

38 In fairness it should be recognized that these limitations have been generally admitted by the supporters of the new classical school, but in a manner and context whose purpose is to prove the superiority of their approach and the 'fatal defects' of alternative approaches (e.g. Lucas and Sargent, 1979; Barro, 1981; McCallum, 1979).

39 Lucas's pleas (1980b) for the Friedmanite programme are difficult to understand. It is true that his model (1972b) leads to a preference for a systematic rather than an arbitrary rule, and that the latter has effects only because of expectation errors that it provokes. But even from this viewpoint the result is not robust. Azariadis (1981) has shown, within the framework of Lucas's model, that from the viewpoint of economic welfare an arbitrary monetary policy could be superior to one of monetary norm.

40 A series of works are devoted to this question: cf., e.g., Fischer (1977, 1980); Taylor (1979, 1980); Hahn (1982).

41 The use of econometric models for short-term unconditional forecasts is not questioned by this reasoning since the problem of forecasting must be distinguished from that of simulation. In the case of simulation an external perturbation, i.e. the modification of statistical series representing one or many exogenous variables, implies a new series of decisions, and the decision-making role of the agent is not invariant with respect to his environment.

42 It has been shown above that the neutrality of money proposition should be distinguished from that of the homogeneity of excess demand functions. The latter is a necessary ingredient of a model based on rationality, but the former is *very specific* even in the framework of a purely neoclassical model.

References

Ackerlof, G. A. (1979) 'The case against conservative mcroeconomics: an inaugural lecture', *Economica*, vol. 46, August.

Ackerlof, G. A. (1980) 'A theory of social custom, of which unemployment may be one consequence', *Quarterly Journal of Economics*, vol. XCIV, June.

Alchian, A. (1970) 'Information costs, pricing and resource unemployment', in E. Phelps *et al.*, *Microeconomic Foundations of Employment and Inflation Theory*, W. W. Norton.

Arrow, K. J. (1959) 'Toward a theory of price adjustment', in M. Abramovitz (ed.), *The Allocation of Economic Resources*, Stanford University Press.

Arrow, K. J. (1978) 'The future and the present in economic life', *Economic Inquiry*, vol. XVI, April.

Arrow, K. J. (1980) 'Real and nominal values in economics', *The Public Interest*, special issue.

Arrow, K. J. and Hahn, F. H. (1971) *General Competitive Analysis*, Holden Day/Oliver & Boyd.

Azariadis, C. (1981) 'A reexamination of natural rate theory', *American Economic Review*, vol. 71, December.

Barro, R. J. (1976) 'Rational expectations and the role of monetary policy', *Journal of Monetary Economics*, vol. 2, January.

Barro, R. J. (1979) 'Second thoughts on Keynesian economics', *American Economic Review*, vol. 69, May.

Barro, R. J. (1981) 'The equilibrium approach to business cycles', in R. J. Barro, *Money, Expectations and Business Cycles: Essays in Macroeconomics*, Academic Press.

Barro, R. J. and Grossman, H. I. (1971) 'A general disequilibrium model of income and employment', *American Economic Review*, vol. 61, March.

Barro, R. J. and Grossman, H. I. (1976). *Money, Employment and Inflation*, Cambridge University Press.

Begg, D. K. H. (1982) *The Rational Expectations Revolution in Macroeconomics*, Phillip Allan.

Benassy, J. P. (1975) 'NeoKeynesian disequilibrium theory in a monetary economy', *Review of Economic Studies*, vol. 42, October.

Benassy, J. P. (1976) 'The disequilibrium approach to monopolistic price setting and general monopolistic equilibrium', *Review of Economic Studies*, vol. 43, February.

Benassy, J. P. (1977) 'On quantity signals and the foundations of effective demand theory', *Scandinavian Journal of Economics*, vol. 79, April.

Benassy, J. P. (1980) 'Developments in non-Walrasian economics and the microeconomic foundations of macroeconomics, CEPREMAP, November.

Benassy, J. P. (1983) *The Economics of Market Disequilibrium*, Academic Press.

Blanchard, O. J. (1976) 'The non-transition to rational expectations', mimeo, Massachusetts Institute of Technology.

Böhm, V. (1978) 'Disequilibrium dynamics in a simple macroeconomic model', *Journal of Economic Theory*, vol. 17, April.

Böhm, V. (1981) 'Inventories and money balances in a dynamic model with rationing', Caress Working Paper, no. 81-15.

Böhm, V. and Levine, J. P. (1979) 'Temporary equilibria with quantity rationing', *Review of Economic Studies*, vol. 46, April.

Burmeister, E. (1980) 'On some conceptual issues in rational expectations modelling', *Journal of Money, Credit and Banking*, vol. 12, Part II, November.

Clower, R. W. (1965) 'The Keynesian counter-revolution: a theoretical appraisal', in F. H. Hahn and F. Brechling (eds), *The Theory of Interest Rates*, Macmillan.

Davidson, P. (1977) 'Money and general equilibrium', *Economie Appliquée*, vol. XXX, October.

Debreu, G. (1974) 'Excess demand functions', *Journal of Mathematical Economics*, vol. 1.

Dehez, P. (1982) 'Stationary Keynesian equilibria', *European Economic Review*, vol. 19, October.

Dehez, P. and Drèze, J. (1982) 'On supply-constrained equilibria', Core discussion paper, no. 8249.

Drazen, A. (1980) 'Recent developments in macroeconomic disequilibrium theory', *Econometrica*, vol. 48, March.

Drèze, J. (1975) 'Existence of an exchange equilibrium under price rigidities', *International Economic Review*, vol. 16, July.

Fair, R. C. (1978) 'A criticism of one class of macroeconomic models with rational expectations', *Journal of Money, Credit and Banking*, vol. 10, November.

Fischer, S. (1977) 'Long-term contracts, rational expectations and the optimal money supply rule', *Journal of Political Economy*, vol. 85, February.

Fischer, S. (1979) 'Capital accumulation on the transition path in a monetary optimising economy', *Econometrica*, vol. 47, November.

Fischer, S. (1980) 'On activist monetary policy with rational expectations', in S. Fischer (ed.), *Rational Expectations and Economic Policy*, NBER/University of Chicago Press.

Fisher, F. M. (1981) 'Disequilibrium, awareness and the perception of new opportunities', *Econometrica*, vol. 49, March.

Fitoussi, J. P. and Georgescu-Roegen, N. (1980) 'Structure and involuntary unemployment', in E. Malinvaud and J. P. Fitoussi (eds), *Unemployment in Western Countries*, Macmillan.

Friedman, B. M. (1979) 'Optimal expectations and the extreme information assumptions of rational expectations models', *Journal of Monetary Economics*, vol. 5, January.

Friedman, M. (1968) 'The role of monetary policy', *American Economic Review*, vol. 58, March.

Friedman, M. (1970) 'A theoretical framework for monetary analysis', *Journal of Political Economy*, vol. 78, March–April.

Glustoff, E. (1968) 'On the existence of a Keynesian equilibrium', *Review of Economic Studies*, vol. 35, July.

Grandmont, J. M. (1973) 'on the short-run equilibrium in a monetary economy', in J. Drèze (ed.), *Allocations Under Uncertainty, Equilibrium and Optimality*, Macmillan.

Grandmont, J. M. (1977) 'Temporary general equilibrium theory', *Econometrica*, vol. 45, April.

Grandmont, J. M. (1983). *Money and Value; A Reconsideration of Classical and Neoclassical Monetary Theories*, Cambridge University Press.

Grandmont, J. M. and Laroque, G. (1973) 'Money in the pure consumption loan model', *Journal of Economic Theory*, vol. 6, August.

Grandmont, J. M. and Laroque, G. (1975) 'On money and banking', *Review of Economic Studies*, vol. 42, April.

Grandmont, J. M. and Laroque, G. (1977) 'On temporary Keynesian equilibrium', in G. C. Harcourt (ed.), *The Microeconomic Foundations of Macroeconomics*, Macmillan.

Grossman, H. J. (1980) 'Rational expectations, business cycles and government behavior', in S. Fisher (ed.), *Rational Expectations and Economic Policy*, University of Chicago Press.

Haavelmo, T. (1950) 'The notion of involuntary economic decisions', *Econometrica*, vol. 18, January.

Hahn, F. H. (1965) 'On some problems of proving the existence of equilibrium in a monetary economy', in F. H. Hahn and F. P. R. Brechling (eds), *The Theory of Interest Rates*, Macmillan.

Hahn, F. H. (1977a) 'Keynesian economics and general equilibrium theory: reflections on some current debates', in G. C. Harcourt (ed.), *The Microeconomic Foundation of Macroeconomics*, Macmillan.

Hahn, F. H. (1977b) 'Exercises in conjectural equilibria', *Scandinavian Journal of Economics*, vol. 79, April.

Hahn, F. H. (1977c) 'Unsatisfactory equilibria', IMSS Technical Report no. 247, Stanford University.

Hahn, F. H. (1978) 'On non-Walrasian equilibrium', *Review of Economic Studies*, vol. 45, February.

Hahn, F. H. (1980a) 'Unemployment from a theoretical viewpoint', *Economica*, vol. 47, August.

Hahn, F. H. (1980b) 'Monetarism and economic theory', *Economica*, vol. 47, February.

Hahn, F. H. (1980c) 'General equilibrium theory', *The Public Interest*, special issue: *The Crisis in Economic Theory*.

Hahn, F. H. (1982) *Money and Inflation*, Basil Blackwell.

Hart, O. (1979) 'A model of imperfect competition with Keynesian features', *Economic Theory Discussion Paper* no. 29, Cambridge University.

Heller, W. P. and Starr, R. M. (1979) 'Unemployment equilibrium with myopic complete information', *Review of Economic Studies*, vol. 46, April.

Hicks, J. (1937) 'Mr Keynes and the classics: a suggested interpretation', *Econometrica*, vol. 5, April.

Hicks, J. (1939) *Value and Capital*, Clarendon Press.

Hicks, J. (1965) *Capital and Growth*, Clarendon Press.

Hicks, J. (1977) *Economic Perspectives*, Clarendon Press.

Hicks, J. (1979) 'Review of E. R. Weintraub', *Microeconomic Foundations: The Compatibility of Microeconomics and Macroeconomics*, in *Journal of Economic Literature*, vol. 17, December.

Hildenbrand, K. and Hildenbrand, W. (1978) 'On Keynesian equilibria with unemployment and quantity rationing', *Journal of Economic Theory*, vol. 18, August.

Howitt, P. (1979) 'Evaluating the non-market-clearing approach', *American Economic Review*, vol. 69, May.

Kantor, R. (1979) 'Rational expectations and economic thought', *Journal of Economic Literature*, vol. 17, December.

Keynes, J. M. (1936) *The General Theory of Employment Interest and Money*, vol. VII of *The Collected Writings*, Macmillan for the Royal Economic Society.

Klein, L. R. (1947, 1966) *The Keynesian Revolution*, Macmillan.

Kuenne, R. E. (1963) *The Theory of General Equilibrium*, Princeton University Press.

Kurtz, M. (1982) 'Unemployment equilibrium in an economy with linked prices', *Journal of Economic Theory*, vol. 26, January.

Leijonhufvud, A. (1968) *On Keynesian Economics and the Economics of Keynes*, Oxford University Press.

Leijonhufvud, A. (1981) *Information and Coordination; Essays in Macroeconomic Theory*, Oxford University Press.

Lipsey, R. G. (1978) 'The place of the Phillips curve in macroeconomic models', in A. R. Bergstrom *et al.* (eds), *Stability and Inflation*, John Wiley.

Lucas, R. E. (1972a) 'Economic testing of the natural rate hypothesis', in O. Eckstein (ed.), *The Econometrics of Price Determination*, Board of Governors of the Federal Reserve System, Washington DC.

Lucas, R. E. (1972b) Expectations and the neutrality of money', *Journal of Economic Theory*, vol. 4, April.

Lucas, R. E. (1973) 'Some international evidence on output–inflation trade-offs', *American Economic Review*, vol. 63, June.

Lucas, R. E. (1976) 'Econometric policy evaluation: a critique', in K. Brunner and A. H. Meltzer (eds), *The Phillips Curve and Labor Markets*, North Holland.

Lucas, R. E. (1977) 'Understanding business cycles', in K. Brunner and A. H. Meltzer (eds), *Stabilization of the Domestic and International Economy*, vol. 5 of Carnegie-Rochester Series on Public Policy, North Holland.

Lucas, R. E. (1980a) 'Methods and problems in business cycle theory', *Journal of Money, Credit and Banking*, vol. 12, part 2, November.

Lucas, R. E. (1980b) 'Rule, discretion and the role of the economic advisor', in S. Fisher (ed.), *Rational Expectations and Economic Policy*, University of Chicago Press for the NBER.

Lucas, R. E. (1981) 'Tobin and monetarism: a review article', *Journal of Economic Literature*, vol. 19, June.

Lucas, R. E. and Rapping, L. A. (1970) 'Real wages, employment and inflation', in E. Phelps *et al.*, *Macroeconomic Foundations of Employment and Inflation Theory*, W. W. Norton.

Lucas, R. E. and Sargent, J. (1979) 'After Keynesian economics', *Federal Reserve Bank of Minneapolis Quarterly Review*, vol. 3, April.

Malinvaud, E. (1977) *The Theory of Unemployment Reconsidered*, Basil Blackwell.

Malinvaud, E. (1980a) 'Macroeconomic rationing of employment', in E. Malinvaud and J. P. Fitoussi (eds), *Unemployment in Western Countries*, Macmillan.

Malinvaud, E. (1980b) *Profitability and Unemployment*, Cambridge University Press and Maison des Sciences de l'Homme.

Malinvaud, E. and Younes, Y. (1977) 'Some new concepts for the microeconomic foundations of macroeconomics', in G. Harcourt (ed.), *The Microeconomic Foundations of Macroeconomics*, Macmillan.

McCallum, B. T. (1978) 'Price levels adjustments and the rational expectations approach to macroeconomic stabilisation policy', *Journal of Money, Credit and Banking*, vol. 10, November.

McCallum, B. T. (1979) 'The current state of the policy ineffectiveness debate', *American Economic Review*, vol. 69, May.

McCallum, B. T. (1980a) 'Rational expectations and macroeconomic stabilisation policy: an overview', *Journal of Money, Credit and Banking*, vol. 12, part 2, November.

McCallum, B. T. (1980b) 'Hahn's theoretical viewpoint on unemployment: a comment', *Economica*, vol. 47, August.

Modigliani, F. (1944) 'The monetary mechanism and its interaction with real phenomena', in A. Abel (ed.), *The Collected Essays of Franco Modigliani*, vol. 1: *Essay in Macroeconomics*, MIT Press.

Modigliani, F. (1977) 'The monetarist controversy, or should we forsake stabilization policies', *American Economic Review*, vol. 67, March.

Mortensen, D. T. (1970) 'A theory of wage and employment dynamics', in E. Phelps *et al.*, *Microeconomic Foundations of Employment and Inflation Theory*, W. W. Norton.

Muellbauer, J. and Portes, R. (1978) 'Macroeconomic models with quantity rationing', *Economic Journal*, vol. 88, December.

Neary, P. and Stiglitz, J. E. (1983) 'Towards a reconstruction of Keynesian economics: expectations and constrained equilibria', *Quarterly Journal of Economics* (forthcoming).

Negishi, T. (1961) 'Monopolistic competition and general equilibrium', *Review of Economic Studies*, vol. 28.

Negishi, T. (1977) 'Existence of an underemployment equilibrium', in G. Schwödiauer (ed.), *Equilibrium and Disequilibrium in Economic Theory*, D. Reidel.

Negishi, T. (1979) *Microeconomic Foundations of Keynesian Macroeconomics*, North Holland.

Patinkin, D. (1956, 1965) *Money, Interest and Prices*, Harper and Row.

Phelps, E. (1970) 'Money, wage dynamics and labor market equilibrium', in E. Phelps *et al.*, *Microeconomic Foundations of Employment and Inflation Theory*, W. W. Norton.

Phelps, E. *et al.* (1970) *Microeconomic Foundations of Employment and Inflation Theory*, W. W. Norton.

Pippard, B. (1980) 'Instability and chaos: physical models of everyday life', mimeo, Cambridge University.

Radner, R. (1968) 'Competitive equilibrium under uncertainty', *Econometrica*, vol. 36, January.

Radner, R. (1972) 'Existence of equilibrium plans, prices and price expectations in a sequence of markets', *Econometrica*, vol. 40, March.

Sargent, T. J. (1973) 'Rational expectations, the real rate of interest and the natural rate of unemployment', *Brookings Papers on Economic Activity*, vol. 2.

Sargent, T. J. (1976) 'A classical macroeconomic model for the United States', *Journal of Political Economy*, vol. 84, April.

Sargent, T. J. and Wallace, N. (1975) 'Rational expectations, the optimal monetary instrument and the optimal money supply role', *Journal of Political Economy*, vol. 83, April.

Sargent, T. J. and Wallace, N. (1976) 'Rational expectations and the theory of economic policy', *Journal of Monetary Economics*, vol. 2, April.

Shiller, R. J. (1978) 'Rational expectations and the dynamic structure of macro-economic models', *Journal of Monetary Economics*, vol. 4, January.

Solow, R. M. (1979) 'Alternative approaches to macroeconomic theory: a partial view', *Canadian Journal of Economics*, vol. 12, August.

Solow, R. M. (1980) 'On theories of unemployment', *American Economic Review*, vol. 70, March.

Sonnensheim, H. (1973) 'Do Walras's identity and continuity characterize the class of community excess demand functions?', *Journal of Economic Theory*, vol. 6, August.

Taylor, J. B. (1975) 'Monetary policy during the transition to rational expecta-tions', *Journal of Political Economy*, vol. 83, October.

Taylor, J. B. (1979) 'Staggered wage setting in a macroeconomic model', *American Economic Review*, vol. 69, May.

Taylor, J. B. (1980) 'Aggregate dynamics and staggered contracts', *Journal of Political Economy*, vol. 88, February.

Tobin, J. (1980) *Asset Accumulation and Economic Activity*, Basil Blackwell.

Tobin, J. (1981) 'The monetarist counter-revolution today – an appraisal', *Economic Journal*, vol. 91, March.

Tobin, J. and Buiter, K. (1976) 'Long-run effects of fiscal and monetary policies on aggregate demand', in J. Stein (ed.), *Monetarism*, North Holland.

Weintraub, E. R. (1979) *Microeconomic Foundations: The Compatibility of Microeconomics and Macroeconomics*, Cambridge University Press.

PART I
What is Wrong with IS–LM?

2

IS–LM: An Explanation

JOHN HICKS

The *IS–LM* diagram, which is widely, but not universally, accepted as a convenient synopsis of Keynesian theory, is a thing for which I cannot deny that I have some responsibility. It first saw the light in a paper of my own, 'Mr Keynes and the Classics' (1937), but it was actually written for a meeting of the Econometric Society in Oxford in September 1936, just eight months after the publication of *The General Theory* (Keynes, 1936). (There I used different lettering, but here I keep that which has become conventional.) And this is not my only connection with it; I also made use of it in some chapters (11-12) of my book *The Trade Cycle* (1950), and again in a paper that appears as 'The classics again' in my *Critical Essays* (1967).[1] I have, however, not concealed that, as time has gone on, I have myself become dissatisfied with the *IS–LM* diagram. I said, in my contribution to the Festschrift for Georgescu-Roegen, that 'that diagram is now much less popular with me than I think it still is with many other people' (1976, pp. 140-1). In the reconstruction of Keynesian theory that I published at about the same time (1974), it is not to be found. But I have not explained the reasons for this change of opinion, or of attitude. I shall try, in this paper, to do so.

This article was originally written for presentation to the Marshall Society in Cambridge, England, in November 1979 and was repeated at a symposium at the European University Institute, Florence, Italy, in May 1980. It has undergone considerable changes between, and since, those presentations, as a result of the discussions that took place on those occasions, and for other reasons. The present version is reprinted from *Journal of Post-Keynesian Economics*, vol. III, Winter 1980–81, by permission of M. E. Sharpe, Inc., White Plains, New York 10603.

I

I must begin with the old story. 'Mr Keynes and the Classics' was actually the fourth of the relevant papers that I wrote during those years. The third was the review of the *General Theory* that I wrote for the *Economic Journal*, a first impression which had to be written under pressure of time, almost at once on first reading of the book. But there were two others that I had written before I saw the *General Theory*. One is well known, my 'Suggestion for Simplifying the Theory of Money' (1935a), which was written before the end of 1934. The other, much less well known, is even more relevant. 'Wages and Interest: the Dynamic Problem' (1935b)[2] was a first sketch of what was to become the 'dynamic' model of *Value and Capital* (1939). It is important here because it shows (I think quite conclusively) that that model was already in my mind before I wrote even the first of my papers on Keynes.

I recognized immediately, as soon as I read the *General Theory*, that my model and Keynes's had some things in common. Both of us fixed our attention on the behaviour of an economy *during a period* – a period that had a past, which nothing that was done during the period could alter, and a future, which during the period was unknown. Expectations of the future would nevertheless affect what happened during the period. Neither of us made any assumption about 'rational expectations'; expectations, in our models, were strictly exogenous.[3] (Keynes made much more fuss over that than I did, but there is the same implication in my model also.) Subject to these *data* – the given equipment carried over from the past, the production possibilities within the period, the preference schedules, and the given expectations – the actual performance of the economy within the period was supposed to be determined, or determinable. It would be determined as an equilibrium performance, with respect to these data.

There was all this in common between my model and Keynes's; it was enough to make me recognize, as soon as I saw the *General Theory*, that his model was a relation of mine and, as such, one that I could warmly welcome. There were, however, two differences, on which (as we shall see) much depends.

The more obvious difference was that mine was a flexprice model, a perfect competition model, in which all prices were flexible, while in Keynes's the level of money wages (at least) was exogenously determined. So Keynes's was a model that was consistent with unemployment, while mine, in his terms, was a full-employment model.

I shall have much to say about this difference, but I may as well note, at the start, that I do not think it matters much. I did not think, even in 1936, that it mattered much. *IS–LM* was in fact a translation of Keynes's non-flexprice model into my terms. It seemed to me already that that could be done; but how it is done requires explanation.

The other difference is more fundamental; it concerns the length of the *period*. Keynes's (he said) was a 'short period', a term with connotations derived from Marshall; we shall not go far wrong if we think of it as a year. Mine was an 'ultra-short period'; I called it a week. Much more can happen in a year than in a week; Keynes has to allow for quite a lot of things to happen. I wanted to avoid so much happening, so that my (flexprice) markets could reflect propensities (and expectations) as they are at a moment. So it was that I made my markets open only on a Monday; what actually happened during the ensuing week was not to affect them. This was a very artificial device, not (I would think now) much to be recommended. But the point of it was to exclude the things that might happen, and must disturb the markets, during a period of finite length; and this, as we shall see, is a very real trouble in Keynes.

In the rest of this article, I shall take these two issues separately, beginning with the fixprice–flexprice question, which is the easier.

II

It will readily be understood, in the light of what I have been saying, that the idea of the *IS–LM* diagram came to me as a result of the work I had been doing on three-way exchange, conceived in a Walrasian manner. I had already found a way of representing three-way exchange on a two-dimensional diagram (to appear in due course in chapter 5 of *Value and Capital*). As it appears there, it is a piece of statics; but it was essential to my approach (as already appears in 'Wages and Interest: the Dynamic Problem') that static analysis of this sort could be carried over to 'dynamics' by re-definition of terms. So it was natural for me to think that a similar device could be used for the Keynes theory.

Keynes had three elements in his theory: the marginal efficiency of capital, the consumption function, and liquidity preference. The market for goods, the market for bonds and the market for money: could they not be regarded in my manner as a model of three-way exchange? In my three-way exchange I had two independent price parameters: the price of A in terms of C and the price of B in terms of C (for the price of A in terms of B followed from them). These two parameters were determined by the equilibrium of two markets, the market for A and the market for B. If these two markets were in equilibrium, the third must be also.

Keynes also appeared to have two parameters – his Y (income *in terms of wage units*) and r, the rate of interest. He made investment depend on r and saving on Y; so for each value of r there should be a value of Y that would keep saving equal to investment – excess demand on the market for goods then being zero. This gave a relation between r and Y that I expressed as the *IS* curve. The demand for money depended on Y (transactions balances) and on r (liquidity preference). So for any given supply of money (*in terms of wage units*) there should be a relation between r and Y that would keep the money 'market' in equilibrium. One did not have to bother about the market for 'loanable funds', since it appeared, on the Walras analogy, that if these two 'markets' were in equilibrium, the third must be also. So I concluded that the intersection of *IS* and *LM* determined the equilibrium of the system as a whole.

Now this was really, at that stage, no more than a conjecture, for I had not properly shown that the Walras analogy would fit. In Walras, all markets are cleared; but in *IS–LM* (following Keynes) the labour market is not cleared; there is excess supply of labour. Does this, by itself, upset the Walras model? I think that by now it is generally accepted that it does not. It will nevertheless be useful, for what follows, to check the matter over in detail.

In strictness, we now need four markets, since labour and goods will have to be distinguished. But before giving them those names, let us look at the matter in terms of a general Walrasian four-goods model.

We then say that commodities A, B, C and X are being traded, with X as standard (*numéraire*). Prices p_a, p_b, p_c are reckoned in terms of the standard; $p_x = 1$. Demands and supplies on the *ABC* markets are functions of the three prices. The three equations $S_a = D_a$ and so on are sufficient to determine the three prices. Further, since

$$S_x = p_a D_a + p_b D_b + p_c D_c, \quad D_x = p_a S_a + p_b S_b + p_c S_c$$

when the supply and demand equations are satisfied for *ABC*, that for X follows automatically.

There is just this one identical relation between the four equations. We could use it to eliminate the X equation, as just shown, or to eliminate any one of the other equations, while retaining the X equation. Thus the system of three prices for ABC can be regarded as determined by equations for ABC, or by equations for BCX, CAX or ABX.

Thus far Walras. But now suppose that one of the commodities is sold on a fixprice market, where the price is fixed in terms of the standard, but where the equation of supply and demand does not have to hold. The actual amount sold will be equal to the demand or to the supply, whichever is the lower. So let p_a be fixed, with the equation $D_a = S_a$ removed. The remaining (variable) prices can still be determined from the equations $S_b = D_b$, $S_c = D_c$, for the p_a that appears as a parameter in these equations is now a constant. If it turns out that at these prices $S_a > D_a$, it is only D_a that can actually be traded. When calculating S_x and D_x, we must use this *actual* D_a for both D_a and S_a. With that substitution, we have $S_x = D_x$, as before.

And it is still possible, using this construction, to let the equation for the standard, $S_x = D_x$, replace one of the equations otherwise used, as could be done in the all-round flexprice case. For with D_a substituted for S_a, $p_a(S_a - D_a) = 0$ is an identity. The only terms in $S_x - D_x$ that survive, on application of this identity, are those that relate to the flexprice commodities B and C. The sub-system of BCX will then work in the regular Walrasian manner. We can determine p_b and p_c from any pair of the three equations that are left.

In this way, the Walrasian analogy gets over its first hurdle; but there is another, close behind it, which may be considered more serious. We have so far been making demands and supplies depend only on prices; and for the pure case of multiple exchange with flexible prices, that may probably be accepted. But as soon as a fix-price market is introduced, it ceases to be acceptable. It must be supposed that the demands and supplies for B and C will be affected by what happens in the market for A. That can no longer be represented by the price, so it must be represented by the quantity sold. Assuming, as before, that there is excess supply in the A market, this is D_a. So demands and supplies for B and C will be functions of p_b, p_c and D_a. The BCX sub-system would then *not* be complete in itself; but the whole system, with D_a included as a parameter, would still work in the way that has been described.

We would then have three variables to be determined, p_b, p_c, and D_a – and four equations. They are the demand–supply equations for BCX (the X equation being constructed with the *actual* D_a, as before); and there is also the demand equation for D_a, which makes

D_a a function of p_b and p_c. As before, any one of the BCX equations can be eliminated. The system is determined, whichever equation we choose to eliminate.

The model is still very formal; but now it is the same kind of model as the *IS–LM* model. We could represent that as a three-way (ABX) model, in which there is just one price (p_b, which becomes the rate of interest) that is determined on a flexprice market, and one quantity (Y), which plays the part of D_a. I have deliberately taken a case which in the same formal terms is slightly more complicated, since I have admitted two flexprice markets, for B and for C. It may indeed be useful to show that there is, in principle, no difficulty in introducing a second flexprice market – or, for that matter, in introducing several. It could be useful, even for macroeconomic purposes, to introduce a second flexprice market – for instance, a market for foreign exchange.

But that is not the reason I have introduced the extra market. The important use of a four-way model, in this connection, is that it enables us to consider the market for goods and the market for labour separately. And when we take them separately, quite interesting things happen.

One could construct a model in which only the market for labour was a fixprice market, and in which not only the rate of interest but also the price (or price level) of finished products was flexible. That would fit very exactly into the scheme that has just been outlined, with demand–supply equations determining D_a (employment) and the two flexible prices p_b, p_c. It is possible that Keynes himself sometimes thought in terms of that sort of model (see, for example, Keynes, 1936, ch. 21); but it cannot be this that *IS–LM* is supposed to represent. For Y is taken to be an index not only of employment, but also of output, so the prices of products also are supposed to be fixed in terms of the standard; and it is hard to see how that can be justified unless the prices of products are derived from the wage of labour by some mark-up rule. But if that is so we have not one, but two, fixprice markets.

Say that A and B are fixprice markets, while C is flexprice. As long as we follow the Walrasian practice of working entirely in terms of price parameters, there is no trouble: p_a and p_b are then fixed, so that all demands and supplies are functions of the single variable p_c. p_c is determined on the market for C (or, equivalently, on the market for X) as before. And the actual amounts of A and B that are traded are D_a or S_a, D_b or S_b – whichever, at the equilibrium p_c, turns out to be the lower.

But now suppose that, as before, we change the parameters, making demands and supplies functions of D_a and D_b (assuming that there is excess supply in both markets), not of p_c only. One would at first say that at a (provisionally given) p_c, D_a would be a function of D_b and D_b of D_a; and there need be nothing circular about that. There are just these two 'curves' in the $(D_a D_b)$ plane (like supply and demand curves); at their intersection, the equilibrium is determined.

It must be this that, in the *IS–LM* model, is supposed to happen. We are now to take A to be the labour market, C the market for loanable funds (as before), and B the market for finished products (consumption goods and investment goods not being, so far, distinguished). p_a is the fixed money wage; p_b, the fixed price level of the finished products; p_c, the rate of interest, the only price that is left to be determined on a flexprice market.

How, then, do we identify the 'curves'? One, which makes D_b (effective demand for products) a function of D_a (employment), is easy to find in Keynes. D_b depends on D_a, since the consumption component of D_b increases when employment increases (the consumption function), while the investment component depends on the rate of interest, provisionally given. There is no trouble about that. But what of the other 'curve' – the dependence of D_a on D_b, of employment on effective demand? Keynes took it for granted that they must go together, but the matter needs looking into. For it is here that there is a danger of going seriously wrong by neglecting time.

III

It is not true, of course, that time has been wholly neglected. As I said at the beginning, all the prices and quantities that have figured in the analysis must belong to a period; the past (before the period) and the future (beyond the period) have always been playing their regular parts. What has been neglected is the flow of time within the period. It is here that the length of the period is important.

In my own version ('Wages and Interest: the Dynamic Problem' or *Value and Capital*), the period ('week') was kept very short, so that little could happen within it. The actual outputs of products, and probably also the actual input of labour, would be largely predetermined. What could vary, considerably, would be prices. So for the study of price formation on flexprice markets, the 'week' had something to be said for it.[4] But that was not what Keynes was interested in; so he had to have a longer period.

It is not unreasonable to suppose that the prices that are established in flexprice markets, during a 'week' (or even at a point of time) do reflect the expectations of traders, their liquidity positions and so on. That is to say (it is equivalent to saying), we may fairly reckon that these markets, with respect to these data, are in equilibrium. And one could go on, as we have in fact been seeing, even while maintaining the 'week' interpretation, to admit that there are some markets that are fixprice markets, in which demands and supplies do not have to be equal. Then it is only to the markets that are flexprice markets that the equilibrium rule applies. Now it would be quite hard to say, in terms of such a model, that effective demand would determine employment. It is so tempting to say that there can be no output without labour input, so that an increase in demand must increase employment (as Keynes effectively did). But the question is not one of the relation between input and output, in general; it is a question of the relation between current demand and current input, both in the current period. It is at once shown, on the 'week' interpretation, that current output is largely predetermined; while, if the price of output is fixed, current demand may be greater or less than current output (stocks being decumulated or accumulated). How, then, is current input to be determined? We can only make it determinate, as a function of current demand, if we can bring ourselves to introduce some *rule*, according to which the extent of excess demand (or supply) in the current period will affect the employment that is offered, again in the current period. If we have such a rule, we can complete the circle, and show, in the current period, effective demand and employment simultaneously determined.

It is quite a question whether we would be justified, in general, in imposing such a rule.[5] For the effect on current input of excess demand or supply in the product market is surely a matter of the way in which the excess is interpreted by decision-makers. An excess that is expected to be quite temporary may have no effect on input; it is not only the current excess but the expectation of its future that determines action. It may be useful, on occasion, to suspend these doubts, and so to make models in which current input depends on excess demands (or supplies) in the product markets according to some rule. But one can hardly get a plausible rule while confining attention to what happens within a single period. So it would seem that the proper place for such a proceeding is in sequential models, composed of a succession of periods, in each of which the relevant

$$\frac{\$Y}{LM} = \frac{1}{L^2}$$

$$\frac{\$Y}{L} = \boxed{\frac{M}{\alpha^2}}$$

parameters have to be determined; there is then room for linkages between the periods, and so for lags. I have myself made some attempts at the construction of such models.[6] I think they have their uses, but they are not much like *IS–LM*.

If one is to make sense of the *IS–LM* model while paying proper attention to time, one must, I think, insist on two things: (1) that the period in question is a relatively long period, a 'year' rather than a 'week'; and (2) that, because the behaviour of the economy over that 'year'[7] is to be *determined* by propensities and such-like data, it must be assumed to be, in an appropriate sense, *in equilibrium*. This clearly must not imply that it is an all-round flexprice system; the exogenously fixed money wage and (as we have seen) the exogenously fixed prices of products must still be retained. But it is not only the market for funds, but also the product market, that must be assumed to be in equilibrium.

Though the prices of products are fixed, it is not necessary to suppose that there is disequilibrium in the product market. Even at the fixed price and fixed wage, when these are maintained over the relatively long period, it will pay producers to adjust supply to demand, as far as they can. For a loss is incurred in producing output that cannot be sold, and a profit is forgone when output that could profitably be sold is not produced. There are problems of adjustment, of which sequential analysis can take account; but there may be purposes for which it is legitimate to leave them to one side. We should then assume that the product markets, during the 'year', are in equilibrium and remain in equilibrium. And since it is to be continuing equilibrium, maintained throughout the 'year', this must mean that plans (so far as they relate to the proceedings of the year) are being carried through without being disturbed.

It is not, I think, inconsistent to suppose that the product markets are in equilibrium, while the labour market is not in equilibrium. For although there are some possibilities for adjusting supply to demand in the case of unemployment on the labour market (even while prices and wages remain unchanged), as by withdrawal of elderly labour from the market, or by departure of migrants, they are surely less than the corresponding possibilities in the market for products. A model that permits excess supply in the labour market, but no product market disequilibrium, is not inconsistent.

Once we allow ourselves to assume that product markets remain in equilibrium, things become easier. For once we assume that production plans, during the period, are carried through consistently, we have the relation between current input during the period, and current output during the period (which has been made equal to effective demand within the period) for which we have been looking. There are some difficulties about production processes that were begun before the commencement of the period, and others that will not be completed at the end of the period, but these, perhaps, may be overlooked. We can then proceed to the two 'curves' in the $(D_a D_b)$ plane, by which employment and effective demand are simultaneously determined.

The goal is reached, but at a considerable price. For how, after all, can this equilibrium assumption be justified? I do not think it can be justified for all purposes, maybe not for the most important purposes; but I have come to think that there is one purpose for which it may sometimes be justified. I have described this purpose in chapter 6 of my book *Causality in Economics* (1979); an abstract of the argument of that chapter may be given here.

We are to confine attention to the problem of explaining the past, a less exacting application than prediction of what will happen or prescription of what should happen, but surely one that comes first. If we are unable to explain the past, what right have we to attempt to predict the future? I find that concentration on explanation of the past is quite illuminating.

We have, then, facts before us; we know or can find out what, in terms of the things in which we are interested, did actually happen in some past year (say, the year 1975). In order to explain what happened, we must confront these facts with what we think would have happened if something (some alleged cause) had been different. About that, since it did not happen, we can have no factual information; we can only deduce it with the aid of a theory, or model. And since the theory is to tell us what would have happened, the variables in the model must be determined. And that would seem to mean that the model, in some sense, must be in equilibrium.

Applying these notions to the *IS–LM* construction, it is only the point of intersection of the curves that makes any claim to representing what actually happened (in our '1975'). Other points on either of the curves – say, the *IS* curve – surely do not represent, make no claim to represent, what actually happened. They are theoretical constructions, which are supposed to indicate what *would have happened* if the rate of interest had been different. It does not seem farfetched to suppose that these positions are equilibrium positions, representing the equilibrium that corresponds to a different rate of interest. If we cannot take them to be equilibrium positions, we cannot say much about them. But, as the diagram is drawn, the *IS* curve passes through the point of intersection; so the point of intersection appears to be a point on the curve; thus it also is an equilibrium position. That, surely, is quite hard to take. We know that in 1975 the system was not in equilibrium. There were plans that failed to be carried through as intended; there were surprises. We have to suppose that, for the purpose of the analysis on which we are engaged, these things do not matter. It is sufficient to treat the economy, as it actually was in the year in question, as if it were in equilibrium. Or, what is perhaps equivalent, it is permissible to regard the departures from equilibrium, which we admit to have existed, as being random. There are plenty of instances in applied economics, not only in the application of *IS-LM* analysis, where we are accustomed to permitting ourselves this way out. But it is dangerous. Though there may well have been some periods of history, some 'years', for which it is quite acceptable, it is just at the turning points, at the most interesting 'years', where it is hardest to accept it.

What I have been saying applies, most directly, to the *IS* curve; what of the other?

In elementary presentations of the *IS-LM* model, the *LM* curve is supposed to be drawn up on the assumption of a given stock of money (the extension to a stock of money given in terms of wage units comes in only when the level of money wages is allowed to vary, so I shall leave it to one side). It is, however, unnecessary to raise those puzzling questions of the definition of money, which in these monetarist days have become so pressing. For I may allow myself to point out that it was already observed in 'Mr Keynes and the Classics' that we do not need to suppose that the curve is drawn up on the assumption of a given stock of money. It is sufficient to suppose that there is (as I said)

a given monetary system – that up to a point, but only up to a point, monetary authorities will prefer to create new money rather than allow interest rates to rise. Such a generalised (*LM*) curve will then slope upwards only gradually – the elasticity of the curve depending on the elasticity of the monetary system (in the ordinary monetary sense). (p. 157)[8]

That is good as far as it goes, but it does not go far enough. For here, again, there is a question of time reference; and it is a very tricky question. The relation that is expressed in the *IS* curve is a flow relation, which (as we have seen) must refer to a period, such as the year we have been discussing. But the relation expressed in the *LM* curve is, or should be, a stock relation, a balance sheet relation (as Keynes so rightly insisted). It must therefore refer to a point of time, not to a period. How are the two to be fitted together?

It might appear, at first sight, that we must proceed by converting the stock relation into a relation that is to hold for the period – treating it, in some way, as an average of balance sheet relations over the period. But this has to be rejected, not merely because it is clumsy, but because it does not get to the point. It has been shown that, if we adopt the equilibrium interpretation, on the *IS* side the economy must be treated *as if* it were in equilibrium over the period; that means, on the *IS* side, that the economy must remain in flow equilibrium, with demands and supplies for the flows of outputs remaining in balance. It would be logical to maintain that on the *LM* side the economy must be treated similarly. There must be a *maintenance* of stock equilibrium.

I have examined the relation between stock equilibrium and flow equilibrium in chapter 8 of my *Capital and Growth* (1965), where I have shown that the maintenance of stock equilibrium over the period implies the maintenance of flow equilibrium over the period; so it is a sufficient condition for the maintenance of equilibrium over time, in the fullest sense. A key passage is the following:

Equilibrium over time requires the maintenance of stock equilibrium; this should be interpreted as meaning that there is stock equilibrium not only at the beginning and end of the period, but throughout its course. Thus, when we regard a 'long' period as a sequence of 'short' periods, the 'long' period can only be in equilibrium over time if every 'short' period within it is in equilibrium over time. Expectations must be kept self-consistent; so there can be no revision of expectations at the junction between one 'short' period and its successor. The system is in stock equilibrium at each of these junctions; and is in stock equilibrium with respect to these consistent expectations. That can only be possible if expectations – with respect to demands that accrue within the 'long' period – are *right*. Equilibrium over time thus implies consistency between expectations and realisations within the period. It is only expectations of the further future that are arbitrary (exogenous) as they must be. (pp. 92–3)[9]

That is the formal concept of full equilibrium over time; I do not see how it is to be avoided. But for the purpose of generating an *LM* curve, which is to represent liquidity preference, it will not do without amendment. For there is no sense in liquidity, unless expectations are uncertain. But how is an uncertain expectation to be realized? When the moment arrives to which the expectation refers, what replaces it is fact, fact that is not uncertain.

I have suggested, in my most recent book (1979), a way of cutting the knot, but I do not have much faith in it.

We must evidently refrain from supposing that the expectations as they were before April (some date in the middle of the 'year') of what is to happen after April, were precise expectations, single-valued expectations; for in a model with single-valued expectations, there can be no question of liquidity. And we must also refrain from the conventional representation of uncertain expectations in terms of mean and variance, since that makes them different in kind from the experiences which are to replace them. There is, however, a third alternative. Suppose we make them expectations that the values that are expected, of the variables affecting decisions, will fall within a particular range. This leaves room for liquidity, since there are no certain expectations of what is going to happen; but it also makes it possible for there to be an equilibrium, in the sense that what happens falls within the expected range. A state of equilibrium is a state in which there are no surprises. What happens (during the period) falls sufficiently within the range of what is expected for no revision of expectations to be necessary. (p. 85)

As far as I can see, that is the only concept of equilibrium over time[10] that leaves room for liquidity.

IV

I accordingly conclude that the only way in which *IS–LM* analysis usefully survives – as anything more than a classroom gadget, to be superseded, later on, by something better – is in application to a particular kind of causal analysis, where the use of equilibrium methods, even a drastic use of equilibrium methods, is not inappropriate. I have deliberately interpreted the equilibrium concept, to be used in such analysis, in a very stringent manner (some would say a pedantic manner), not because I want to tell the applied economist, who uses such methods, that he is in fact committing himself to anything that must appear to him to be so ridiculous, but because I want to ask him to try to assure himself that the divergences between reality and the theoretical model that he is using to explain it are no more than divergences that he is entitled to overlook. I am quite prepared to believe that there are cases where he is entitled to overlook them. But the issue is one that needs to be faced in each case.

When one turns to questions of policy, looking toward the future instead of the past, the use of equilibrium methods is still more suspect. For one cannot prescribe policy without considering at least the possibility that policy may be changed. There can be no change of policy if everything is to go on as expected – if the economy is to remain in what (however approximately) may be regarded as its *existing* equilibrium. It may be hoped that, after the change in policy, the economy will somehow, at some time in the future, settle into what may be regarded, in the same sense, as a new equilibrium; but there must necessarily be a stage before that equilibrium is reached. There must always be a problem of traverse. For the study of a traverse, one has to have recourse to sequential methods of one kind or another.[11]

Notes

1 The date of this latter paper is really 1958, when it appeared, in an earlier version, in the *Economic Journal* as a review of Patinkin. I still believe that the use I made of *IS-LM* in that paper is perfectly legitimate. I am much less sure about the version in *The Trade Cycle* (1950).

2 The paper is reprinted in the supplement that was added to the second edition of my *Theory of Wages* (1963).

3 It is true that when I came to 'Mr Keynes and the Classics' I did propose to make investment depend on current output (just as Kaldor was to do, three years later, in his 'Model of the Trade Cycle', 1940). But I have never regarded this as an essential part of the *IS-LM* construction. I have fully accepted, in later work, that a capital stock adjustment principle, or some equivalent, is a better expression of what one had in mind. But whatever view one takes about this, it is still the case that it has never been intended, in any of the versions for which I am responsible, that investment changes should be entirely explicable by changes in output, of whatever sort. Even in my *Trade Cycle* book (1950), there was autonomous investment. There was always a residual element, depending on expectations, and many other things, which could vary independently.

4 No more than something. I have myself become pretty critical of the *Value and Capital* temporary equilibrium method when applied to flow markets. (I do not question its validity for the analysis of markets in stocks.) See chapter 6 of my *Capital and Growth* (1965).

5 My mind goes back to a conversation I had, a few years ago, with a distinguished economist, who might at an earlier date have been reckoned to be a Keynesian. I was saying to him that I had come to regard J. S. Mill as the most undervalued economist of the nineteenth century. He said, 'Yes, I think I understand. *Demand for commodities is not demand for labour.* It is true, after all.'

6 In particular, in *Capital and Growth* (1965, chs 7-10).

7 The *year* must clearly be long enough for the firm to be 'free to revise its decisions as to how much employment to offer' (Keynes, 1936, p. 47, n. 1).

8 In the reprint of this paper in my *Critical Essays* (1967), the passage appears on p. 140.

9 I have made a few minor alterations in wording to make it possible to extract the passage quoted from the rest of the chapter.

10 I should here make an acknowledgement to G. L. S. Shackle, who in much of his work has been feeling in this direction.

11 I have paid no attention, in this paper, to another weakness of *IS-LM* analysis, of which I am fully aware; for it is a weakness that it shares with the *General Theory* itself. It is well known that, in later developments of Keynesian theory, the long-term rate of interest (which does figure, excessively, in Keynes's own presentation and is presumably represented by the *r* of the diagram) has been taken down a peg from the position it appeared to occupy in Keynes. We now know that it is not enough to think of the rate of interest as the single link between the financial and industrial sectors of the economy; for that really implies that a borrower can borrow as much as he likes at the rate of interest charged, no attention being paid to the security offered. As soon as one attends to questions of security, and to the financial intermediation that arises out of them, it becomes apparent that the dichotomy between the two curves of the *IS-LM* diagram must not be pressed too hard.

The modern 'post-Keynesian' view of interest takes its origin from R. F. Kahn (1953). But I have done a good deal of work on it myself, in chapter 23 of *Capital and Growth* (1965), in lecture 3 of 'The Two Triads' (1967), in the second chapter of *The Crisis in Keynesian Economics* (1974) and in the section on Keynes in *Economic Perspectives* (1977, pp. 77ff).

References

Hicks, J. R. (1932) *The Theory of Wages*, London, Macmillan (2nd edn, 1963).

Hicks, J. R. (1935a) 'Suggestion for simplifying the theory of money', *Economica*, vol. 3.

Hicks, J. R. (1935b) 'Wages and interest: the dynamic problem', *Economic Journal*, vol. 3.

Hicks, J. R. (1937) 'Mr Keynes and the classics', *Econometrica*, vol. 5.

Hicks, J. R. (1939) *Value and Capital*, Oxford University Press.

Hicks, J. R. (1950) *The Trade Cycle*, Oxford University Press.

Hicks, J. R. (1965) *Capital and Growth*, Oxford University Press.

Hicks, J. R. (1967) *Critical Essays in Monetary Theory*, Oxford University Press.

Hicks, J. R. (1974) *The Crisis in Keynesian Economics*, New York, Basic Books.

Hicks, J. R. (1976) 'Some questions of time in economics', in A. M. Tang *et al.* (eds), *Evolution, Welfare and Time in Economics*, Lexington, Mass., Lexington Books.

Hicks, J. R. (1977) *Economic Perspectives*, Oxford University Press.

Hicks, J. R. (1979) *Causality in Economics*, New York, Basic Books.

Kaldor, N. (1940) Model of the trade cycle', *Economic Journal*, vol. 50.

Kahn, R. F. (1953) 'Some notes on liquidity preference', *Manchester School*.

Keynes, J. M. (1936) *The General Theory of Employment, Interest and Money*, New York, Harcourt Brace.

3

What was the Matter with IS–LM?

AXEL LEIJONHUFVUD

I

At a conference on Recent Developments in Macroeconomics, elementary *IS–LM* might be a somewhat unexpected topic. *IS–LM*, after all, has been around for a while. It ruled research for 30 years or more, and, in the teaching of macroeconomics, a better mousetrap has still to be invented. For the last 15 years or so, however, it has been out of favour even with many economists who do not quite know what to put in its place. And in the last decade, theoretical research in macroeconomics has moved away from this frame of reference.

Why are we bent on abandoning *IS–LM*? This would seem to be a question to which we ought to have a clear answer. An answer is needed for the appraisal of 'Recent Developments'. Do fixprice temporary general equilibrium models solve (or successfully avoid) the problems we had with *IS–LM*? Do rational expectations models?

Well – what were those problems?

II

Different people are apt to have different answers to that question. Every teacher of macroeconomics has his own list of 'troubles' with *IS–LM*. But almost all of those one hears frequently mentioned are

The argument of this paper is a subsidiary theme of my 'The Wicksell Connection: Variations on a Theme'; cf. Leijonhufvud (1981).

surely remediable deficiencies. Taking inventory of the most popular complaints does not seem a promising tack, therefore.

My title does *not* ask what's *wrong* with *IS-LM*. We are not looking for some simple error or omission. Omissions would have been remedied long ago. Fatal error is inconsistent with the long dominance of the framework. Yet, somehow, *IS-LM* does not do what a good model is supposed to do; it is not dependable in producing the right answers to questions in the hands of students (for example), who may not yet understand all that much economics but do know their algebra. It is a good vehicle for demonstrating certain relationships, which is why we continue to use it. But some questions are more easily understood or analysed without it than with it. In the end, it is probably not a short-cut to understanding macroeconomics; for knowing when to use it and when not to rely on it seems to be more difficult than the subject matter itself. Even the best economists can go wrong with *IS-LM* on occasion.

In my opinion, *IS-LM* has served us ill in three long-lasting controversies.

1   In the *Keynes and the classics* controversy, *IS-LM* produced, in the end, widespread agreement on the wrong answer; namely, that Keynes was merely doing orthodox economics with rigid wages (cf., e.g., Leijonhufvud, 1969, Lecture 1).[1]
2   *IS-LM* was used to deny that the issues of the *loanable funds versus liquidity preference* controversy were of serious consequence to general macrotheory.[2] This was a mistake.
3   In the course of the *monetarist* controversy, *IS-LM* has proved a less than helpful framework for producing agreement between the two sides on what the empirically important issues are.[3]

I will try not to bore the reader with a rehash of my views on controversy 1. Some observations on the second point will be made. But this paper will deal mainly with the Monetarist controversy, as seen through *IS-LM* glasses darkly.

III

There are, speaking somewhat simplistically, two broad approaches to macroeconomics today. In one, which I have elsewhere called the 'spanner-in-the-works' approach, co-ordination failures are explained as the consequence of rigidities in the economic system which prevent it from adjusting appropriately to parametric disturbances. For the individual agents of the system, the obstacle to appropriate adjustment may be coercion or past commitment to a (possibly implicit) contract or to a particular structure of physical capital. When this approach is being followed, it is usually not an important issue whether agents do or do not correctly perceive the potential gains from trade that they are in any case prevented from exploiting. Since this is so, the standard conceptual apparatus of static equilibrium theory – which assumes that agents have full information about their opportunities – may as well be utilized. Economists of this persuasion are consequently less likely to question the adequacy of standard neo-Walrasian theory as a micro-foundation for macroeconomics, and also less likely to see any reason why *IS–LM* should not serve perfectly well, at least for the proper care and feeding of undergraduates.

In the other approach, which we may cheerfully call the 'mud-in-the-eye' approach, co-ordination failures are explained as the consequence of the failure of agents correctly and completely to perceive the opportunities present in the system. Thus, 'stickiness' of certain prices, for example, is interpreted as being due not to constraints on price-setters, but instead to their ignorance of changes in relevant market conditions. Economists who try to follow this approach find that they make lots of trouble for themselves, for all the nuts and bolts and tricks of standard models are apt to be fashioned on the assumption that agents do know market conditions. So this group has problems with static price theory and is also likely to have problems with *IS–LM*.

Perhaps it would be better to talk of 'emphases' rather than 'approaches', for the two are obviously not mutually exclusive. In pursuing, for instance, the incomplete information approach as far as it will go, one need not be committed to the belief that the world is free of institutional or other rigidities of significant consequence.

Here, however, the question of the title will be discussed altogether from the incomplete information perspective.

IV

It is sometimes complained that *IS–LM* is 'too static'. As we will see later, however, one might, with at least equal justice, voice the complaint that 'it is not as static as it seems'. *IS–LM*, as it is most frequently utilized, is neither static nor dynamic. It is a 'short-run period model' – the accepted term for a static model with which one tries to do dynamic analysis. We had better clarify its status in relation to the two concept pairs 'static–dynamic' and 'long run–short run'.

The most widely accepted definition of dynamics in economics is the one due to Sir John Hicks: when the *quantities* that appear in our model must be *dated*, we are doing dynamics. For present purposes at least, I would like to amend the Hicksian definition to read: when we must *date* the *decisions* taken by various agents, we are doing dynamics. In statics, then, we need not date decisions – *because it does not matter in what sequence they are made*.

The temporal order of decisions is of analytical significance if, and only if, transactors have to act on incomplete information. In models where agents are assumed to have complete information, all choices are made at the same time. The multi-period general equilibrium model is the best example. It is 'dynamic' by Hicks's definition, since an infinite number of future periods adds as many dimensions to its commodity space. It is 'static' by the present definition, since the opportunities and preferences defined over this space pose just one choice for each agent and since the simultaneous market reconciliation of the choices of all agents is provided for. Everything is decided simultaneously at the origin of time in this construction.

The well-known 'cobweb' model illustrates the opposite case. Here, consumers and producers are assumed to take turns making decisions. On odd-numbered dates, consumers get to set a demand price on the output that has been produced. On even-numbered dates, producers must choose their outputs for the next period. The system oscillates because, at the time when producers have to commit themselves, they do not have, nor are they able to anticipate, the information most pertinent to the output decision: namely, the price that it will fetch. If we provide the producers with sufficient additional information – for example by putting a futures market into the model, or by assuming rational expectations that will substitute for such a market – they will find the market equilibrium directly.[4] The dynamic behaviour of the system becomes of no interest. The exact sequence of events no longer matters. The static supply-and-demand cross tells us everything we want to know.

One further illustration will help to suggest approximately where one might draw the line between 'complete' (or 'full') and 'incomplete' information. Arrow and Debreu generalized the metastatic neo-Walrasian model to deal with a probabilistically uncertain future. In their famous contingency market model, it is also true that all choices are made at the origin of time. I would like to subsume uncertain knowledge of this kind, therefore, under 'complete' information. But can this be justified?

In the Arrow–Debreu model, agents plan for all possible futures. No matter what the future brings, they have anticipated it perfectly and have concluded the contracts that are optimal to this contingency. All they learn, therefore, as the future moves into the present, is what particular Markovian railroad track the world is fated to run out. In a more fundamental sense, they have nothing to learn. They do not learn, for example, what it is like to grow old; that is, they do not 'discover' anything about themselves (and their preferences) that they had not already anticipated. In particular, they do not learn anything about the economic system that they did not already know. Their *understanding* does not change.[5]

Processes of this type are *equilibria* in the sense suggested by Hahn, in that further experience with market interaction will not teach agents anything that significantly alters their beliefs.[6] We may note also that the rational expectations approach, which assumes that agents fully understand the world that they inhabit, has produced a class of equilibrium models of the business cycle. Lucas explicitly interprets business cycles as the period-by-period revelation of a particular Arrow–Debreu contingent-claim time-path (cf. Lucas, 1980). And preceding both Hahn and Lucas, we have Hicks (1965): 'Equilibrium over time requires ... (that) there can be no revision of expectations at the junction between one "short" period and its successor' (pp. 92–3; also cited by Hicks in chapter 2 above).

The older theories of business cycles were generally not equilibrium theories by these criteria. It is for the representation of these 'dynamic' or 'disequilibrium' theories that *IS–LM* has been so much utilized. In trying to understand these theories from the incomplete information standpoint, it may then be a good idea to examine the *sequence* of interactions that lead up to *IS–LM* solution states.

V

In the 'long run' of price theory, all adjustments have taken place. In the 'short run', some adjustments 'have not had time' to be completed. Originally, in Marshall, the distinctive characteristic of the short run was that stocks need not be stationary but that net investment or disinvestment may be going on. Except for the adjustment of stocks, all activities were 'equilibrated' in the Marshallian short run. More recently, new short-run notions have begun to proliferate in the literature to fit all sorts of incomplete adjustment cases.

For macroeconomics, Marshall's long run does not seem to be the most useful full-adjustment benchmark. Since, most of the time, we are dealing with growing economies, the stationarity condition is inappropriate. An economy travelling on an equilibrium growth-path is 'fully adjusted' as far as the co-ordination of economic activities is concerned. If we are to be able to define what 'goes wrong' with the adjustment of the system, we need a clear conception of what 'full adjustment' would entail. So what should this benchmark be like?

The suggestion here, of course, is that it should be complete or *full information.* This term should *not* evoke notions of perfect foresight or costless information: rather, it should convey the sense of a situation in which agents are not going to learn anything new or surprising from continued market interaction.[7] In a full information state, agents have learned all that can be (profitably) learned about their environment and about each other's behaviour. In economies that are not hampered by rigidities, adjustments will then be complete; people are not going to change their behaviour. Full information states are equilibria in this sense. By the same token, incomplete information states are, of course, 'disequilibria', in the sense that, when people proceed to interact in markets on the basis of the information they possess, some of them will discover that they are acting on incorrect (and unprofitable) premises.

It would be a mistake, I feel, to press the badly used and badly worn Marshallian 'long run'/'short run' terms into the further service of covering also the 'full information state'/'incomplete information state' concepts.[8] Marshall had in mind the actual creation and installation, or depreciation and wearing out, of physical capital as the adjustments needed to bring about a stationary state. These are processes that necessarily take a *long time* – 'real', calendar time. We are concerned not with stationarity, but with the co-ordination of activities. The degree to which co-ordination is achieved depends upon the state of knowledge and convergence to full co-ordination on the speed of learning. Learning can be sometimes fast and sometimes slow.

To illustrate the point, consider the complaint voiced with some frequency by Keynesians in the course of the monetarist controversy: 'The trouble with Friedman is that he takes propositions that we all agree are true in the long run and uses them as if they were true in the short run.' What does it mean? What we all agree to be true in the long run is that money is neutral. In the long run, therefore, nominal income is proportional to the money stock. Friedman has a monetarist theory of nominal income in the short run. Keynesians object to it because they do not think money stock policy is as effective and reliable as this would imply.[9]

Friedman might presumably say the same thing about Lucas (or Sargent, Wallace, and Barro): 'The trouble with Lucas is that he takes propositions that I agree are true in the long run . . .', etc. What would this mean? In Friedman's theory, the long-run Phillips curve is vertical, so that monetary policy has only price level effects in the long run. In Lucas's theory, anticipated monetary policy is neutral right away. Friedman would object because he does not believe anticipated monetary policy to be without consequence for real variables in the short run.

When Sam played it again (fans of *Casablanca* will remember), his words were

. . . the fundamental things apply
As time goes by.

The trouble here is that the 'fundamental things' might apply without much time at all going by.[10] It depends upon how much people understand and what information they receive. In the two cases just mentioned, Friedman's transactors are assumed to *know more* than Keynesians think is reasonable, and to *know less* than Lucas thinks it reasonable to assume for his transactors.

This last statement could stand some more explanation. But here we are not interested in the transmission of monetary impulses for its own sake, but only in order to find out what is the matter with *IS-LM*. There are a number of things to be done before we can return to the transmission question and look at it from the *IS-LM* angle.

VI

Full-information macroeconomics (FIM) would be a useful branch of the subject. We may not be terribly fascinated with a kind of macroeconomics in which little, if anything, ever goes wrong. But FIM would be useful as a benchmark construction. Its main purpose would be to define the adjustments that must take place if the system is to adapt fully following some disturbance, such as a shift of the investment function or a change in the money supply. Knowing this is helpful in trying to define exactly what is the trouble assumed to occur in various macro-theories in which much, if not everything, always goes wrong.

Use of FIM constructions, on the other hand, does not commit us to the belief that the system will always or normally adapt smoothly and rapidly no matter what the disturbance; nor does it force us to preclude the very rapid convergence of the economy on full-information equilibrium in certain cases. We do not want invariably to associate the notion of an FIM state with either the short run or the long.

For present purposes, we want an FIM model that will match the structure of a simple *IS-LM* model. For present purposes, also, it is not necessary (fortunately) to derive and justify the properties of the FIM model in any detail. It will be all right to 'suppose' a system with certain FIM properties, and then look at it through its *IS-LM* version. Our FIM model should, of course, have a reasonable family resemblance to Hicks's classical model. So, we suppose the following:

$$X = f(N, \underline{K}) \tag{1}$$

$$N^d = f_N^{-1}(w/p) \tag{2}$$

$$N^s = g(w/p) \tag{3}$$

$$N^d = N^s \tag{4}$$

The notation is too familiar to need explanation. The first four equations state that *labour supply and derived demand for labour* in a competitive, one-commodity system *determine output, employment, and the real wage rate* in FIM states.

$$I = I(r) \tag{5}$$

$$S = \underline{X} - C(\underline{X}, r) \tag{6}$$

$$S = I \tag{7}$$

Saving and investment determine the rate of capital accumulation and the real interest rate.

$$M^d = \underline{k}p\underline{X} \tag{8}$$

$$M^s = \underline{M} \tag{9}$$

$$M^s = M^d \tag{10}$$

Money supply and money demand determine the price level. For

certain purposes, we will substitute a more common liquidity preference function,

$$M^d = p \times L(X, r) \tag{8'}$$

for the constant velocity function (8). For the time being, however,
we are supposing that, in comparisons between FIM states, velocity
will be found unrelated to the real rate of interest.

In this paper, we will discuss only two macroeconomic questions:
(1) What are the effects of a change in the money supply? and
(2) What are the effects of a decline in the marginal efficiency of
capital (MEC)? For brevity, we will refer to the two parametric shifts
as the 'monetary shock' and the 'real shock'.

The comparative statics of the above FIM model are so simple as
to be obvious. The relevant results might be summarized as follows.

1 *Monetary shocks have no real effects.* Only the price level is
affected; note in particular that the real interest rate is not. Conceivably, it may be a long, long run before we get neutrality, but FIM
comparative statics should skip by all intervening incomplete information states in silence.

2 *Real shocks have no monetary consequences.* A decline in the
MEC is interpreted here as a worsening of the terms on which a
society can trade present goods for future goods – the terms being
judged according to the best information available to that society.
(For simplicity, think of a decline in the rate of embodied techno-
logical progress.) The rational adaptation entails a lower rate of
capital accumulation, a transfer of resources to consumption goods
industries, and a lower real rate of interest. It does not entail unemployment, of course, or (in this FIM model) a decline in the price
level.[11]

VII

The macroeconomics we actually teach, of course, bears no clear
relationship to full-information macro. Instead of the static properties of some FIM model, the beginning student may be given one or
the other of two crosses to bear. The first one uses a Keynesian
savings–investment cross to determine (real) income. Call it 'model
A'. The second employs a given money stock and a 'Cambridge $\underline{k}$'
money demand to determine (nominal) income.[12] Call it 'model T'.

$$pS = p[X - C(X)] \quad \text{(A1)} \qquad\qquad M^d = \underline{k}pX \tag{T1}$$

$$pI = p\underline{I} \qquad \text{(A2)} \qquad M^s = \underline{M} \qquad \text{(T2)}$$

$$pS = pI \qquad \text{(A3)} \qquad M^d = M^s \qquad \text{(T3)}$$

Why do we start students off this way? Are these gadgets supposed to be easier to understand than an FIM model? Whether the student is fed A or T as his first introduction to macro, he has had a switch pulled on him before he even gets started. In our FIM model, *contra* model A, savings and investment have nothing to do with the level of income, whether real or nominal, and, *contra* model T, money supply and demand determine the price level and not real income or the product of the two. Full-information macro may have little direct bearing on problems of unemployment and short-run stabilization policy; but why does 'relevant' macroeconomics start off by replacing FIM (5)–(7) with model A, or else by replacing FIM (8)–(10) with model T?

As suggested in the previous section, it is not really a very good answer to say that FIM is long-run and model A (say) short-run. That leaves the student on his own to try to figure out why savings and investment determine income in the short run but the rate of interest in the long run.[13]

Since A and T both differ from FIM, our answer should be that certain information failures (or rigidities) are taken for granted – so much so, in fact, that they are built into elementary models as if they were inescapable features of the real world. The monetarist controversy started off, in effect, with a confrontation between models A and T. To understand the theoretical issues in that controversy, then, it would seem desirable, as a first step, to explain how A and T, respectively, depart from a full-information (all things flexible) model. This would tell us what the information problems (rigidities) are that are presumed to be ever-present – or ignored as implausible – by each side.

Model T is the simplest. In the rigidities (R) version, to the extent that prices (wages) are sticky, a change in the money stock will affect real output, X, and not just prices, p. In the incomplete information (IIM) version, anticipated changes in money affect prices, but unanticipated ones affect real income as well.

For model A, the R-version would state: to the extent that intertemporal prices (i.e. the interest rate) do not adjust to a change in perceived intertemporal production opportunities (i.e. MEC), changes in investment will lead to changes in aggregate money income. The corresponding IIM argument would run: whereas changes in the realizable rate of profit that are generally recognized will affect only the interest rate and the growth path, unrecognized such changes will affect money income. Except that model A is more extreme than that – it asserts that (R) the interest rate *never* responds or (IIM) the market *never* knows what is going on, so that the rational FIM adjustment (which leaves income unchanged) can be excluded as a possibility from the model.[14] Model T is more reasonable in that, specified as a theory of nominal income, it leaves the extent to which the FIM response is approximated an open question.

Two long-established stylized facts lend plausibility to A and T, respectively, as candidates for the first thing the student should learn in macroeconomics. For model A, we have the fact (SF1) that investment and GNP are positively correlated over business cycles with investment showing a larger amplitude than other components of income. For model T, of course, we have (SF2) the positive correlation between the money stock and nominal income. The monetarist controversy started out as a statistical contest over the dependability of these stylizations. Although no economist alive will confess to belief in either model A or model T, the issues for round 1 of the controversy are produced by putting the two on a collision course: the relative stability of the consumption–income and the money–income relations; the appropriate empirical components to be included in 'autonomous expenditures' or in the money supply, respectively; the 'autonomy' of investment and the 'exogeneity' of the money stock; the effectiveness of fiscal and monetary policy actions and the predictability of their consequences.

Econometric contention over these issues did nothing to bring out the information failures implicit in the debate.

VIII

From A to T, our student graduates to *IS–LM*. By linking A and T by the real rate of interest, r, we obtain the simplest version – a model of nominal income:

$$pS = p\,[X - C(X, r)] \quad \text{(AT1)} \qquad M^d = p \times L(X, r) \quad \text{(AT4)}$$

$$pI = pI(r) \quad \text{(AT2)} \qquad M^s = \underline{M} \quad \text{(AT5)}$$

$$pS = pI \quad \text{(AT3)} \qquad M^d = M^s \quad \text{(AT6)}$$

On this loftier plane, new riddles appear. In the comparative statics of our FIM model, real and monetary phenomena were independent of one another. In *IS–LM*, as usually taught, real disturbances have monetary consequences and vice-versa – unless extreme assumptions are made about the elasticities of *IS* and *LM*. Is it plausible that this two-way interdependence also stems from information failures of some sort?

Round 2 of the monetarist debate necessarily had to lead on to consideration of these interdependencies as well. An A-theorist who relies on (SF1) to argue that changes in autonomous expenditures cause income movements must also explain away (SF2) as showing endogenous movements in the money stock.[15] A T-theorist similarly has to explain away (SF1). *IS-LM* gives us a handle of sorts on the interaction of real and monetary phenomena, so it became, rather naturally, the framework for debating these interaction issues.

The *IS-LM* model is used, in this type of context, as if one were doing comparative statics with a genuinely static model. Real disturbances (or fiscal policy actions) are represented as shifting *IS*, while *LM* stays put; monetary disturbances (i.e. policy) as shifting *LM*, while *IS* stays put. The issues of round 1 were gone over again in this framework and Crowding Out and Gibson's Paradox added.[16] *IS-LM* curve-shifting will suggest that the values of the elasticities of the two curves are crucial to the issues of the monetarist debate. Many of the participants accepted this suggestion. The discussion tended to presume, moreover, that these elasticities are stable properties of the system, that the results of time-series regressions give information on these steady-state elasticities, and that qualitative results from *a priori* static choice theory have a bearing on the issues in sufficing by themselves to exclude extreme values.

There are two extremist possibilities. The 'fiscalist' extreme would postulate a vertical *IS* and/or a horizontal *LM*; the monetarist extreme, a horizontal *IS* and/or a vertical *LM*. Putting it this way tends to suggest that, surely, all moderate men of sound judgement will take a position somewhere in the middle. The trouble is that this moderate position (like the fiscalist extreme) implies that real impulses *always* must affect income and that monetary impulses *always* must change the economy's rate of growth. It implies that the rational FIM adjustments can never happen. And the monetarist extreme will imply that real impulses *never* change income and that monetary impulses *never* disturb the growth path. In either case, 'sometimes' is the (econometrically troublesome) possibility that is being excluded by construction. This steady-state version of *IS-LM* is a model that will not allow representation of an economy that adapts more or less well to shocks depending upon the state of information.

Note that, *if* it were to be the case that these short-run interactions of real and monetary phenomena are due to incomplete
information on the part of agents, then the steady-state elasticities
view is seen to be misleading. What the response to a particular
impulse will be then depends upon the state of information and not
just on steady-state behavioural parameters. What counts is the
extent to which the nature and extent of the shock is recognized
or unrecognized, anticipated or unanticipated, perceived as permanent or as transitory. The same impulse need not produce the same
response every time it is repeated.

In order to re-examine the interaction of real and monetary
phenomena in the *IS–LM* model, start back with A and T, with the
propositions that are fundamental to each. Money income, in model
A, will decline *if and only if* intended saving exceeds intended investment (so that we have an excess supply (ES) of commodities). In
model T, money income will decline *if and only if* the prevailing
state is one of excess demand (ED) for money. So far the two are
consistent. But we have two contrasting hypotheses about causation.
In A, a decline in investment produces the ES of commodities. In T,
a reduction in the money supply produces the ED for money. If we
scrutinize the A story through the suspicious eyes of a T-believer and
then let an A-believer have his turn with the T story, we obtain two
questions about 'transmission':

1   Why should real disturbances be expected to cause an excess
    demand for money and thus a change in the nominal income
    level (and, if money prices and/or wages are inflexible, a change
    in activity levels)?[17]
2   Why should monetary disturbances be expected to cause savings
    and investment intentions to diverge (and thus to change nominal
    income, etc.)?[18]

Let us begin with the second of these questions.

IX

The effects of an increase in the money supply are usually demonstrated by shifting *LM* rightwards. With *IS* assumed to stay put ('in
the short run'), money income rises and the interest rate declines.
What kind of transmission mechanism does this suppose?

In order to discuss the *sequence* of events, we supplement our
simple *IS–LM* model with an excess demand table (table 1).[19] We

Table 1

	L	X	B	M
(1) FIGE$_1$: M^S increased	0	0	0	0
(2) Impact effects: r declines	0	0	ED	ES
(3) Inflationary pressure: pX rises	0	ED	0	ES
(4) Nominal income 'equilibrium'	?	0	0	0

count four goods: labour (L), commodities (X), securities (B) and money (M). The *IS-LM* story of the once-over money injection should begin with the following course of events. (1) We assume the initial state to be a full-information general equilibrium (FIGE) – all excess demands (EDs) are zero and the demands and supplies from which these EDs are computed are generated by full-information individual conceptual experiments and aggregation over transactors. (2) We assume a disturbance that creates excess reserves in the banking system. The banks expand, creating an ES of money and an ED for securities. The ED that implicitly corresponds to the explicitly specified ES of money is found to be 100 per cent in the bond market, rather than distributed over all non-money markets, because the banking system is assumed to demand nothing but securities. Note, however, that we know that the ED distribution at impact of the disturbance must be as specified in the table also for another reason. Whenever *IS* is assumed to be shifted by the disturbance, the impact effect must be zero in the commodities markets. Holding *IS* constant when *LM* is shifted, consequently, is a *strong* assumption. (3) Next, interest rates decline in response to the excess demand for bonds and until this ED becomes zero; demand prices for assets rise relative to their current rental values and relative to their initial supply prices; planned investment thus exceeds savings, so that the state of the economy at this stage is one of money ES and commodity ED. (4) Looking at the third row of table 1, A- and T-believers will agree on what must happen next: money income will rise.

That finishes phase 1 of the *IS-LM* tale. It takes us from the initial FIGE at $(\hat{Y}_0, \hat{r})$ in figure 1 to the *IS-LM* 'short run' at $(\underline{Y}, \underline{r})$. But this cannot be a full STOP. There has to be a further GO at $(\underline{Y}, \underline{r})$ because in the comparison of initial and terminal equilibria money must be seen to be neutral. This requires that we end up in some FIGE$_2$ with the same relative prices as in FIGE$_1$ – e.g. at $(\hat{Y}_1, \hat{r})$ in figure 1.

Phase 2 of the story might run as follows. When at stage (4) nominal income rises, some part of this is an increase in p but some

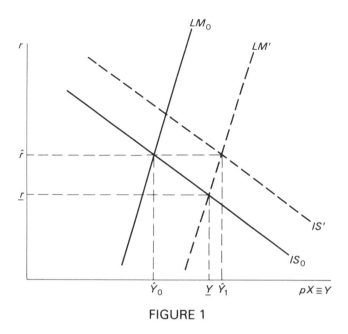

FIGURE 1

part of it initially takes the form of an increase in real output, X, and employment. For concreteness we may suppose that these departures from 'natural' full-information activity levels are due to a temporary information asymmetry between employers and employed. Suppose that firms learn the truth about the new price level *before* workers do. Observing the demand prices for their output going up in relation to money wages, firms find that they can hire labour at a reduced real wage. Workers whose perceptions of the inflation are lagging believe they are being hired at somewhat improved real wage rates. Consequently, the two sides of the market will agree (at some money wage between $\hat{w}_0$ and $\hat{w}_1$) to a volume of employment exceeding the FIGE one. (5) As prices (and nominal rentals) increase, aggregate demand in money terms will come proportionally to exceed the level indicated by IS_0 at whatever the interest rate happens to be. So IS shifts rightwards.[20] (6) In this process, workers discover that real wages are not what they supposed them to be. The initial overshooting of output and employment is corrected, so that, with X declining back to $\hat{X}$, prices increase further. The process ends up with a new FIM state with the monetary impulse having affected only nominal magnitudes.[21] In terms of the *IS–LM* diagram, both schedules are shown to have shifted to precisely the same extent.

Once the sequence is spelled out in this way, it is obvious that the analysis definitely does assume incomplete information. It is these ignorance assumptions, moreover, rather than the steady-state interest elasticities of money demand or investment, that count in explaining the position of the system at stages intermediate between FIGEs. It also becomes apparent that *IS–LM* can be a cumbersome, inappropriate framework for representing theories that make non-standard assumptions about the knowledge of transactors and, consequently, about the time-phasing of events.

In the above sequence, incomplete information is implied at two points. In phase 1 we have it at stage (3), where the real interest rate, and therefore the relative prices of assets and their services, changes away from its FIM values. Then, in phase 2 incomplete information is assumed at stage (4), where activity levels and not just nominal values rise. If we replace the first one by a full-information assumption, the result is an approximation to Friedman's Theory of Nominal Income, where the first information imperfection is minimized but the second is admitted. In an *IS–LM* representation of the resulting theory, the effects of a once-over money injection are shown by *simultaneously* shifting *both IS* and *LM* outward to the same extent. The phase 1 sequence is short-circuited. If we replace also the second IIM assumption by a full-information one, we obtain the rational expectations theory of the fully anticipated once-over money injection. No relative prices and no activity levels are affected; only nominal values change. Phase 2 also is short-circuited. The system jumps directly from FIGE$_1$ to a full STOP at FIGE$_2$, without passing any *IS–LM* GO *en route*. 'Long-run propositions become true in the short run.'

Some 20 to 30 years ago, Keynesian doubts about the effectiveness of monetary policy were commonly couched in *IS–LM* terms: *IS* was interest-inelastic and *LM* very elastic, so that shifts in *LM* (*IS* staying put) could be seen not to have much effect on nominal income. There have been really two monetarist counter-arguments to this 'fiscalist' position, and it would probably have been helpful if the two had been more clearly distinguished than has been the case. *Monetarist counter no. 1* takes the sequencing of table 1 for granted, and therefore concedes the appropriateness of posing the issue in terms of the *IS–LM* elasticities. Thus, in the early days of the controversy, the monetarists were concerned to show or argue that each link in this particular transmission mechanism was more robust than Keynesians believed. In particular, they argued, first, that no 'liquidity trap' was ever absolute; monetary policy was never quite a case of 'pushing on a string', but the central bank would always bring about the situation in row (2) of the table. Second, they argued that Keynesians tended to underestimate the interest elasticity of aggregate expenditures in large part because of too narrow an interpretation of 'the interest rate'. In Keynesian theory, the term tended to signify 'borrowing cost'; in a world where elasticities of substitution between various asset types are high, the more appropriate interpretation of the phrase 'a fall in the interest rate' is that of 'a rise in the demand prices of durables relative to their rental values'. Going from row (2) to row (3) of table 1, therefore, we should find a strong increase in the effective demand for output. This is because relative prices change everywhere in the economy. Monetary policy, in this account of the transmission mechanism,[22] is effective because of the pervasive non-neutrality of its 'short-run' effects.

The *monetarist counter no. 2* denies the above sequence and has the economy going directly from row (1) to row (3), omitting (or downplaying very much) row (2).[23] How is that story to be told? Assume a large subset of transactors who have accurate information on the supply of high-powered money and who understand that an increase in the money supply eventually must raise prices. As soon as the intentions of the central bank to expand base money become known, these agents will increase their demand for commodities at the old prices and the full-information interest rate. At the same time, the increased supply of credit by the banking system is offset by the increased demand on the part of those who anticipate a rise in prices. The rate of interest does not move, and never plays any role in the transmission of the monetary impulse. We get to row (3) without it.[24] In the analysis where the standard sequence is followed, the lowering of the rate of interest (at row (2)) serves, we may conclude, to cajole *those agents who do not know what is going on* into none the less increasing their spending. When agents do know, there is no 'transmission problem' and the whole notion of a 'transmission mechanism' becomes somewhat meaningless.

This illustrates a more general proposition that the rational expectations literature is making exceedingly familiar: namely, that fully informed agents have no need for a price mechanism to inform them about what is happening. Prices merely reflect what they already know.

X

The other question concerning the interaction of real and monetary phenomena asked why a change in the marginal efficiency of capital

Table 2

	L	X	B	M
(1) FIGE$_1$: MEC declines	0	0	0	0
(2) Impact effects: *r* declines	0	ES	ED	0
(3) Deflationary pressure: p^x declines	0	ES	0	ED
(4) Nominal income 'equilibrium'	?	0	0	0

(MEC) should produce a change in money income and perhaps also in employment. We take the case of a decline in MEC and we construe this to mean, in FIM terms, that the economy faces the problem of traversing to a new full-information general equilibrium on a lower growth path with a lower real rate of interest. In *IS-LM*, of course, the analysis is usually begun by shifting *IS* left, keeping *LM* put. Again, this procedure imposes a particular *sequence* of events; this sequencing implicitly rests on certain incomplete information assumptions, and hence is no more immutable than these assumptions are.

Once more, we may use an excess demand table (table 2) to examine phase 1 of the sequence. (1) We start with the initial full-information general equilibrium. (2) Perceived returns to investment decline. Firms decrease their demands for capital goods and their net issue of securities. The impact effects show that *IS* has shifted with *LM* constant (since ED for money is zero). (3) Next – in the loanable funds sequence of events[25] – the interest rate declines in response to the excess demand for bonds and finds the level at which this ED is zero; with a lower rate of interest the amount of money demanded at the initial level of money income will increase. (4) Row (3), therefore, will show an ES of commodities and an ED for money. T-theorists and A-theorists will agree that the spending of money on commodities must decline until the excess demand for money in terms of commodities is zero.[26] (5) If money wages fail to fall in proportion to this decline in nominal aggregate demand, there will be unemployment in the state portrayed in row (4).

That would be phase 1 of the usual *IS-LM* tale. It takes us from the initial FIGE$_1$ at $(\hat{X}_1, \hat{r}_0)$ in figure 2 to the *IS-LM* unemployment state at $(\underline{X}, \underline{r})$.[27] Note that a significant interest elasticity of money demand is crucial to the story. Unless an excess demand for money emerges, at row (3), there will be no deflationary pressure on the level of money income and, consequently, no unemployment (whether or not money wages are sticky).

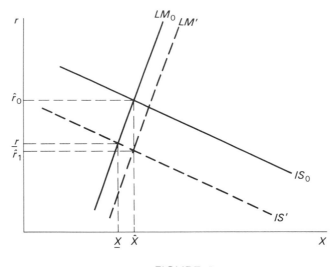

FIGURE 2

So liquidity preference in this sense of the interest elasticity of money demand is a *sine qua non* to any Keynesian theory of employment fluctuations.[28] The reader may recall that Modigliani came to a different conclusion in his influential 1944 assessment of Keynesian theory. Liquidity preference, Modigliani argued, was not an essential part of Keynes's story. Instead, 'the low level of investment and employment are both the effect of the same cause, namely a basic maladjustment between the quantity of money and the wage rate' (Modigliani, 1944, pp. 224-5).[29] This conclusion fits monetarist theory, where unemployment arises either from a reduction of the money stock or from money wages rising faster than the money stock. But as a characterization of a Keynesian theory where unemployment arises in response to an unfavourable shift of MEC, Modigliani's conclusion is simply incorrect. It is the result of an investigation of the pure statics of the *IS–LM* model. If the *comparative statics* of *IS–LM* imposes a certain sequencing of events, the *pure statics*, naturally, ignores sequence – and causation – altogether. Consequently, it mis-identifies 'what goes wrong' – what rational adaptation to changing circumstances agents fail to see – in the Keynesian theory.

There are two ways (not necessarily mutually exclusive) in which the crucial excess demand for money can be made to develop at the critical juncture of row (3) of the story.

The first relies on the speculative demand for money. We assume a money demand function, $M^d = f(p^X, r - r^*)$, which does not significantly depend upon the absolute level of the interest rate, r, but only on the difference between r and the perceived 'normal' rate, r^*. If, then, we suppose an adverse change in the MEC taking place, while speculators fail to realize that a lower rate of return will be normal from now on, the system will fail to make the traverse smoothly. An excess demand for money will develop, as in table 2, and income and presumably employment will decline.[30] If, on the other hand, the decline in MEC is correctly perceived and seen to be permanent, r^* will be re-evaluated accordingly, and the downward adjustment of the growth rate and of the real rate of return will proceed without creating deflationary pressure on the income level – as in our FIM model. In this version of the model, whether or not the real shock has monetary consequences is seen to depend on the state of information.

The second way to generate the table 2 story is the more common one. We assume $(8')$, $M^d/p = L(X, r)$, to be the steady-state money demand function and rely on the interest elasticity of a Baumol–Tobin transactions demand to produce an excess demand for money as the interest rate declines. In this instance, the real shock will always produce a change in the price level, also in comparisons between FIM states. By the same token, the *IS–LM* solution at $(\underline{X}, \underline{r})$ of figure 2 is seen to be a temporary position of the system. There should be a phase 2 to the sequence. In response to the unemployment of stage (5), money wages and prices fall, thereby increasing the real value of the money stock until excess demand for money is zero. In the *IS–LM* figure 2, this is shown as *LM* shifting right until the new equilibrium, $FIGE_2$, is reached at $(\hat{X}, \hat{r}_1)$.[31]

In this second story of an *IS* shift, we are supposing that people can know the real rate of return in the system so that there are no differences of opinion giving rise to a speculative demand for money. Agents all perceive the decline in MEC correctly; it is only that (when fully informed) they demand larger real balances when the return on alternative assets has fallen. But this adjustment down the steady-state demand for money function for a known decrease in the rate of profit should produce an entirely predictable decline in velocity. And, in turn, if everyone knows the extent of the required deflation, why should reservation wages and prices be sticky? If they are not, then unemployment need not develop in the move from the initial to the terminal FIGE. The system would not pass through the point $(\underline{X}, \underline{r})$ in the course of its adaptation to the decline in MEC.

Once more, we conclude that, with a bit more information at their disposal, agents would short-circuit the particular sequence assumed in the usual *IS–LM* exercise. In that case, *IS* and *LM* have to be shown as shifting simultaneously.

XI

The liquidity preference (LP) hypothesis of the interest rate mechanism maintains that the interest rate is governed by the excess demand for money: $\Delta r = f(M^d - M^s)$. It gives rise to a different sequence of events following a decline of the marginal efficiency of capital. The characteristic LP sequence is shown in table 3. The impact effect of the MEC shift is, as before, an ES of commodities and an ED for bonds. Since, according to the LP hypothesis, the rate of interest will fall *if and only if* we have an ES of money, there is no interest rate response. Row (2) shows an intertemporal disequilibrium – saving exceeds investment – but intertemporal prices will not change. The Keynesian system that incorporates the LP hypothesis is altogether incapable of adjusting rationally to disturbances that require a change in the rate of capital accumulation.[32] The appropriate price mechanism, it is assumed, will *never* work. The loanable funds hypothesis, in contrast, asserts that the interest rate is governed by the ES of securities: $\Delta r = g(B^s - B^d)$. This price mechanism will work with well-informed speculators and will not do the job, of course, if speculators are ill-informed. The difference between the LP Keynesian and the loanable funds (LF) Keynesian models is that between a system that cannot work properly and one that can, and

Table 3

	L	X	B	M
(1) MEC declines	0	0	0	0
(2) Output falls	0	ES	ED	0
(3) *r* falls	(ES)	0	ED (?)	ES
	(ES)	0	0	0

presumably often does, work, but cannot be counted on to do so without fail. That difference is not a trivial theoretical issue.

The LP sequence contains another issue that is not trivial. Comparison of rows (2) and (3) shows, first, that spending (of money on commodities) declines although the excess demand for money is zero and, second, that the decline in money income proceeds to produce an excess supply of money. This contradicts every possible quantity theory of nominal income, whereas the LF Keynesian model is consistent with quantity theory reasoning.

Keynes summarized his departures from classical theory in two propositions: (1) saving and investment determine income – not the interest rate, as the classics believed; (2) liquidity preference and the money supply determine the interest rate – and not the price level, as the classics believed. Both propositions stem directly from the LP hypothesis (which remains the core of British Cambridge Keynesianism). They can be read off, in LP sequence, from table 3.

Alvin Hansen, who was extremely influential in shaping the American Keynesian tradition, decided that Keynes's summary propositions were simple analytical mistakes and therefore meaningless. Savings and investment, Hansen argued, determine neither income nor the interest rate: they give us the *IS* schedule. And money supply and demand, of course, give us the *LM* schedule. Everything has to be determined simultaneously. This is another argument that treats the model *as if* it were a purely static one. And, again, it misses the point – an important point.

XII

The simplest version of *IS-LM* can be produced by linking models A and T by the rate of interest.[33] But model A (especially) and model T are incomplete-information models. Their solutions portray market interactions that are, at least on the part of some group of transactors, based on misapprehension of the opportunities potentially present. It is to invite misunderstandings, therefore, to treat *IS-LM* solutions as if they were the static, short-run equilibria familiar from price theory.

One must pay attention to the sequencing of events in order to understand the theoretical reasons why the system is supposed not to be in full-information general equilibrium and also in order to understand the interaction of real and monetary phenomena in the system.

IS–LM, handled as if it were a static construction, will pay no attention to the sequence of events. This use of the apparatus produced a nonsensical conclusion to the *Keynes and the classics* debate: namely, that Keynes had revolutionized economic theory by advancing the platitude that wages too high for full employment and rigid downwards imply persistent unemployment. It failed to capture essential elements of Keynes's theory: namely, that the typical shock is a shift in investors' espectations and that it is the failure of intertemporal prices to respond appropriately to this change in perceived intertemporal opportunities that prevents rational adaptation to the shock. The same 'as if static' method produced the conclusion that *liquidity preference versus loanable funds* was not a meaningful issue; that it does not matter whether the system is or is not potentially capable of adjusting intertemporal prices appropriately in response to changes in intertemporal opportunities.

The popularity and staying power of the *IS–LM* apparatus, especially in classroom teaching, rests not on its static but on its comparative static uses, however. In the course of the monetarist debate, this method was employed to bolster the suggestion that the steady-state interest elasticities of the two schedules were central – or even *the* central – issues in contention. If the interest elasticity of *IS* is pretty far from infinite and that of *LM* pretty far from zero, standard curve-shifting exercises suggest that real disturbances should have monetary effects and monetary disturbances have real ones – although these interdependencies do not occur in our FIM theory. When reasonable assumptions are made about the interest elasticities of excess commodity and money demand, the *IS–LM* model seemingly will not allow the interest rate to adjust appropriately 'in the short run'. Monetary disturbances are shown to have real (allocative) effects because the interest rate changes – when in FIM it should not. Real disturbances have monetary (income) consequences – because the rate of interest does not change as far as (in FIM) it should.[34]

The reason why *IS–LM* seemingly will not allow equilibration in the short run, of course, is that it is habitually assumed that the disturbances in question will shift one reduced form and leave the other one put. Whether this procedure is justified or not is a question of some importance. Supply and demand analysis, as Marshall noted, is a useful tool in so far as the forces that shift one schedule do not also tend to shift the other. The same is true in this case. *IS–LM* as a modelling strategy – i.e. first concentrating on obtaining the two reduced forms and then getting the answers by manipulating them – is really predicated on the procedure being justified. If, in response to the standard disturbances, *IS* and *LM* both shift, this modelling strategy makes little sense. When both shift more or less simultaneously, preoccupation with the elasticities is on the whole a mistake.

But FIM analysis shows that both schedules should shift – ultimately. The use of *IS-LM* 'as if' it were a comparative static apparatus is thus seen to involve the lag-assumption that one shifts before the other, that there will be a well-defined 'short run' solution half-way in the process – and that macroeconomic policy-makers have their natural being in this halfway house. This imposed sequencing or lag structure rests on assumptions of incomplete information on the part of various groups of agents.

So, is the procedure of shifting *LM*, keeping *IS* constant – or vice versa – justified? The answer is: sometimes; perhaps often; but not necessarily or always. And that, very largely, is what is the matter with *IS-LM*.

Notes

1 My own disaffection with *IS-LM*, obviously, starts here.
2 *Loanable funds v. liquidity preference* started out, of course, as part and parcel of the *Keynes and the classics* debate. Following its wrongful dismissal from among the major issues of the latter, it has lived an independent and somewhat fitful existence as a sometime preoccupation of a small number of specialists in monetary general equilibrium theory. It is convenient to treat it as a separate set of issues here.
3 Thus Professor Tobin would maintain, for example, that the magnitude of the interest elasticity of the *LM* reduced form is a critical issue between the two camps, while Professor Friedman maintains that it is not decisive in determining whether you are a 'monetarist' or not.
4 Students used to be told that the cobweb model oscillates 'because production takes time'. But the time-consuming nature of physical processes is significant only in so far as it is associated with an information lag.
5 It is a world in which economic theory need not be taught and where the only economic research needed would be of the simplest fact-finding variety. What a threatening picture to paint on the wall!
6 This is loosely paraphrased. For the original statement, cf. Hahn (1973).
7 Disappointments or surprises of a sort may still occur. But they should then be in the nature of lottery outcomes (or harvest results), where it is too late for the winner or loser to do anything about it. Also, the outcome should not change the agent's willingness to play the game or the strategies he uses in doing so.
8 Most of all, of course, we want to avoid calling the mathematical solution to an incomplete information model a 'short-run equilibrium'.
9 This is not the only objection to Friedman's theory that is suggested when this loosely worded complaint is aired. But it will do for our illustrative purpose here.

10 Love at first sight is one example – a case of irrational expectations. In the drearier area of rational expectations, the example would be Money at first sight.

11 If we replace (8) with (8′), however, a decline in MEC will produce not only a decline in the growth rate and a decrease in the real rate of interest, but also an increase in the amount of real balances demanded and hence a decline of the price level.

12 There is some recklessness here in the use of 'determine'. But the beginning student should not be bothered by 'missing equations' when first trying to fathom the familiar diagrams.

13 Beginning macroeconomics can be made even more challenging for him by suggesting that the reason for 'switching' what savings and investment are made to determine lies, somehow, in the short-run stickiness of money wages.

14 Worse than that. Model A clearly allows us to eliminate the p's everywhere. Then it asserts, in addition, that shifts in investment must change *real* income, implying that the imperfection admitted as a possibility in model T is inescapably present also in A.

15 For our simple AT model to serve this purpose, its fifth equation had better be changed into $M^s = M(\underline{B}, r)$, with B denoting the monetary base.

16 Gibson's Paradox is the positive correlation of the interest rate and price level over business cycles. Tooke's stylized fact would be a better name for it, since Tooke was the first to pose it as an empirical challenge to monetary theories of nominal income movements. In the *IS–LM* setting, movements of the *LM* locus with *IS* stable should give rise to negative correlation between the interest rate and nominal income. In this discussion of *IS–LM* we will leave this (SF3) aside.

17 Empirically, do real disturbances cause income movements? Always, sometimes, or never? The Keynesian answer is that they *always* do (although Cambridge Keynesians would insist, as we will see, that they do so without creating an ED for money in the process). Monetarists think 'never' is the better conjecture.

18 Empirically, do they? Always, sometimes, or never? In the various macro-theories stemming from Wicksell (which include the Austrian and Keynesian theories), it is presumed that monetary impulses do work this way. In modern monetarism it is presumed that they will always create an ED for commodities but *not* by disturbing the growth path. The clearest contrast, on this score, is that between Hayek and Friedman.

19 Also known as a one-armed bandit. For four 'lemons' in a row, the machine will pay the general equilibrium jackpot.

20 If we had chosen to draw figure 1 with real income, X, rather than nominal income, $pX \equiv Y$, on the horizontal axis, this part of the story would be told in terms of rising prices gradually reducing real balances back to their initial level. *LM* would be shown to shift back rather than *IS* also shifting out. For present purposes, having the diagram in terms of nominal income seems pedagogically preferable. Doing the exercise in real income has the advantage of highlighting the point of the Archibald–Lipsey critique of Patinkin, namely, that real balance effects result from evaluating nominal balances at disequilibrium prices. If and when we can assume that money balances are

evaluated at equilibrium prices, we regain the valid classical dichotomy, that is to say, the FIM 'independence' of real phenomena on monetary ones.

21 ... except in so far as the transitory period of producing at false prices has also left a legacy of disequilibrium stocks of capital (as in Hayekian over-investment theory).

22 It is an account that I tend to associate especially with the work of Brunner and Meltzer in the 1960s. But cf. also Friedman and Schwartz (1963).

23 I am thinking here of the later position of Friedman, according to which the central bank has no influence over the real rate of interest, liquidity effects on the real rate are insignificant and evanescent, and the interest elasticity of money demand is irrelevant to the effectiveness of monetary policy. In my opinion, as is clear from the text, the *IS-LM* representation of this theory should show both *IS* and *LM* shifting together at the impact of a monetary disturbance. The elasticities are then irrelevant. However, Friedman has (I think) muddied the waters by suggesting that the *IS* schedule should perhaps be drawn horizontal. Cf. for example Friedman (1976).

24 Passing through the monetarist black box that is so often the object of complaints.

25 For the contrast between loanable funds and liquidity preference, see section XI below.

26 Note that the liquidity preference theory of interest rate determination predicts, instead, that in the state depicted in row (3) the interest rate will rise.

27 We have chosen to put real income, X, on the horizontal axis in this exercise.

28 Liquidity preference in the sense of the hypothesis that the ED for money governs the interest rate is better dispensed with, however; cf. section XI.

29 Cf. also Leijonhufvud (1969, pp. 14ff.), where 'Keynes' special case' – as Modigliani called the liquidity trap possibility – is also considered.

30 Note that, since this unemployment disequilibrium is due to the inconsistency of the beliefs of entrepreneurs (with respect to MEC) and of securities markets investors (with respect to r^*), it is not to be cured by persuading wage-earners that the (FIM) level of wages is too high.

31 Deflation helps in this instance because the new FIM state that the system should reach requires larger real balances. In the earlier exercise, where the excess demand for money developed for speculative reasons, the FIM money demand function was supposed to be interest-inelastic so that the new FIM equilibrium required the same wage and price level as the old one.

32 Model A – the 'Keynesian cross' – properly portrays a system with the dynamic properties of table 3.

33 ... and looking elsewhere for the 'missing equation(s)' that will determine the price and output components of nominal income.

34 This maladjustment of the interest rate is the theme of my 'The Wicksell Connection' (1981).

References

Friedman, M. (1976) 'Comment', in J. L. Stein (ed.), *Monetarism*, Amsterdam.

Friedman, M. and Schwartz, A. (1963) 'Money and business cycles', *Review of Economics and Statistics*, supplement, February.

Hahn, Frank H. (1973) *On the Notion of Equilibrium in Economics*, Cambridge.

Hicks, J. R. (1965) *Capital and Growth*, Oxford.

Leijonhufvud, A. (1969) *Keynes and the Classics: Two Lectures*, London.

Leijonhufvud, A. (1981) 'The Wicksell connection: variations on a theme', in A. Leijonhufvud, *Information and Coordination: Essays in Macroeconomics*, Oxford.

Lucas, Robert E. Jr (1980) 'Methods and problems in business cycle theory', *Journal of Money, Credit and Banking*, vol. 12, part 2, November.

Modigliani, F. (1944) 'Liquidity preference and the theory of interest and money', *Econometrica*; reprinted in F. A. Lutz and L. W. Mints (eds), *Readings in Monetary Theory*, Philadelphia, 1951. Quotation from this reprinting.

PART II
The Fixprice Approach to Macroeconomics

4

Notes on Growth Theory with Imperfectly Flexible Prices

EDMOND MALINVAUD

Should one reconsider the theory of economic growth at this time when a better understanding of fixprice temporary equilibria has been achieved? Such is the question to be discussed here.

The most developed formalizations that are now available for the process of economic growth assume a sequence of Walrasian temporary equilibria. These formalizations are certainly interesting for anyone who wants to grasp some of the logical problems raised by the functioning of our economies; they should not be dismissed, since they are an essential building block of our theoretical construction. But do they provide a valid first approximation for a representation of the real world?

To argue for a positive answer it is clearly not enough to point out that all prices are flexible in the long run; one should also prove that the actual growth path does not deviate much from the one that would result if adjustments of prices were instantaneous and excess demands or supplies were never to appear. Such a proof is difficult to give, and indeed a long tradition of economic thinking takes it for granted that, in some important respects, economic growth crucially depends on price disequilibria that are sustained over prolonged periods. This explains why the distinction between fixprice and flexprice theories, which now proves so useful for the study of short-run phenomena, may have been first introduced by J. Hicks on the occasion of a book entitled *Capital and Growth* (1965).

It will be suggested here that a reconsideration of the theory of growth could be rewarding, because some very relevant issues still need clear explanations, which might hopefully follow from the study of the dynamics of fixprice equilibria. This paper does not claim to do more than put forward such a suggestion; the modest

93

formalization that will be introduced to support the argument will remain more or less inappropriate, I am afraid, for a good theory of the phenomena under discussion.

Incomplete adjustment of prices

The starting point is to note once again that prices are not fully flexible. Hence, deviations exist at any time between the actual price system and what this system ought to be if a balanced growth path would occur from that time on.

I shall not try here to be precise about what this 'notional' balanced growth would be, or about the corresponding notional price system. On the one hand, the question has been clarified by an extensive literature, starting from the Solow aggregate model to the many multi-sectoral mathematical growth models that have been discussed during the past 20 years (see Burmeister and Dobell, 1970). On the other hand, the sophistication of this paper is too low to require a precise definition. It is sufficient to make a factual observation: to an extent that varies as between countries and as between decades, significant excess demands or supplies exist for some goods or types of labour, and significant price disequilibria also exist (for instance, the wage rate for the same occupation may be higher in some industries than in others).

Neither shall I discuss the fundamental reasons why such disequilibria are observed. This is certainly an interesting question for economists, but it is not the one I want to consider here. I may, however, note that the explanation will certainly give some role to two features that should also play an important part in a full description of economic growth: an efficient use of physical capital often implies constant modes of operation and is therefore responsible for some rigidities in production; economic agents often find it to be mutually advantageous to go into long-term contracts, which again cause some rigidities.

Nor shall I discuss whether the fixed-price temporary general equilibrium is the appropriate concept for a representation of the instantaneous state of the economy. I shall take it to be so, but I accept the view, expressed for instance by A. Coddington (1978), that the concept is valid only when the imbalances are not too large, that is, when the costs of information and of quick adaptations dominate over the losses due to the fact that otherwise advantageous opportunities are not searched for and seized.

Students of economic growth will easily accept two ideas put forward in this paper, namely that some disequilibria may be sustained over rather long periods, and that the existence of these disequilibria significantly reacts on the growth process, to speed it up, slow it down or change its course.

We naturally think of excess demands or supplies. We know that scarcities play, or have played in some periods, an important role in some countries; this fact stimulates special types of behaviour, as was argued notably by J. Kornai (1979). We know that unemployment and the excess capacity margin have tended to be higher at some times than at others; this explains part of the changes that were observed concerning workers' migrations, participation rates allotted to the labour force and investment.

But we should pay still more attention to price disequilibria. During long historical periods wage rates and profit rates have been systematically lower in some industries than in others; most economists believe that the size of the differences has a lot to do with the speed of modernization, causation links running in both directions. Progress in statistics tends to substantiate the view, commonly held by economic historians, that the excess of the rate of return on productive capital over that on financial capital is not the same everywhere and at all times; after some progress still to be made in the econometrics of investment, the view should also be substantiated that this excess has a significant role in explaining the speed of capital accumulation.

Once the potential role of such disequilibria has been realized, the question naturally comes to mind as to how they ought to be represented in the macroeconomic models on which growth theory is based. The answer looks rather obvious and consists only in putting together a few concepts that are very familiar to analysts of actual economic evolution.

Some of these concepts, like a measure of unemployment, are commonly found in current macroeconomic models, and I shall not consider them at this stage. But I want to argue for the explicit introduction of two variables measuring, respectively, excess capacity and profitability: two disequilibrium concepts concerning, first, quantities and, second, prices.

Indeed, an essential part of any theory of economic growth should be the representation of investment, and it seems to me that both excess capacity and profitability have an important role to play in this representation.

The balanced growth theories of the Solow type need not consider investment behaviour. In a world with perfect foresight, without uncertainties or irreversibilities, with perfect markets that are permanently cleared, the volume of capital adapts to the changing needs of production, in conformity with the saving and working behaviour of the people; given the production function, this volume of capital can be written as a function of the prices (price of output, cost of labour and cost of capital); an investment equation can of course be obtained from this capital demand equation, but it can hardly claim to describe any specific behaviour.

The matter is different when one considers a world in which business men are confronted with an uncertain future. Assuming the prices for current transactions and the interest rates for current loans to be well defined, one must recognize that many uncertainties still remain. Investment behaviour then has a high degree of autonomy. To describe precisely what is systematic in this behaviour, one ought to explain first how expectations are formed from the current situation and past evolution, and then what level of investment is chosen considering both the current situation and the expectations about the future; the investment equation, connecting this volume directly to the current situation and past evolution, should be the final outcome of the explanation.

If relative prices should appear for the same reason as they appear in the investment equation of the Solow-type theories, some arguments, such as excess capacity and profitability, should be added.[1] Indeed, when excess capacity is large, the existing capital is too important for the present size of the market, and, other things being equal, it should also be seen as relatively important for the expected future size of the market. But if profitability is high, businessmen, who know that their expectations concern an uncertain future, should be ready to run the risk of having excess capacities, whereas they would not take this risk if profitability was low.

Excess capacity, which is regularly considered in the current analysis of business conditions, is often said to be too elusive a concept to find its place in a theoretical model. I wonder why. Like many other macroeconomic indicators, it may require for its measurement some agreed rules, which may be somewhat conventional. But this is a common situation.

The problem probably results from the fact that the productive capacity of interest in general depends on the price system: it is this existing capacity that entrepreneurs would find it profitable to operate at the prevailing prices in the short run if demand for their products were as large as they could wish. This capacity would not depend on small changes of prices if the technology were 'putty-clay' or 'clay-clay' and if, on each piece of equipment, the operating cost were smaller than the value of the product. In other cases capacity must be defined with respect to a reference price system. But there is no fundamental impossibility of doing so. In particular, when the investment equation is considered, I suggest that profitability appears as an argument together with excess capacity; if a decrease in profit margins induces some scrapping, this is an added reason for a low rate of change of the capital stock, besides the reluctance of business-men to take risks. Of course, an accurate analysis would then require a careful specification of the relationship between investment, capital, productive capacity and scrapping; but this can be done, even though I shall not do it here.

The definition of profitability may actually raise more difficult problems than that of excess capacity. It must probably be measured by the ratio between some expected surplus resulting from produc-tion and the value of the capital engaged in this production. But, what expected surplus? Clearly, it should refer to the surplus over what would be earned by this capital if it were not engaged in production: perhaps short-term lending as an alternative to some current operating decisions like inventory accumulation; financial investment as an alternative to productive investment.

This measure of profitability should then be something like the 'expected pure profit rate'. It ought to have some relationship with the q ratio studied by J. Tobin,[2] which is also a measure of the disequilibrium in prices; but I shall not discuss this relationship here.

The reconsideration of the theory of growth should explicitly deal with the fact that prices are sticky, so that their adjustment remains incomplete and price disequilibria may be sustained during rather long periods. A correct representation of this fact requires that price adjustments are themselves represented.

My own view on how this ought to be done has already been put in print (Malinvaud, 1980, pp. 20–1 and 52–3). I believe that the econometric explorations into the actual dynamics of prices and wages must be our main guide. I agree that such explorations do not always lead to clear-cut results and that the transposition of these results by simple equations to be put in theoretical models will make the latter look very ad hoc; but I do not see any better solution.

Any growth theory should of course make it clear by how much its results depend on the specific hypotheses that have been chosen concerning price adjustments. A kind of sensitivity analysis should protect against the risk of errors owing to too-special specifications.

Keynesian stationary states

Starting from the preceding ideas, I should like to demonstrate that an interesting reconsideration of the theory of growth is feasible. In so doing I shall make a very modest start at such a reconsideration and put just one question: is economic growth subject to a cumulative process that would explain why some countries during some historical periods have experienced an apparently self-sustained growth while others, or the same ones at different times, were trapped in stagnation?

The question has, of course, many aspects. Even restricting attention to the process of capital accumulation, I cannot claim more than to provide a partial and provisional answer.

Like most students of growth, I shall consider only the real economy and pay no attention to money or financial operations. I shall moreover make a drastic hypothesis: namely that the economy is permanently in a state of excess supply. This hypothesis will make the formalization easier than it would otherwise be. Moreover, if we are going to choose a simple hypothesis for building a non-monetary theory about the role of disequilibria on economic growth, assuming a situation of general excess supply is probably the best we can do; it is not without relevance and does not place money to the forefront.

To represent capital accumulation in a fully aggregated model, we shall assume that technology is putty-clay, is not subject to any technical progress and has constant returns to scale (economies of scale and embodied technical progress would of course affect any cumulative process that we can find).

If y is (net) output, $\bar{y}$ productive capacity, K capital and L labour, the constraint on production will be

$$L = yg(k) \quad \text{with } k = K/\bar{y} \tag{1}$$

and

$$y \leqslant \bar{y} \tag{2}$$

In other words, $g(k)$ is the labour requirement by unit of output; it is a (decreasing) function of the capital–output ratio (at full capacity).

(Its derivative g' is *minus* the marginal rate of substitution between labour and capital at full capacity.)

We shall not consider the investment equation right away but shall first define a *Walrasian stationary state* for reference in what follows. Output will of course be equal to capacity and labour input L to the constant labour supply $\bar{L}$. The (real) wage rate will then be w and the (real) interest rate, r. They will be respectively equal to the marginal productivities of labour and capital in a Walrasian state; hence

$$\frac{r}{w} = -g'(k) \tag{3}$$

$$r = \frac{-g'(k)}{g(k) - kg'(k)} \tag{4}$$

which imply

$$wg(k) + rk = 1. \tag{5}$$

To keep the analysis very simple we shall assume that, when (net) investment is zero, as is required by the hypothesis of a stationary state, aggregate demand is the sum of an autonomous component x (about which I shall say more later on), and of labour income wL; hence the equation

$$y = wL + x. \tag{6}$$

Equations (1), (3), (4) and (6) give one degree of freedom in the simultaneous determination of y, k, x, w and r for a given $L = \bar{L}$. One may easily characterize the changes of the first four of these variables as functions of the changes of the last one, along this one-dimensional family of Walrasian stationary states, at least if one considers only infinitesimal changes dy, dk, dx, dw and dr.

Let α, β and σ be respectively the labour share, the capital share and the elasticity of substitution at full capacity:

$$\alpha = wg(k) \qquad \beta = rk = 1 - \alpha$$

$$\sigma = \frac{-g'(k)\,[g(k) - kg'(k)]}{kg(k)\,g''(k)}. \tag{7}$$

Then differentiation of (1), (3), (4) and (6) leads to

$$\frac{dy}{y} = \frac{-\beta\sigma}{\alpha}\frac{dr}{r} \qquad \frac{dk}{k} = -\sigma\frac{dr}{r}$$

$$\frac{dx}{y} = \beta\left(1 - \frac{\sigma}{\alpha}\right)\frac{dr}{r} \qquad \frac{dw}{w} = \frac{-\beta}{\alpha}\frac{dr}{r}. \tag{8}$$

Along the family of Walrasian stationary states, y, k and w increase as the interest rate decreases. The relation between autonomous demand x and the real rate of interest r depends on the sign of $\alpha - \sigma$: if the labour share is larger than the elasticity of substitution, then a decrease in the rate of interest must be accompanied by a decrease in autonomous demand, because the increase in labour income is then larger than the increase in productive capacity; the opposite relation holds if the elasticity of substitution is larger than the labour share.

Similarly, we can define Keynesian stationary states, for constant and exogenously given values of r, w and x. These states will serve as a reference for the discussion to be made subsequently.

Considering that the real prices, r and w, as well as 'autonomous' demand x, remain constant when excess supply prevails on both markets is of course disputable. This hypothesis will be examined later on. Similarly, we shall have to ask for which set of values of r, w and x can Keynesian stationary states appear.

The states to be considered are characterized by excess capacity: $\bar{y} > y$. If firms choose to keep this excess capacity, it is because of a net profitability:

$$\pi = \frac{y - wL}{K} - r > 0. \tag{9}$$

More precisely, the assumption is made that the capacity is found to be satisfactory if

$$a\frac{\pi}{r} - b\left(1 - \frac{y}{\bar{y}}\right) = 0 \tag{10}$$

where a and b are two positive numbers. The argument for such an assumption has been developed in *Profitability and Unemployment* (Malinvaud, 1980, pp. 29–36): since firms are uncertain as to the future demand for their products, they choose a capacity that is the higher as profitability is itself higher.[3]

An assumption as to the optimal capital–output ratio in such an economy with excess capacity must also be made. When firms choose k for a given capacity $\bar{y}$ and given average expected demand y, they consider the cost of a 'marginal' productivity investment, $r\bar{y}\,dk$ and the labour cost that will be saved, $-wyg'\,dk$. Hence, the optimal k is such that

$$\frac{r}{w} = -\frac{y}{\bar{y}}g'(k). \tag{11}$$

Equations (1), (6), (9), (10) and (11) define a system that must be

satisfied by a Keynesian stationary state. This system can be somewhat simplified by elimination of π, K and L. Indeed, the equations
in (12) are obtained as follows: the first one by eliminating L
from (1) and (6), the second one by eliminating π, K and L from (1),
(6), (9) and (10), the third one by rewriting (11):

$$
\left.
\begin{aligned}
&[1 - wg(k)]\, y = x \\[2mm]
&ak\bar{y} + bk(\bar{y} - y) = \frac{ax}{r} \\[2mm]
&r\bar{y} + wyg'(k) = 0.
\end{aligned}
\right\} \tag{12}
$$

This system may be viewed as determining y, $\bar{y}$ and k from given
values of x, w and r, under the assumption that a Keynesian stationary
state will result.

It will be convenient to consider it in differential form, in other
words to work with a linear approximation of the system in a neighbourhood of one particular Keynesian stationary state. Moreover,
this state will be assumed to be close enough to a Walrasian stationary
state for another approximation to be made: namely that, in the
coefficients of the linear approximation, the values of the variables
are assumed to fulfil the equations prevailing in a Walrasian stationary
state.

Taking (7) into account in the differentiation of (12), we obtain

$$
\left.
\begin{aligned}
&\beta \frac{dy}{y} + \beta \frac{dk}{k} = \alpha \frac{dw}{w} + \frac{dx}{y} \\[2mm]
&\beta \left(1 + \frac{b}{a}\right)\frac{d\bar{y}}{y} - \frac{\beta b}{a}\frac{dy}{y} + \beta \frac{dk}{k} = \frac{dx}{y} - \beta \frac{dr}{r} \\[2mm]
&\frac{d\bar{y}}{y} - \frac{dy}{y} + \frac{1}{\alpha\sigma}\frac{dk}{k} = \frac{dw}{w} - \frac{dr}{r}.
\end{aligned}
\right\} \tag{13}
$$

This system can be solved for dk, dy and $d(\bar{y} - y)$ and is then
rewritten as

$$
\left.
\begin{aligned}
&\frac{dk}{k} = \alpha\sigma \left[(1 + \alpha\gamma)\frac{dw}{w} - (1 - \beta\gamma)\frac{dr}{r}\right] \\[2mm]
&\frac{d(\bar{y} - y)}{y} = -\gamma \left[\alpha \frac{dw}{w} + \beta \frac{dr}{r}\right] \\[2mm]
&\frac{dy}{y} = \frac{\alpha}{\beta}[1 - \beta\sigma(1 + \alpha\gamma)]\frac{dw}{w} + \alpha\sigma(1 - \beta\gamma)\frac{dr}{r} + \frac{1}{\beta}\frac{dx}{y}.
\end{aligned}
\right\} \tag{14}
$$

with

$$\gamma = \left[\beta \left(1 + \frac{b}{a} \right) \right]^{-1}. \tag{15}$$

One finds that, in the family of Keynesian stationary states, the capital–output ratio at full capacity is an increasing function of the real wage rate and a decreasing function of the real interest rate. It is more interesting to note that excess capacity is a decreasing function of both the real wage and real interest rates. Output is an increasing function of autonomous demand and of the real interest rate. It is also an increasing function of the real wage rate if the elasticity of substitution is not too large; more precisely if

$$\sigma < \frac{a + b}{a + \beta b} \tag{16}$$

(the right-hand side is larger than one). The unfamiliar role of the elasticity of substitution in the output equation is easily explained by the first of equations (12): factors that stimulate capital deepening have a depressing effect because they lower the labour input in a stationary state; hence, other things being equal, they tend to depress labour income.

We must now consider the conditions on the variables w, r and x for the existence of such a Keynesian stationary state. These conditions are of course that the solution of (12) leads to excess supplies on both markets.

It will be enough here to consider which changes of w, r and x from a Walrasian stationary state may lead to a Keynesian stationary state. The second of equations (14) immediately shows that appearance of a permanent excess supply of goods depends only on changes of w and r. Those leading to such excess supply are in the direction given by

$$\alpha \frac{dw}{w} + \beta \frac{dr}{r} < 0. \tag{17}$$

We must similarly examine which changes may lead to permanent excess supply of labour. It is equivalent to look for changes under which

$$\frac{dL}{L} = \frac{dy}{y} + \frac{kg'}{g} \frac{dk}{k} < 0. \tag{18}$$

The required inequality on dw, dr and dx, derived from equations (14), may be written as

$$\frac{dx}{y} + \mu \frac{dw}{w} + v \frac{dr}{r} < 0 \tag{19}$$

with

$$\mu = \alpha - \beta\sigma(1 + \alpha\gamma) \qquad v = \beta\sigma(1 - \beta\gamma). \tag{20}$$

The coefficient v is of course positive and μ is also positive if the elasticity of substitution is not too large, more precisely if

$$\sigma < \frac{\alpha(a + b)}{a + \beta b} = \omega. \tag{21}$$

It is also easy to check that μ/v is larger than α/β precisely when σ is smaller than α.

The three possible cases for the conditions on dx, dw and dr are illustrated in figures 1-3 drawn in the (w, r) plane. The point W is supposed to correspond to a Walrasian stationary state, the line D to the changes of w and r that leave the excess supply of goods equal to zero, the line D_L to the changes that leave the excess supply of labour equal to zero; the dotted line is the new position taken by D_L in case a positive change dx is brought to autonomous demand. The region for Keynesian stationary states is in all three cases the one that is below both D and D_L.

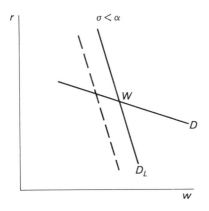

FIGURE 1

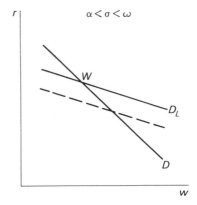

FIGURE 2

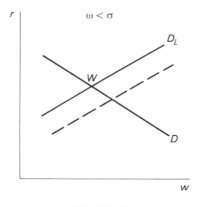

FIGURE 3

One is not surprised to find that an increase in autonomous demand reduces the region for Keynesian unemployment. The final effects of changes in the real wage and interest rates must be understood through their effects on consumption, that is on labour income, since net investment is null in any stationary state.

There are two possible depressing effects on labour income: either a reduction of the real wage rate w or a reduction of labour input. A decrease of the labour requirement per unit of output is associated with a decrease of r/w and is the stronger as the elasticity of substitution σ is larger. A too low real interest rate is depressing because of its impact on the labour requirement. A too low real wage rate is depressing because of its impact on the price of labour, unless its impact on the labour requirement dominates, as would be the case if the elasticity of substitution were high.

The Keynesian depression that is described by the preceding model has its origin in a permanent deficiency of aggregate demand. But the question may be raised to know whether it is realistic to assume that the exogenous variables, and in particular the prices, will stay constant in such a depression.

The model operates with real magnitudes only. One may think that the simultaneous decrease of the nominal wage rate and the price level, or rather a slower increase than would realistically occur in the otherwise stationary Walrasian state, will stimulate economic activity through the well-known real wealth effects. This is indeed true in the short run if part of the consumers' wealth is in nominal assets; but even in this case it is not sufficient in the long run, as I have shown in *Profitability and Unemployment* (Malinvaud, 1980):

a Keynesian stationary state will still be reached, in which the consumers will have a smaller real wealth than in the corresponding Walrasian stationary state.

The first exogenous variable in the model is the so-called autonomous demand, which is essentially government demand and also that part of consumption that comes from the net transfers from government to households. Whether this would be kept permanently too small in face of a deficient aggregate demand is, of course, a question. There is not more to be said at this stage, except to note that the question will be considered again in the next section of this paper.

If a spontaneous pressure to raise the real wage rate were to exist, the Keynesian depression would not be sustained. Such a pressure could of course come from political forces or from trade union activity. As for economic forces, they are likely to work in the wrong direction in most cases. Econometric studies seem to show that a given degree of slack on the labour market reacts more on the wage rate than the same degree of slack on the goods market would do on the price level; hence, except when the rate of unemployment is much smaller than the degree of excess capacity, the nominal wage rate should tend to drift downward more quickly than should prices. If anything, the hypothesis of a constant real wage rate appears to be too optimistic in most cases.

Whether the real interest rate should be kept constant in a positive model of the Keynesian depression is a question that reminds us of the debates that occurred when the General Theory was discussed in the 1940s. Let me simply note here that, in order to stimulate aggregate demand, one usually thinks of lowering interest rates; but our analysis concludes that, in all cases, if such a policy were maintained and if a new stationary state were achieved, then it would correspond to a still deeper depression. There is clearly here a contradiction between short-term and long-term effects.

This shows the limitations of a comparative analysis that is restricted to stationary states. Short-term dynamics can no longer be neglected. Hence, we are going to turn our attention to it. Actually, I now want to examine the impact of a policy of low interest rate intended to stimulate or sustain economic growth.

A self-sustained growth?

Analysts of economic growth have been led to think of cumulative processes that would generate virtuous or vicious circles. The argument has not been made very accurate so far,[4] but runs about as follows. A good initial profitability stimulates investment, hence later both productivity and competitiveness on foreign markets; this in turn is responsible for high profits and high profitability; and so on. The role of international competition in such an argument is of course important in practice and may be necessary to explain the characteristics of the growth process experienced in some countries. But it is a relevant theoretical question to ask whether, even in a closed economy, a cumulative process could not be generated by the causation chain running from profitability to investment to productivity to profitability.

The full discussion of a dynamic model that would aim at correctly representing this causation chain would be too complex to be taken up in this paper. I shall only introduce this discussion by a heuristic examination of the consequences that would follow if, starting from a Keynesian stationary state, the economy would experience a profitability boom initiated by a sudden decrease of the real interest rate.

This examination is interesting also with respect to a close scrutiny of the thesis advocating a policy of low interest rates. According to A. Leijonhufvud (1968, esp. section V.2), substantiating this thesis was an important motivation of Keynes throughout his writings. This is an extra reason why I find it appropriate to consider it here and to make the hypothesis of generalized excess supply.

Starting from a Keynesian stationary state ruled by equations (1), (6), (10) and (11) and corresponding to given values of x, w and r, let us assume a sudden change δr on the interest rate while x and w remain unchanged.

This will have two immediate effects that appear on equations (9) and (11): profitability π will increase, and the desired full capacity capital–output ratio k will increase. Hence investment will positively react for two reasons: the increase of profitability will stimulate construction of capacities (capital-widening), and the decrease of the capital cost will stimulate substitution of capital for labour (capital-deepening).

The exact equations ruling this investment boom might be discussed here. An accurate representation of the short-term dynamics would require a careful specification of the various lags involved in the changes of the volume and composition of capital. This would make the theory quite complex, as everyone knows.

We shall be satisfied here with a simple formulation in continuous time with instantaneous but partial adaptation of capital to the current economic conditions. Such a formulation may be good enough as a framework for reflections about the growth process, even though it would obviously be inappropriate for a precise study of business cycles.

Net investment will then be written as

$$i = k\dot{\bar{y}} + \bar{y}\dot{k} \tag{22}$$

$\dot{\bar{y}}$ and $\dot{k}$ being the speeds of variation of $\bar{y}$ and k. Writing here v for the current degree of capacity utilization $y/\bar{y}$ and $\hat{k}$ for the desired full-capacity capital–output ratio, we shall assume that productive capacity changes depend positively on profitability π and negatively on excess capacity, whereas changes in k depend on the difference between the desired and actual values of this variable. These assumptions are specified by

$$\dot{\bar{y}} = \left[a\frac{\pi}{r} - b(1-v) \right] \bar{y} \tag{23}$$

$$\dot{k} = \lambda(\hat{k} - k) \tag{24}$$

$$\frac{r}{w} = - vg'(\hat{k}) \tag{25}$$

where λ is a (small) positive number (one notes that equation (23) is consistent with the previous hypothesis that equation (10) holds for stationary states).

The dynamic system is then defined by equations (23)–(25) together with (1), (9) and a new equation replacing (6), namely

$$y = wL + x + k\dot{\bar{y}} + \bar{y}\dot{k}. \tag{26}$$

This system is rather complex and will not be discussed precisely here. An appendix to this chapter is devoted to it.

The argument in the appendix shows that one condition is necessary and sufficient for the system to have an admissible solution in the neighbourhood of a Keynesian stationary state that is close enough to a Walrasian stationary state. This condition then implies that the growth path converges to a Keynesian stationary state. It is precisely

$$a + b + \alpha\lambda\sigma < r. \tag{27}$$

Let us discuss the implications of the dynamic system that we built in order to represent the investment boom following a sudden decrease of the real interest rate. In order to do so, let us first examine the resulting evolution when inequality (27) holds, then wonder what can be said when the opposite inequality is true, and finally look at the meaning of condition (27).

Figure 4 shows what type of evolution will be followed, when (27) holds, by the three main variables of the model: the productive capacity $\bar{y}$, the full-capacity capital–output ratio k, the actual output y (the real wage rate w and autonomous demand x are assumed to be constant all the way through). The initial investment boom concerns both the building of new capacities and a substitution of capital for labour; output then suddenly increases. But the speed of investment later declines, so that the output level also declines. After a while there may even be some decrease in productive capacity. In any case, the level of output is eventually smaller than it was initially, before the decrease of the interest rate.

When the opposite inequality to (27) holds, the dynamic system can no longer be considered to apply because it would describe the evolution of an unstable temporary equilibrium, that is, of a temporary equilibrium whose realization can no longer be realistically assumed. This is indeed a case in which the multiplier process, which is supposed to operate within the temporary equilibrium, becomes explosive.

Indeed, for the determination of this equilibrium, k and $\bar{y}$ are considered to be predetermined by past evolution. But output, investment and other variables are assumed to be simultaneously determined. In particular, equations (22)–(25), together with (9), may be considered to define investment as a function of output and

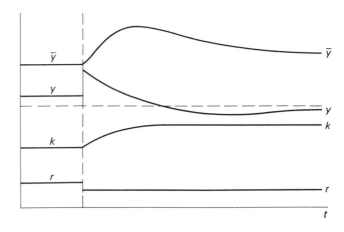

FIGURE 4

the predetermined variables. One may see that the partial derivative of this function actually is

$$\frac{\partial i}{\partial y} = (a + b + \alpha\lambda\sigma)\, k. \tag{28}$$

Similarly, equations (1), (22) and (26) may be considered to determine output as a function of investment and predetermined variables, the relevant partial derivative then being

$$\frac{\partial y}{\partial i} = \frac{1}{rk}. \tag{29}$$

By a well-known argument, stability of the multiplier process requires the product of the two preceding partial derivatives to be smaller than one, which is precisely inequality (27).

If the opposite inequality holds, investment tends to react too strongly to contemporaneous changes in output for any equilibrium to be possible after the decrease in interest rate, except at a lower level of output,[5] which is of course paradoxical. In other words, we may say that, in this case, there is indeed a cumulative process, increases in investment and output reinforcing each other; but this process operates instantaneously and destroys the feasibility of a temporary equilibrium.

In order to understand the meaning of this result, one must of course remember the specification of the model and the fact that a number of lags have been neglected. If these lags were taken into account, the cumulative process would no longer be instantaneous. We may then consider that the opposite inequality to (27) represents the condition for the existence of a virtuous circle involving profitability–investment–productivity. If this interpretation is accepted, the following inequality

$$a + b + \alpha\lambda\sigma > r \tag{30}$$

may be viewed as the condition for the existence of vicious and virtuous circles.

In the left-hand side of this inequality, we find the three parameters, a, b, and λ, that describe the speed of reaction of investment to its factors: profitability, pressure of demand, and excess of the desired over the actual full-capacity capital–output ratio. High values of these parameters may be responsible for the appearance of a cumulative process. We note that a high elasticity of substitution can also lead to such a result.

Before we leave inequality (30), we must still note that the value of the right-hand side depends on the assumption that consumption is equal to real labour income. This is made apparent by equation (29), which suggests also how (27) and (30) would have to be changed if other hypotheses were chosen for the formalization of savings behaviour.

One might dwell on the model of the preceding sections and modify it so as to try to take a better account of various considerations. In particular, one may remark that the time profiles presented in figure 4 depend on the hypothesis that the real wage w and autonomous demand x remain constant, no matter what course is followed by other variables. This is indeed disputable.

Concerning the real wage rate in particular, the investment boom will increase the demand for labour: simultaneously, the rise of labour productivity will make it socially inadmissible to maintain a fixed real wage rate. In other words, there seem to be good reasons for believing in a drift of real wages, a drift that would of course change the evolution of the variables.

How this should be formalized is not very clear. One rather simple solution is to admit that the wage share must remain constant. This certainly exaggerates the short-term flexibility of the wage rate, since it is a well established fact that the wage share decreases in the early phases of economic booms. But it may be admissible for a study of the medium-term dynamics. In any case, it is a convenient alternative to the hypothesis of a constant real wage.

Although the dynamic system so defined differs from the one studied in the preceding sections, its implications are very similar: inequality (27) still holds as the condition for stability of the multiplier process; convergence to a Keynesian stationary state still holds when this condition is met and when, moreover, inequality (16) applies, that is, when the elasticity of substitution is not too large.

But it is more interesting to wonder whether the model studied really catches what was implied in the heuristic ideas of virtuous and vicious circles when they were put forward by analysts of modern growth. In this respect the following argument may be ventured.

In Western Europe the decades of the 1950s and 1960s were marked by a rapid increase of autonomous demand. The political choice in favour of the 'welfare state' induced the building of many public equipments and a quick development of transfers. This trend, possibly reinforced by an 'autonomous' drive towards higher real wages, resulted in a permanent risk of excess pressure on productive capacities. Faced with this common situation, the various countries did not behave in the same way.

Perhaps favoured by the conditions prevailing in the immediate postwar period, some countries experienced high profitability, low real interest rates, a fast growth of productive capacities and a quick substitution of capital for labour. Hence, on the one hand the increase of demand could be matched; on the other hand the investment boom did not result in excess capacity. Roughly speaking, we may say that only the first phases of figure 4 can be illustrative of such an evolution.

Other countries, on the contrary, found themselves, time and again, facing an excess demand, which could be checked only by a deflationary policy. Investment remained sluggish and productivity increased only slowly, profitability being on the whole rather low. The analysis of the preceding sections cannot be considered to apply since the excess supply hypothesis cannot be maintained.

Still, the fact that two such distinct courses of events could occur against similar non-economic conditions is explained by the phenomenon that I wanted to stress here: adaptations of relative prices remain incomplete, so that favourable or unfavourable price disequilibria may be sustained over rather long periods; this in turn strongly reacts on economic growth. Moreover, to the extent that a deficiency of aggregate demand is not to be feared in the medium-term future, one easily finds arguments for a deliberate policy of low interest rates.

Appendix

The dynamic process defined by equations (1), (9) and (23)–(26) may be reduced to the following system on the four endogenous variables $v, \bar{y}, k$ and $\hat{k}$:

$$k\dot{\bar{y}} = \left\{ \left[\frac{a}{r} + bk - \frac{aw}{r} g(k) \right] v - (a+b)k \right\} \bar{y} \tag{31}$$

$$\dot{k} = \lambda(\hat{k} - k) \tag{32}$$

$$0 = r + wg'(\hat{k}) v \tag{33}$$

$$k\dot{\bar{y}} + \bar{y}\dot{k} = [1 - wg(k)] v\bar{y} - x. \tag{34}$$

Starting from a stationary state corresponding to values given to the exogenous variables w, r and x, we shall consider the evolution that would follow if these variables would be subject to once-for-all small changes $\delta w, \delta r$ and δx. Instead of working on the variables v, $\bar{y}$, $\hat{k}$ and k, we shall work on their deviations from the stationary state δv, $\delta \bar{y}$, $\delta \hat{k}$ and δk; we shall note that $\dot{\bar{y}} = \delta \dot{\bar{y}}$ and $\dot{k} = \delta \dot{k}$.

Moreover, we shall consider the linear approximation to system (31)–(34) in the neighbourhood of the stationary state, which will itself be assumed to be close to the Walrasian stationary equilibrium ($v = 1$).

The linear approximation permits calculus of δv and $\delta \hat{k}$ as functions of $\delta \bar{y}$, δk, δw, δr and δx. Indeed, (33) gives

$$\frac{\delta \hat{k}}{k} = \alpha \sigma \left(\delta v + \frac{\delta w}{w} - \frac{\delta r}{r} \right) \tag{35}$$

α and σ being defined by equations (7). Similarly, equations (31), (32) and (34) lead to

$$\left[\beta \left(1 - \frac{a}{r} \right) - bk \right] \delta v - \lambda \delta \hat{k} + (r + \lambda)\, \delta k + \beta \frac{\delta \bar{y}}{y}$$

$$= \alpha \left(1 - \frac{a}{r} \right) \frac{\delta w}{w} - \beta \frac{a}{r} \frac{\delta r}{r} + \frac{\delta x}{y}. \tag{36}$$

From (35) and (36), one easily derives

$$A\delta v = -(r + \lambda) \frac{\delta k}{k} - r \frac{\delta \bar{y}}{y} + (B - A) \frac{\delta w}{w} + (A - C) \frac{\delta r}{r} + \frac{1}{k} \frac{\delta x}{y} \tag{37}$$

$$A \frac{\delta \hat{k}}{k} = -\alpha \sigma (r + \lambda) \frac{\delta k}{k} - \alpha \sigma r \frac{\delta \bar{y}}{y} + \alpha \sigma B \frac{\delta w}{w} - \alpha \sigma C \frac{\delta r}{r} + \frac{\alpha \sigma}{k} \frac{\delta x}{y} \tag{38}$$

in which

$$A = r - a - b - \alpha \sigma \lambda \tag{39}$$

$$B = \frac{1}{\beta}(r - a - b\beta) \tag{40}$$

$$C = r - b. \tag{41}$$

Equations (31) and (32) then lead to a dynamic system relating directly the two endogenous variables $\delta \bar{y}$ and δk to the exogenous variables δw, δr and δx. Indeed, linearization of these equations give the following system:

$$\frac{\dot{\bar{y}}}{y} = (a + b)\, \delta v - \frac{a\alpha}{\beta} \frac{\delta w}{w} - a \frac{\delta r}{r} \tag{42}$$

$$\frac{\delta \dot{k}}{k} = \lambda \frac{\delta \hat{k}}{k} - \lambda \frac{\delta k}{k}. \tag{43}$$

Substitution of (37) and (38) then gives

$$A\frac{\dot{\bar{y}}}{y} = -r(a+b)\frac{\delta\bar{y}}{y} - (a+b)(r+\lambda)\frac{\delta k}{k} + \frac{\alpha}{\beta}\,[br + (a+\beta b)\sigma\lambda]\,\frac{\delta w}{w}$$

$$-(ar+\alpha b\sigma\lambda)\frac{\delta r}{r} + \frac{a+b}{k}\frac{\delta x}{y} \tag{44}$$

$$A\frac{\dot{k}}{k} = -\alpha r\sigma\lambda\frac{\delta\bar{y}}{y} - \lambda(r-a-b+\alpha\sigma r)\frac{\delta k}{k} + \alpha\sigma\lambda B\frac{\delta w}{w}$$

$$-\alpha\sigma\lambda C\frac{\delta r}{r} + \frac{\alpha\sigma\lambda}{k}\frac{\delta x}{y}. \tag{45}$$

The behaviour of the solution to this system depends on the characteristic roots, whose sum S and product P are easily seen to be given by

$$AS = -r(a+b) - \lambda(r-a-b+\alpha\sigma r) \tag{46}$$

$$A^2 P = \lambda(a+b)\,[r(r-a-b+\alpha\sigma r) - \alpha r\sigma(r+\lambda)] \tag{47}$$

which may also be written as

$$-AS = r(a+b) + \lambda A + \alpha\sigma\lambda(\lambda + r) \tag{48}$$

$$A^2 P = r\lambda(a+b)\,A. \tag{49}$$

It is clear that, when A is positive, the sum of the roots is negative and their product positive. Hence, when δw, δr and δx are held constant, the solution of the system converges to constant values of $\bar{y}$ and k, which implies constant values of v and $\hat{k}$ also.

One may, moreover, see that the two roots are real, since (48) and (49) lead to

$$A^2(S^2 - 4P) = [\lambda A - r(a+b)]^2 + \text{positive terms}. \tag{50}$$

Hence, the time profile of the difference between $\bar{y}$ (or k) and its limit value is the sum of two exponentials converging to zero.

If we assume again δr and δx to be exogenous but δw to vary in such a way that $wg(k)$ remains constant, we must replace in (44) and (45) the ratio $\delta w/w$ by $-g'\delta k/g$, or equivalently by $\beta\delta k/\alpha k$. This replacement changes the coefficients multiplying $\delta k/k$ and therefore also the characteristic roots. One finds that (48) and (49) must then be replaced by

$$-AS = r(a+b) + \lambda(1-\sigma\beta)(A + \alpha\sigma\lambda) + a\alpha\sigma\lambda \tag{51}$$

$$A^2 P = r\lambda\,[(a+b) - \sigma(a+b\beta)]\,A. \tag{52}$$

When A is positive and inequality (16) holds, which implies $\sigma\beta < 1$, S is negative and P positive. Hence, the dynamic system is again stable.

Notes

1 In *Profitability and Unemployment* (Malinvaud, 1980) I tried to provide a justification for the investment equation (pp. 29–37). I then used the most extreme form of a production function in which absolutely no substitutability between labour and capital is recognized. This explains why only excess capacity and profitability appear. Under more realistic hypotheses relative prices should play a greater role and, notably, the relative cost of capital with respect to labour should appear.

2 See for instance the articles by J. Ciccolo and G. Fromm, and by B. Malkiel, G. von Fürstenberg and H. S. Watson, in the *Journal of Finance*, May 1979.

3 The existence of excess capacity in a stationary state should not be viewed as paradoxical. This state must be considered as a first approximation for the stationary stochastic process that would appear if uncertainties were explicitly introduced in the formulation. Indeed, some uncertainty is assumed to remain at the level of individual firms.

4 The best presentation of the argument is probably that given by Beckerman (1966).

5 This is so at least for the linear system approximating our essentially non-linear model in the neighbourhood of a Keynesian stationary equilibrium. Considering feasible equilibria outside of such a neighbourhood would lead us much too far into a mathematical discussion.

References

Beckerman, W. (1966) 'The determinants of economic growth', in P. D. Henderson (ed.), *Economic Growth in Britain*, London.

Burmeister, E. and Dobell, A. R. (1970) *Mathematical Theories of Economic Growth*, New York.

Coddington, A. (1978) Review of E. Malinvaud's *The Theory of Unemployment Reconsidered*, in *Journal of Economic Literature*, February.

Hicks, J. R. (1965) *Capital and Growth*, Oxford.

Kornai, J. (1979) 'Resource-constrained versus demand-constrained systems', *Econometrica*, July.

Leijonhufvud, A. (1968) *On Keynesian Economics and the Economics of Keynes*, Oxford.

Malinvaud, E. (1980) *Profitability and Unemployment*, Cambridge.

5

Conjectural Stock and Flow Responses to Market Rationing: An Analysis of Output and Employment Multipliers in Non-Walrasian Equilibria

PANAYOTIS G. KORLIRAS

Introduction

It has long been recognized that 'a model which can serve as an adequate foundation of a monetary theory ... must distinguish between abstract exchange opportunities at some notionally called prices and actual transaction opportunities' (Hahn, 1965, p. 197). This distinction stems from the fundamental role of money, which is to serve as a means of payment. In a monetary economy, and thus in a proper monetary theory, the possibility of barter, that is the possibility that goods buy goods, must be excluded. This in turn requires that 'money be offered or demanded as one of the commodities entering into every trade'. It follows that money, far from being a mere 'veil', imposes an important restriction in the working or functioning of a monetary economy. For each agent–transactor, 'the total value of goods demanded cannot in any circumstances exceed the amount of money held by the transactor at the outset of the (trading) period' (Clower, 1967, pp. 208, 209). This restriction must be clearly distinguished from the general principle that 'no agent can plan a greater expenditure on goods and services than the receipts he plans to obtain from the sale of goods and services.' This is an 'accounting constraint', which, properly interpreted to include lending and borrowing, is merely taken as a basic assumption in economic theory (Arrow and Hahn, 1971, pp. 20–1). If one's earnings plans are not realized, then spending plans can be effectively constrained by a 'liquidity constraint'. This is where the difference between 'abstract' and 'actual' transaction opportunities becomes crucial.

Beginning with attempts to re-interpret Keynes (Clower, 1965, Leijonhufvud, 1968), a non-Walrasian theory has gradually developed, the principal characteristic of which is the abandonment of the Walrasian *tâtonnement* and the assumption that transactions can take place even at non-market-clearing prices. In such cases, the markets will have to operate at non-zero excess demands, and thus the buyer or seller who happens (on the basis of his original plans) to be in the long side of the market will have to be 'rationed'. This quantity market rationing constitutes the analytical basis for distinguishing between 'equilibrium' and 'disequilibrium' models.

The literature on non-market-clearing models with quantity rationing is quite extensive; on the level of a generalized theory we already have a comprehensive monograph (Barro and Grossman, 1976), as well as a stimulating application of that approach to the theory of unemployment (Malinvaud, 1977). Such recent theoretical work aims at re-interpreting the 'principle of multiplier', which is perhaps the most interesting (and best known, too) aspect of Keynesian economics, while at the same time it provides a fertile ground for re-examining the concept of general equilibrium in a monetary economy. As two recent survey articles point out (Muellbauer and Portes, 1978; Korliras, 1980), the type of non-Walrasian equilibrium that may result in such a framework clearly depends on the sort of microeconomic reactions or responses to market rationing. It is the purpose of this paper to examine that issue in detail, and to show that the magnitude of the 'real' output and employment multipliers can vary according to the agents' conjectural responses to rationing. The adjective 'conjectural' is used here on purpose; our aim is to link alternative responses to market rationing with expectations or 'conjectures' – indeed, in such a way that the 'informational imperfections' or underpinnings of disequilibrium models become obvious. In this respect, our attention in this paper will be concentrated on 'flow' and 'stock' reactions to rationing, mostly in the context of (competitive) 'fixprice' models, while price-setting will be considered briefly in the final section.

I

The simplest model of quantity rationing is based on Clower's illustration of the consequences of his 'dual decision hypothesis'. In this model, the entire economy is assumed to be characterized by a 'representative household' and a 'representative firm'. The firm is owned by the household, who receives all the profits (π) realized by the sale of the firm's output (y) to the household, while the latter provides the firm with the necessary labour input (l) in order to produce output. This simple prototype model is a miniature version of a general equilibrium system, in which both households and firms behave rationally, in the sense that their decisions are the outcomes of an optimization problem. Thus, the household attempts to

$$\text{max. } u(y^d, l^s) \quad \text{s.t. } py^d = wl^s + \pi$$

while the firm attempts to

$$\text{max. } \pi = py^s - wl^d \quad \text{s.t. } y^s = f(l^d) \quad \text{or} \quad y = f(l).$$

Rational behaviour for the firm means that profit maximization occurs at a point on the production function f such that its slope is equal to the slope of the line g (see figure 1), which in turn is equal to the real wage rate w/p, assumed as temporarily given. For the household, utility maximization occurs where the same line g is tangent to the highest possible indifference curve (h). In figure 1 we depict a market-clearing or Walrasian equilibrium (W-equilibrium) such that the household's and the firm's plans are mutually consist-

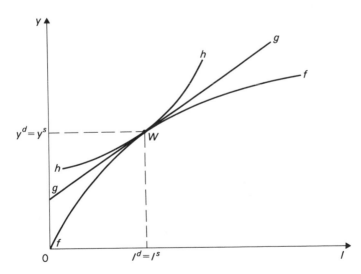

FIGURE 1

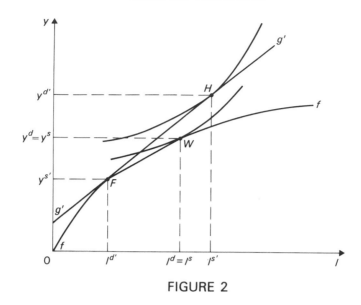

FIGURE 2

ent and thus realized. It is obvious that this W-equilibrium is also Pareto optimal.

In figure 2 we can see what happens if the system's relative price is different from its market-clearing value. Here we have a real wage rate $(w/p)'$ higher than the W-equilibrium w/p, so that the g' line is steeper than the g line consistent with W. As a result, the household's optimal decisions are given by the coordinates of H, which are $y^{d'}$ and $l^{s'}$; the firm's optimal decisions are given by the coordinates of point F which are $y^{s'}$ and $l^{d'}$. In this case we have

$$py^{d'} = wl^{s'} + \pi \quad \text{and} \quad \pi = py^{s'} - wl^{d'}$$

so that

$$p(y^{d'} - y^{s'}) + w(l^{d'} - l^{s'}) = 0 \quad \text{(Walras's law)}$$

We then assume that prices and wages change according to the respective excess demands in the output and labour markets:

$$\dot{p} = \alpha(y^{d'} - y^{s'}) \quad \dot{w} = \beta(l^{d'} - l^{s'}) \quad \alpha > 0, \beta \geqslant 0$$

As a result, in the situation shown in figure 2, prices will rise while (money) wages will fall, so that the real wage will decline. The g' line will change; it will become flatter until it becomes tangential to point W, like the g line in figure 1. The non-zero excess demands will be eliminated, and the system will converge to its market-clearing W-equilibrium. It is easy to see that the attainment of a Walrasian equilibrium is possible even if money wages are rigid, provided that prices respond properly to the sign and the magnitude of the excess demand for goods.

It is a well-known and elementary principle of economic theory that the coordinates of such points as H and F describe merely 'preferred' actions or intended purchases and sales at the going vector of prices (p, w). In other words, the excess demand functions in this framework are *ex ante* concepts, in the sense that 'the actual purchases and sales may differ from those that the theory of the decisions of agents tells us would be the purchases and sales regarded as proper by the agents at (the given) vector of prices' (Arrow and Hahn, 1971, p. 19). It is true, of course, that, if the real wage happens to be equal to the slope of the g line in figure 1, then the mutually consistent plans of the household and the firm make their 'preferred' actions realizable. But in the non-zero excess demands case of figure 2, it is questionable whether the *ex ante* excess demands can be relied upon in order to bring the system to its market-clearing W-equilibrium. It is at this point that Clower introduced his 'dual decision hypothesis'. Assuming that 'no purchase order is "validated" unless it is offset by a sale order that has already been executed', the dual decision hypothesis rests on the idea that, 'if realized current receipts are considered to impose any kind of constraint on current consumption plans, planned consumption as expressed in effective market offers to buy will necessarily be less than desired consumption as given by the (*ex ante*) demand functions of orthodox analysis' (Clower, 1965, pp. 289, 287). Here we have the case of effective income or liquidity constraints, which become binding only when the system operates at non-market-clearing or non-W-equilibrium prices. Thus, if transactions take place at the real wage implied by line g', we will then observe that households are rationed in the labour market.

This sort of market rationing will have to be resolved in some way, and the simplest way is to assume that 'actual' employment $(\bar{l})$ is the minimum of the 'desired' quantities of labour demanded and supplied at the going real wage rate, or

$$\bar{l} = \min(l^d, l^s).$$

For the household that had initially planned to buy y^d on the assumption that it would sell l^s (figure 3), the result of this labour market rationing will be that realized labour income, at given w/p, is less than what the household had anticipated. Therefore, its actual or 'effective' demand for output $\bar{y}^d$ will be less than its initially desired or 'notional' demand, y^d. The dual decision hypothesis says that the household, in its utility maximization problem, takes into consideration the effective income constraint caused by the labour market rationing, and comes up with a 'new' optimal level of output demand which is in accordance with this constraint. Thus,

'notional': $\quad py^d = wl^s + \pi; \quad \pi = py^s - wl^d; \quad y^s = f(l^d)$

'effective': $\quad p\bar{y}^d = w\bar{l} + \bar{\pi}; \quad \bar{\pi} = p\bar{y}^s - w\bar{l}; \quad \bar{y}^s = f(\bar{l}).$

Consequently,

$$p(\bar{y}^d - \bar{y}^s) + w(\bar{l} - \bar{l}) = 0 \quad \text{or} \quad y^d > \bar{y}^d = \bar{y}^s = y^s.$$

We notice here that, with the household rationed in the labour market, effective demand for output is less than notional demand but equal to the effective (= notional) supply of output. Prices will have no tendency to change. The fact that we have a positive notional excess demand for output is of no consequence, precisely because it cannot be 'validated' by available income. It remains to be seen if

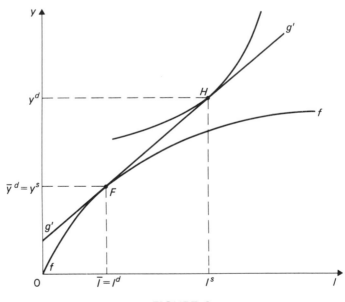

FIGURE 3

money wages have any tendency to change. If the magnitude $l^s - l^d$ causes a fall in money wages, then, despite the zero price change, the real wage rate will decline, pushing the economy towards the W-equilibrium. If, however, money wages are rigid, the economy will remain with 'unemployment' (equal to $l^s - \bar{l}$) at the less than Pareto-optimal point F. This situation is characterized as an 'under-employment equilibrium', or rather a 'quasi-equilibrium'. Although Clower meant this model to explain Keynes's proposition of an under-employment equilibrium, it is more appropriate to call it a 'classical unemployment' case, since unemployment is caused by the fact that money wages are too high rather than by a low level of expenditure (Malinvaud, 1977, pp. 66–7, 85). But as we shall see, this model is incomplete in an important way.

While the excess supply of labour case has been examined so far, the Cloweresque framework can be used to illustrate the opposite case, when the firm is rationed in the labour market. The two cases are, however, not symmetrical. As we see in figure 4, while the firm is rationed, the household can realize its planned supply of labour. Given the labour rationing, the firm will have to operate at point F'. As a result, actual production will be $\bar{y}$, and since the line g'' is not tangent to the production function at point F', the firm will not be maximizing its profits. Actual profits $\bar{\pi}$ will be less than anticipated profits, and it is those smaller profits that will be received by the

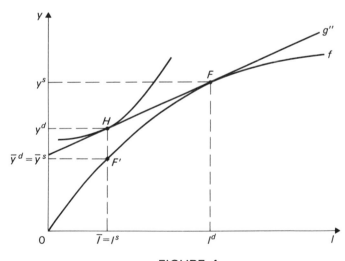

FIGURE 4

household as part of its disposable income. It follows that the house-hold, although not rationed in the labour market, will receive a smaller total income than it anticipated, so that its effective demand for output will again be less than its notional demand. Indeed, here we have:

notional: $py^d = wl^s + \pi;$ $\pi = py^s - wl^d;$ $y^s = f(l^d)$

effective: $p\bar{y}^d = w\bar{l} + \bar{\pi};$ $\bar{\pi} = p\bar{y}^s - w\bar{l};$ $\bar{y}^s = f(\bar{l}).$

Consequently,

$$p(\bar{y}^d - \bar{y}^s) + w(\bar{l} - \bar{l}) = 0 \quad \text{or} \quad y^d > \bar{y}^d = \bar{y}^s < y^s.$$

We thus see that, while in the excess supply of labour case the firm was able to realize all its purchase and sale plans and the household was on the long side in both markets, in the excess demand for labour case the firm is on the long side of both markets but the household cannot realize its notional demand for output plans. In this respect, the two cases are not symmetrical (owing, as it turns out, to the assumption about households earning currently realized profits – see the discussion in Arrow and Hahn, 1971, p. 365). The case shown in figure 4 resembles what can be called an 'under-consumption' equilibrium or disequilibrium at point F', which is also less than Pareto-optimal. Again, since effective demand and supply of output are equal, prices will not change. The economy will remain at point F' as long as money wages are rigid. If, however, money wages are flexible upwards, the excess demand for labour $l^d - l$ will cause real wages to increase, pushing the economy towards a market-clearing W-equilibrium, with both higher levels of employment and output (Korliras, 1976, pp. 275–7).

II

The elementary model of market rationing we have examined so far is, as mentioned earlier, incomplete. It raises a number of issues concerning the household's and the firm's responses to market rationing, issues that cannot be resolved unless we broaden the scope of the agents' choice-theoretic options. Indeed, the possibility of attaining an 'equilibrium' with initial excess supply or excess demand conditions in the labour market rests on the assumption that, in the first case $(l^s > \bar{l})$, the household 'continues to offer to sell labour services according to its notional supply schedule, despite the demand-imposed constraint on its employment', while in the second case $(l^d > \bar{l})$, the firm 'continues to offer to purchase labour services according to its notional demand schedule, despite the supply-imposed constraint on its employment of labour' (Barro and Grossman, 1976, pp. 53, 78). It is clear that such assumptions, although convenient in order to show, for example, that 'classical unemployment' is due to downward wage rigidity, are evidently questionable within the framework of the dual decision hypothesis. If, as a result of their being rationed in the labour market, the consumers cannot purchase as much output as they desire, it is reasonable to doubt whether they will continue to offer the amount of labour services they had initially planned, even at the going real wage rate. The fact that they end up being rationed in the output market as well ought in principle to feed back on their utility maximization problem, possibly leading to a new and lower 'optimal' quantity of labour supply, consistent with the lower level of consumption. The household, on the other hand, may indeed continue to offer to sell its initial notional quantity of labour services (thus maintaining the excess supply in the labour market) if it expects that the current constraints on its employment and consumption are temporary and are likely to disappear in the near future. In such a case, non-static expectations concerning the rationing constraints may induce the households to behave in a way that is transparent in our previous diagrams. For example, the expectation that the employment constraint is only temporary may induce the household to resist the decline in its current consumption, by liquidating part of its (liquid) wealth in order to supplement its temporarily reduced disposable income. As a result, effective demand for output will be greater than effective supply, and prices will tend to increase, so that even with rigid money wages the economy may tend towards a W-equilibrium. Evidently, that depends both on expectations about the degree of temporariness of the current employment constraint, and on the existence of liquid wealth which can serve as a buffer-stock in any attempt to resist a decline in the household's consumption level. If we use Δm to denote the desired liquidation of the household's wealth, we have:

notional: $wl^s + \pi = py^d$

effective: $\Delta m + w\bar{l} + \bar{\pi} = p\bar{y}^d$ if $\bar{l} < l^s$

We then have three alternatives:

$$\bar{y}^d = y^d \quad \text{and} \quad \Delta m > 0 \qquad \text{(liquidation of wealth)}$$

$$\bar{y}^d < y^d \quad \text{and} \quad \Delta m > 0 \qquad \text{(liquidation of wealth)}$$

$$\bar{y}^d < y^d \quad \text{and} \quad \Delta m = 0 \qquad \text{(the case shown in figure 3)}$$

Given the state of expectations and the availability of these buffer-stocks, it does make a difference to the working of the model which one of the above three alternatives is chosen by the household.

A similar argument can be advanced for the case when the firm is rationed in the labour market (see figure 4 and the analysis that follows). It is questionable whether the firm will continue to demand its notional quantity of labour services, since its volume of production and sales has also been reduced. Normally, we would expect the firm to reduce its desired demand for labour services to a level commensurate with the new and lower level of sales, thus not maintaining an upward pressure on money wages. On the other hand, the firm may continue to demand the initial notional-desired amount of labour services if it expects that the rationing in both the labour and the output markets is only temporary and likely to disappear in the near future. Again, non-static expectations may induce the firm to behave differently than the way shown in figure 4. For example, the firm may 'liquidate' (reduce) its stock inventory of finished products in order to satisfy the current demand for output, which potentially stands at a $y^d > \bar{y}^s$ level. If it does so, its sales will exceed current production and as a result profits will also be higher. In turn, these higher profits will be distributed to the consumer who owns the firm, thus enabling the household to realize its notional demand for output. Then we may have not only an excess demand for labour, but also an effective excess demand for output. Thus, the firm's reaction to labour market rationing may be different than the reaction implicit in the simple model underlying figure 4, depending both on expectations and on the existence of stock inventories that can serve as buffer-stocks. If we denote by x the volume of output sales and by Δi the desired liquidation of stocks, we have

notional: $x = y^s(l^d)$

effective: $\bar{x} = \bar{y}(\bar{l}) + \Delta i \quad \text{if} \quad \bar{l} < l^d.$

We then have three alternatives:

$$\bar{x} = x = y^s \quad \text{and} \quad \Delta i > 0 \qquad \text{(liquidation of stocks)}$$

$$\bar{x} < x = y^s \quad \text{and} \quad \Delta i > 0 \qquad \text{(liquidation of stocks)}$$

$\bar{x} < x = y^s$ and $\Delta i = 0$ (the case shown in figure 4).

Again, given the state of expectations and the availability of these stock-inventories, the working of the model will be affected by the choice of one of the above three alternative reactions.

The preceding discussion makes obvious the need to enlarge the scope of the household's and the firm's reaction to market rationing, preferably in the context of a dynamic or intertemporal choice-theoretic model. A rudimentary such model would consist of distinguishing two periods – the present and the future – denoted by subscripts 1 and 2 respectively. At the beginning of the present period, the household carries from the past an amount of liquid wealth m_0 while the firm possesses a stock-inventory equal to i_0. The problem can then be formulated as follows.

For the household: $m_0 + w_1 l_1^s + \pi_1 = p_1 y_1^d + m_1$

$m_1 + w_2 l_2^s + \pi_2 = p_2 y_2^d + m_2$

For the firm: $i_0 + y_1^s = x_1 + i_1; \pi_1 = p_1 x_1 - w_1 l_1^d$

$i_1 + y_2^s = x_2 + i_2; \pi_2 = p_2 x_2 - w_2 l_2^d.$

This formulation enables the household to use intra-period changes in its liquid wealth as a (precautionary–speculative) carry-over element serving as buffer-stock, given the nature of the current market rationing, the desired 'terminal' value of liquid wealth (m_2) and the state of its expectations about the variables relevant to the future period. Obviously, the above changes in liquid wealth can be either positive or negative, so that the possibility of borrowing and lending is included here. Likewise, the firm may use intra-period changes in its stock-inventories, given i_0 and i_2, and given its expectations about the future. In such a model of the firm, inventories play a role analogous to that of liquid wealth or money balances in the model of the household (Muellbauer and Portes, 1978).

This two-period model can only be taken indicatively. In fact, our discussion implies a multi-period intertemporal optimization model for the household and the firm, such that in each period the agents attempt to react to any sort of market rationing by resorting either to a 'flow reaction' or to a 'stock reaction', or to a combination of both. These reactions will be conditioned by the initial and terminal conditions of the buffer-stocks (e.g. m_0, m_2 and i_0, i_2), which can be taken as given parameters of our problem, symbolized by θ_h for the household and θ_f for the firm. Furthermore, the agents' reactions will also be conditioned by their expectations concerning the future, symbolized by E_h and E_f respectively.

We may thus distinguish between two general situations, regarded as particular points on a dynamic time-path of the choice variables. In the first situation, the economy proceeds in an undisturbed temporal sequence of W-equilibria, which in the case of a stationary state results in unchanged and realized notional actions of the household (y^d, l^s) and the firm (y^s, l^d). In the second situation we have cases of market rationing, which can generate the following reactions.

For the household:

$$y^d \geqslant \bar{y}^d = \bar{y}^d(\bar{l}; \theta_h, E_h) \quad \text{and} \quad \Delta m \geqslant 0 \quad \text{if} \quad \bar{l} = l^d < l^s$$

$$l^s \geqslant \bar{l}^s = \bar{l}^s(\bar{y}; \theta_h, E_h) \quad \text{and} \quad \Delta m \leqslant 0 \quad \text{if} \quad \bar{y} = y^s < y^d.$$

For the firm:

$$y^s \geqslant \bar{y}^s = \bar{y}^s(\bar{l}; \theta_f, E_f) \quad \text{and} \quad \Delta i \geqslant 0 \quad \text{if} \quad \bar{l} = l^s < l^d$$

$$l^d \geqslant \bar{l}^d = \bar{l}^d(\bar{y}; \theta_f; E_f) \quad \text{and} \quad \Delta i \leqslant 0 \quad \text{if} \quad \bar{y} = y^d < y^s.$$

The household can be rationed in the labour market, thus facing an effective 'employment constraint' which makes its realized income less than planned. As a result, the household may react only by reducing its demand for output (a 'flow reaction'); or by only liquidating wealth or borrowing in order to realize its notional demand for output (a 'stock reaction'); or, finally, by reducing its effective demand by less than in the case of the pure flow reaction while at the same time resorting to some liquidation of wealth or borrowing (a 'mixed flow–stock reaction'). Alternatively, the household may be rationed in the goods market, facing an effective 'consumption constraint'. Possible reactions include: a reduction in its labour supply (flow reaction); the accumulation of wealth caused by the unsatisfied demand for output, with unchanged labour supply (stock reaction); or mixed stock–flow reaction, a combination of the above. Now the firm may be rationed in the labour market, facing an effective 'labour constraint'. In reaction to that, it can reduce its effective supply of output (flow reaction); maintain its planned supply of output by liquidating its inventories of available finished products (stock reaction); adopt a mixed stock–flow reaction. Alternatively, the firm may be rationed in the goods market, thus facing an effective 'sales constraint'. Possible reactions include: a reduction of its effective demand for labour inputs (flow reaction); accumulation of unsold products as inventories while maintaining its labour demand unchanged (stock reaction); a mixed stock-flow reaction.

These pure stock or flow reactions, as well as the mixed stock–flow reactions to market rationing, are admissible alternatives having the fundamental property that the choice of any one among them depends upon: (1) the objective possibility of resorting to a stock reaction at all, which can open up the discussion of such issues as portfolio management, capital markets, etc.; and, given the above factors, (2) the subjective expectations about the future, which determine, for the household and the firm, the 'conjecturally optimal' type of reaction. It is in this sense that the stock and flow reactions are here characterized as conjectural stock and flow responses to market rationing.

III

Having enlarged the scope of responses to market rationing, we can now handle the most interesting part of our theory, which is the nature and implications of the intra-market 'spillover effects'. It is well known that effective rationing in one market will generate effects that will 'spill' over the other market(s). This possibility of spillover effects, not transparent in the original Cloweresque model, is inherent in the classification of conjectural reactions to market rationing presented in the previous section of this paper. Thus, before we conclude with a closer examination and a further enlargement of the scope of these conjectural responses, we now proceed with a characteristic illustration of spillover effects. In so doing, we shall be essentially exploring the details of the working of the 'principle of the multiplier', in an attempt to have a fresh look at this concept which is so important to macroeconomic theory.

To begin with, we assume that the economy can be described as initially situated in a market-clearing W-equilibrium such that the household's and the firm's desired actions are mutually consistent. In the (y, l) space, this means that points H and F coincide. Then, we assume that this W-equilibrium is disturbed by either endogenous or exogenous shocks. For example, H can shift vertically down if the monetary authorities reduce the money supply, or if the household pays higher taxes, or if the household's liquidity preference is increased. Another example: F can shift downwards if there is a sudden decline in productivity. In general, we can have a variety of disturbances that cause vertical, horizontal or diagonal shifts in H and/or F. It is only when a disturbance causes an exactly similar (in magnitude and direction) dislocation of both H and F that we shall not have multiplier effects. In all other cases, there will be phenomena of effective market rationing which will generate intra-market spillover and multiplier effects. Finally, if any disturbance from an initial W-equilibrium (or, as it turns out, from any initial equilibrium) causes a deviation from it, our analysis based on conjectural responses to market rationing can provide an explanation of the degree to which these spillover effects are 'deviation-amplifying', or are an explanation of the magnitude of the relevant multiplier (Leijonhufvud, 1968, pp. 56–7).

Our characteristic illustration of spillover effects generated by market rationing is shown in figure 5. Here an initial W-equilibrium (y_0, l_0) is disturbed by a downward shift of H into position H', whose coordinates are (y_1, l_0). With F unchanged, the firm will face a sales constraint as it now becomes rationed in the output market. In reaction to this, the firm decides to reduce its demand for labour inputs and operate at point A. Obviously, this reduction of demand for labour will be smaller the more willing the firm is to accept an increase in its stock-inventory of unsold finished products. After the firm has decided to operate at point A, the household, being temporarily at H', will now become rationed in the labour market, where it faces an employment constraint. In reaction to this, the household

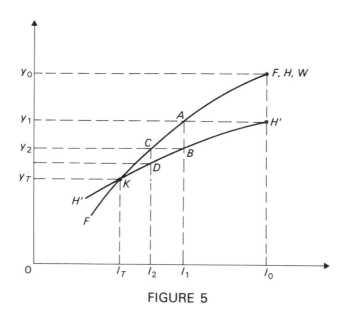

FIGURE 5

decides to reduce its effective demand for output and move to point B. Again, the reduction in output demand will be smaller the more willing (and able) the household is to resort to a reduction of its wealth. To continue the example, after the household has moved to B, the firm faces a new sales constraint, as a result of which it moves to point C. At that point the household faces a new employment constraint, as a result of which it moves to point D. The story continues in a succession of sales and employment constraints which, however, become progressively smaller (in a quantitative sense). The firm reacts to these sales constraints by moving along its 'reaction curve' FF, while the household reacts to these employment constraints by moving along its 'reaction curve' $H'H'$. This contraction process finally stops as our economy converges to point K, with (y_T, l_T). At this point the firm's and the household's plans become mutually consistent, so that K is an equilibrium point with zero effective excess demand in both the labour and the output markets. From a social welfare point of view, this K-equilibrium is inferior to the initial W-equilibrium, but it is an equilibrium situation nevertheless. The process from W to K shows that an initial disturbance equal to $H - H' = y_0 - y_1$ caused an initial rationing in the output market which spilled over to the labour market, which in turn fed back in the output market, and so on. The nature of these intra-market spillover effects was such that the initial disturbance was amplified. When the system has converged to K, we have seen two multiplier effects at work:

an output multiplier (k_y): $y_0 - y_T = ky(y_0 - y_1) = k_y \Delta H$

an employment multiplier (k_e): $l_0 - l_T = k_e(y_0 - y_1) = k_e \Delta H.$

The strength of these multipliers depends on the type of conjectural reaction to market rationing adopted by the household and the firm.

Indeed, in figure 6(a) we see that the firm faces a sales constraint at $\bar{y}$. In reaction to that, it may decide to reduce its demand for labour input accordingly and move to point A. Instead, the firm may decide to reduce its labour demand by less and accumulate unsold output as additional inventories ($\Delta i < 0$), and thus move to point A'. Similarly, in figure 6(b) we see that the household faces an employment constraint at $\bar{l}$. In reaction to that, it can decide to reduce its demand for output and go to point B. Instead, the household may decide to liquidate part of its wealth ($\Delta m > 0$) in order to maintain a high level of output demand and thus go to point B'. Since the kind of employment constraint that the household is going to face depends on the type of reaction (FA or FA') decided by the firm, and since

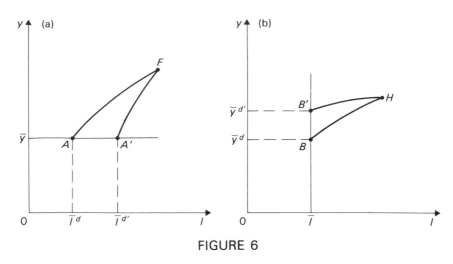

FIGURE 6

the kind of subsequent sales constraint that the firm is going to face depends on the type of reaction (HB or HB') decided by the household, the entire nexus of intra-market spillover effects and the magnitude of the output and employment multipliers also depend on the type of reaction to market rationing decided by the agents. If the firm resorts to a predominantly flow reaction, its reaction will be like the relatively flat FA curve; instead, if it resorts to a predominantly stock reaction, its reaction curve will be like the steeper FA' curve. Similarly, if the household responds to market rationing by resorting to a predominantly stock reaction, its reaction curve will be like the HB', which is steeper than the HB, which implies a predominantly flow reaction.

Figure 7 illustrates the above. Assuming an initial disturbance (ΔH) which caused the separation of H from F, we have two sets of reactions to market rationing. In the first case, both the household and the firm opt for predominantly flow reactions along the FA and HB reaction curves respectively. The economy converges to equilibrium point K, and the output and employment multipliers are given by

$$y_0 - y_T = k_y \Delta H; \quad l_0 - l_T = k_e \Delta H.$$

In the second case, the firm and the household opt for predominantly stock reactions along the FA' and HB' curves respectively. The economy reaches a new equilibrium at point K', and the relevant multipliers are

$$y_0 - y_T' = k_y' \Delta H; \quad l_0 - l_T' = k_e' \Delta H$$

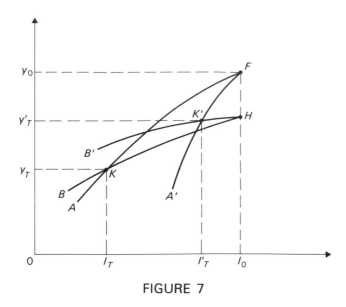

FIGURE 7

so that

$$k'_y < k_y \quad \text{and} \quad k'_e < k_e.$$

Finally, in figure 8(a) and (b) we examine the cases when the firm faces a labour constraint and the household faces a consumption constraint. Thus, with a labour constraint at $\bar{l}$, the firm may opt for a predominantly flow reaction, reducing its supply of output to point A. Instead, it may decide to reduce its stock-inventory of finished products and maintain a higher effective supply of output. This is a predominantly stock reaction corresponding to point A''. Similarly, in figure 8(b) we have a household facing a consumption constraint at $\bar{y}$. In this case, the household may resort to a predominantly flow reaction, reducing its labour supply at point B. Alternatively, it may opt for a predominantly stock reaction, maintaining a higher level of labour supply while accepting an increase in its money holdings, and go to point B''. To use these bifurcated reaction patterns, in figure 9 we assume an initial W-equilibrium to be disturbed, say, by an increase in the money supply, so that H moved vertically above F. At the initially given level of supply of output, the household faces a consumption constraint. If it opts for a stock reaction (i.e. accepting a higher level of 'idle' money balances), it will follow reaction curve HB''. The firm will then face a labour constraint, to which it may also respond with a predominantly stock

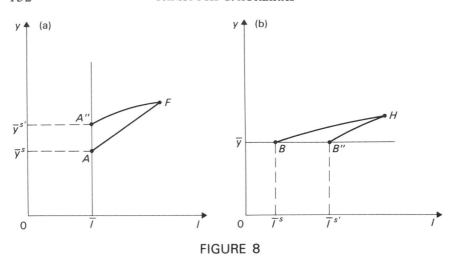

FIGURE 8

reaction along the FA'' curve. We thus see that if both the firm and the household opt for predominantly stock reactions, the economy will converge to an R-equilibrium, which may be called a 'repressed inflation' situation, since there corresponds an *ex ante* excess demand for output although the effective excess demand for output is zero. The increase in the *ex ante* demand for output will have caused a reduction in both production and employment. This case corresponds to what can be called a 'supply multiplier' (Barro and Grossman, 1976, pp. 81–2). If, however, the firm and the household had instead opted for predominantly flow reactions along the FA and HB curves, the economy might not have been able to reach any equilibrium at all. With effective excess demand for output, this would be an 'open inflation' situation. With the flow reaction, the household does not opt for keeping higher 'idle' money balances, and thus effective demand exceeds the effective supply of output. Inflation will, in the end, cause the higher real money balances to their former level, thus causing the entire HB curve to shift downwards. Inflation will stop when H coincides again with F.

IV

In the preceding section, we analysed the working of the 'principle of the multiplier' as a mechanism that depends upon the type of reaction that the household and the firm opt for in case they face an

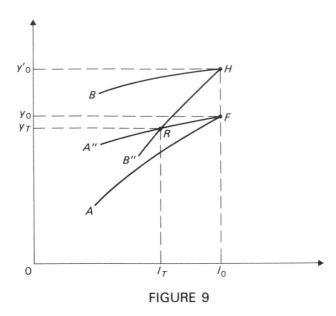

FIGURE 9

effective market rationing. Indeed, the choice between a predominantly stock reaction and a predominantly flow reaction determines the strength of the deviation-amplifying intra-market spillover effects, and thus the magnitude of the relevant output and employment multipliers. It must be noted that, in the case of the under-employment K-equilibrium, stock reactions lead to a smaller contraction of employment compared with flow reactions. In the case of the inflationary R-equilibrium, stock reactions lead to repressed inflation and lower levels of output and employment, while flow reactions lead to open inflation. Although it is not altogether clear which one of the repressed or the open inflation cases represents the higher degree of disorganization, the under-employment case illustrates a more general characteristic of a modern economy. The existence of buffer-stocks may have a stabilizing influence on an economy whose self-regulating and self-organizing mechanisms can (and often do) fail (Leijonhufvud, 1976, pp. 93, 102; Kaldor, 1978, p. 196). It would thus be important for macroeconomic theory to be able to explain the circumstances under which a stock or a flow reaction to market rationing will be chosen by the agents.

At a very general level, we characterized these reactions as 'conjectural', in the sense that they depend on expectations or 'conjectures', given of course the objective possibility of resorting to a stock reaction at all. With 'conjectures', every agent redefines his purchase and sale decisions in the light of 'perceived' market rationing. This in turn means that the re-calculation of 'maximum' utility and profit not only takes into account the effective liquidity constraints owing to market rationing, but also is based on what the agents think about the future. In an intertemporal choice-theoretic framework, in which money balances and stock-inventories can be used as buffer-stocks, the reliance on these stocks must be treated under both a 'precautionary' and a 'speculative' perspective. For example, if a household expects a current employment constraint to be permanent, it would not make much sense to rely on reducing its liquid wealth in order to resist a decline in its effective consumption demand. It would instead be more logical to suppose that this household either reduces its consumption to a level compatible with its reduced labour income (a flow reaction, based on the logic of the permanent income notion), or attempts to reduce its reservation wage in order to increase its employment. Similarly, a firm facing a sales constraint may decide to absorb unsold inventories and maintain its level of operations only if it expects the sales constraint to be temporary. If instead this sales constraint is perceived as permanent, continuous accumulation of inventories is not optimal; the firm will either reduce its labour employment, and thus its output production (flow reaction), or attempt to induce the consumers to buy more output by lowering the sale price of its product.

We could then have a typology of conjectural responses to market rationing, according to which: a stock reaction is more likely to be chosen by the agents if an observed market rationing is perceived to be temporary; a flow reaction is more likely to be chosen if the market rationing is perceived as permanent. Thus, the effects of rationing on the agents' decisions depend on how the resulting constraints are perceived by the agents, or on the kind of 'consciousness on the part of the agents that they are in disequilibrium' (Fisher, 1978, p. 19). It is then obvious that this 'perception' or 'consciousness' depends upon one's expectations about the future, including the agents' expectations as to how the monetary and/or fiscal authorities may react when (they themselves perceive that) the economy develops a tendency towards under-employment or inflation. In fact, changes in the money supply and/or the budget deficit can be and have been used as buffers against the various (random or systematic) disturbances to which a market economy can be subjected. If the agents or the private sector can predict the authorities' reaction, then they can better calculate their own response to market rationing, since they will have a more accurate idea about the temporary or the permanent nature of this rationing. This idea has an affinity with the notion of 'rational expectations', but it does not seem appropriate to use that notion in the analysis of short-run phenomena such as the cases examined in this paper. On the other hand, the conjectural reactions to market rationing do leave enough scope for real output and employment effects of stabilization policy. It would thus seem that the policy-neutrality presumption of the rational expectations hypothesis is not compatible with a non-Walrasian equilibrium (Buiter, 1980, pp. 40–1). Conjectures are formed by experience and by relatively vague ideas about the future. Furthermore, an agent can know what sort of constraint he is subject to, but he can only guess what is happening to others, or how his reaction will affect others. Informational imperfections are an integral part of any disequilibrium theory, in order to explain both the emergence and the intra-market spillover effects of market rationing (Korliras, 1980). Given these informational imperfections, we must not ignore man's imperfect computational capabilities, so that it would be more appropriate to characterize the rationality underlying the conjectures as 'procedural rationality' (Simon, 1976). Finally, in a Walrasian model with no transactions at non-market-clearing prices, the rational expectations assumption might be appropriate, since the agents observe the discrepancies between their conjectures and the outcomes; in a model with effective market rationing, the

agents may be in a situation where they trade what they wish at the terms they expect and yet their wishes may be based on conjectures the falsity of which they could only discover by varying their trades. That is experiment rather than observation would be required to verify conjectures. (Hahn, 1978, p. 12)

To complete our discussion of conjectural responses to market rationing, we must introduce price changes. The models used in this paper are 'fixprice models', in the sense that during each trading period the agents take prices as given parameters in their decision-making. Prices, that is output prices and money wages, do change, but only at the intervals between trading periods, and only as a result of non-zero effective excess demand in the relevant markets. The fixprice method has been proved almost indispensable for the development of disequilibrium theory; it allows unsatisfied buying and selling plans as well as 'stock disequilibria' (such as changes in money balances or inventories) to function as market signals leading to price changes, after these unsatisfied plans have been experienced

(Hicks, 1965, ch. 7; Grandmont, 1977). In generalizing the class of conjectural responses to rationing, we abandon their assumption that agents are price-takers; instead, price-setting is a theoretically promising alternative. If an agent does not encounter a quantity constraint (ration), he can treat prices as parametrically given. If, however, he encounters an effective constraint, he may conjecture that, by lowering the price, he can sell more than he is currently selling or that, by raising the price, he can buy more than he is currently buying. In order to be 'allowed' to have such conjectures, the agent must perceive elastic supply and demand curves; this implies that price-setting models of market rationing intrinsically have a monopolistic competition character, a theoretical trait that may preclude the *a priori* existence of a Walrasian equilibrium. Price setting must, at any rate, be part of the set of conjectural responses to rationing. In fact, the usual definition of a conjecture, in a substantial portion of the related literature, has been limited to the hypothesis that agents react to rationing by price-setting in order to affect their quantity constraints due to rationing (Hahn, 1977). With price-setting, it might be thought easier for the economy to resolve disequilibrium situations. Indeed, in the fixprice models the existence of non-Walrasian equilibria is not unrelated to the assumption that prices do not adjust as fast as quantities. With price-setting, the adjustment of prices is certainly faster, and thus the output and employment multipliers must be smaller; a larger portion of the economy's overall adjustment will be absorbed by price changes so that less will be left to be absorbed by quantity (output and employment) changes. It has, however, been shown by several authors that, even with price-setting conjectures, an economy can get stuck in a non-Walrasian equilibrium (Benassy, 1975; Negishi, 1978; Hahn, 1978).

We can thus conclude that conjectural responses to market rationing are either pure or mixed cases of three types of reaction: a flow reaction, a stock reaction, and a price-setting reaction. Effective market rationing will lead to substantial intra-market spillover effects and thus to substantial output and employment multipliers, if the agents resort to predominantly flow reactions; instead, if there occur mainly price reactions, the real output and employment changes will be smaller. Resorting to predominantly stock reactions represents the intermediate case.

References

Arrow, K. and Hahn, F. (1971) *General Competitive Analysis*, Holden Day.
Barro, R. and Grossman, H. (1976) *Money, Employment and Inflation*, Cambridge University Press.

Benassy, J. P. (1975) 'Neo-Keynesian disequilibrium theory in a monetary economy', *Review of Economic Studies*, October, pp. 503–24.

Buiter, W. (1980) 'The macroeconomics of Dr. Pangloss: a critical survey of the new classical macroeconomics', *Economic Journal*, March, pp. 34–50.

Clower, R. (1965) 'The Keynesian counter-revolution: a theoretical appraisal', in F. Hahn and F. Brechling (eds), *The Theory of Interest Rates*, Macmillan, 1965; reprinted in R. Clower (ed.), *Monetary Theory*, Penguin, 1969, pp. 270–97.

Clower, R. (1967) 'A reconsideration of the microfoundations of monetary theory', *Western Economic Journal*; as reprinted in R. Clower (ed.), *Monetary Theory*, Penguin, 1969, pp. 202–11.

Fisher, F. M. (1978) 'Quantity constraints, spillovers, and the Hahn process', *Review of Economic Studies*, pp. 19–31.

Grandmont, J. M. (1977) 'The logic of the fix-price method', *Scandinavian Journal of Economics*, pp. 168–86.

Hahn, F. (1965) 'On some problems of proving the existence of an equilibrium in a monetary economy', in F. Hahn and F. Brechling (eds), *The Theory of Interest Rates*, Macmillan; as reprinted in R. Clower (ed.), *Monetary Theory*, Penguin, 1969, pp. 191–201.

Hahn, F. (1977) 'Exercises in conjectural equilibria', *Scandinavian Journal of Economics*, pp. 210–26.

Hahn, F. (1978) 'On non-Walrasian equilibria', *Review of Economic Studies*, pp. 1–17.

Hicks, J. R. (1965) *Capital and Growth*, Oxford University Press.

Kaldor, N. (1978) *Further Essays on Economic Theory*, Duckworth.

Korliras, P. (1976) 'On the theory of macroeconomic quasi-equilibria', *Zeitschrift für Nationalökonomie*, pp. 269–86.

Korliras, P. (1980) 'Disequilibrium theories and their policy implications: towards a synthetic disequilibrium approach', *Kyklos*.

Leijonhufvud, A. (1968) *On Keynesian Economics and the Economics of Keynes*, Oxford University Press.

Leijonhufvud, A. (1976) 'Schools, revolutions and research programmes in economic theory', in S. Latsis (ed.), *Method and Appraisal in Economics*, Cambridge University Press, pp. 65–108.

Malinvaud, E. (1977) *The Theory of Unemployment Reconsidered*, Basil Blackwell.

Muellbauer, J. and Portes, R. (1978) 'Macroeconomic models with quantity rationing', *Economic Journal*, December, pp. 788–821.

Negishi, T. (1978) 'Existence of an underemployment equilibrium', in G. Schwödiauer (ed.), *Equilibrium and Disequilibrium in Economic Theory*, Reidel, pp. 497–510.

Simon, H. (1976) 'From substantive to procedural nationality', in S. Latsis (ed.), *Method and Appraisal in Economics*, Cambridge University Press, pp. 129–48.

PART III
Flexprice Approaches to Macroeconomics

6

Consistent Temporary Equilibrium

CHRISTOPHER BLISS

Introduction

In recent years the temporary equilibrium model, which was first enunciated by Hicks (1939) more than 40 years ago, has enjoyed a revival. Indeed, one might say that its importance is being recognized for the first time. The reason for this development is obvious and well known: economic theorists have become increasingly interested in bringing 'macroeconomic' and 'microeconomic' theory closer together, and in constructing models that would incorporate 'Keynesian' features. For this task both the long-run equilibrium models of 'classical' economics and the Walrasian model of general equilibrium as developed by Debreu, Arrow and others are unsuitable. These models assume the existence of too many markets, including futures and contingency markets, and one might say they have too much equilibrium in them.

However the economist knows by instinct and experience that some equilibrium assumptions are necessary in order to reach conclusions. Disequilibrium dynamics is important and is incorporated more and more frequently, but no one has managed to say anything interesting without assuming that some markets at least find some kind of equilibrium. Even so, the temporary equilibrium model goes quite a long way towards side-stepping problems of price adjustment, and could be said to assume that those markets that exist function exceedingly efficiently while recognizing that a full system of forward markets for all goods and services does not exist.

That this approach is not the only one is evidenced by the large literature on 'fixprice' models (see e.g. Malinvaud, 1977). It is not easy at this stage to judge the relative merits of temporary equilibrium models, in which prices are assumed flexible and markets in which they exist perfectly efficient, and fixprice models, which go to the opposite extreme and assume that markets, as agencies for reconciling differences between demands and supplies by price changes, are completely inefficient. Indeed, it seems obvious that neither model describes the world, that each is a tool for looking at certain features of reality in a stylized manner. In spite of this, both approaches have thrown up conclusions that are extraordinarily interesting and suggestive.

A particular feature of the type of temporary equilibrium model that I shall discuss is that it allows one to examine the consequences of economic agents having different and usually inconsistent expectations about prices. To highlight this point it will be assumed that agents have point expectations (i.e., that they act as if they knew for certain what these prices will be), which can be different from one another. If forward markets existed they would present agents with these prices and differences of opinion would be removed. As these markets do not exist, agents can hold on to inconsistent expectations about relative prices in the future. We want to see what consequences flow from this fact. I am eventually going to discuss a special kind of temporary equilibrium, to be called a consistent temporary equilibrium. The definition is best left until later, until I have developed the argument further, but to avoid confusion I should say now that consistency in this sense will carry no implication that price expectations are in any way consistent, or compatible one with the other. They can and will be arbitrary.

One of my main concerns is to throw light on the manner in which a capital market, the market for trading claims on the present against claims on the future, operates in an uncertain world. I shall claim that this market ought to be seen as imposing quantity constraints on agents' actions even if all prices are flexible and markets perfectly efficient. The reason why this conclusion emerges can be explained simply as follows. A basic feature of the competitive perfect market is that agents trade in it 'anonymously'; in other words, only the sums of their supplies and demands matter, not who contributes or how much. Where agents are selling claims on the future (borrowing) and there is no agreement about what various goods will be worth in the future, it makes no sense to assume that these claims are perfect substitutes one for the other. This leads to various problems. One way out of the difficulty is to assume that borrowers can sell only personal claims on the future, of which the obvious example is equity in a firm's profit. The assumption of anonymity is then dropped, but the consequence is that we leave behind fixprice perfect market theory. I wish instead to look at an alternative approach.

It will be assumed that borrowers can issue bonds the supply of which is aggregated to form one side of the capital market. However, as a condition of being allowed to borrow, the agent must conform to a rule of financial prudence. Because lenders know that all bond issues are so constrained, they are willing to accept all bonds as perfect substitutes.

I developed this approach in Bliss (1976). There I explained it in terms of a notional agent called 'the Banker, who vetted loan applications and 'accepted' them (i.e., guaranteed repayment) if they conformed to his view of feasibility according to his price expectations. That story is rather far-fetched. However, I shall retain the notion of the capital market as vetting the plans of borrowers and not allowing borrowing that it is felt would not be repaid. This story is most easily told in terms of the assumption that borrowers' plans become public knowledge, and it is an immediate implication of that assumption that I shall explore in this paper. If one assumes that borrowers' plans are public knowledge, then it must follow that not every temporary equilibrium that could come about is reasonable or convincing. To take an extreme example, suppose that an inspection of borrowers' aggregate plans showed that no firm was going to produce any table salt. Then, even if all present markets and the capital market were clearing, something must shortly change. In particular, agents will alter their price expectations, say, by expecting a higher price for table salt, and this will upset the temporary equilibrium. Putting the matter loosely at this stage, a consistent temporary equilibrium, as I shall use the term, is one that is not upset in this manner. A central concern of the paper will be whether such an equilibrium can be shown to exist.

Before proceeding to details I should forestall an objection that my reader may have in his mind at this point. Surely, it will be said, if a consistent temporary equilibrium is one in which there are no discrepancies between planned supplies and demands, then it is simply the Arrow–Debreu equilibrium, in which there are forward markets for all goods, but arrived at by a different route, without directly assuming that those markets exist.

Formally this objection is not correct. A consistent temporary equilibrium is not necessarily a full Arrow–Debreu equilibrium because agents are not presented with prices for future goods; they are guessing about what those prices will be and their guesses in general differ. This is important, but nevertheless the point has this much force: a consistent temporary equilibrium is a lot more like full intertemporal equilibrium than is simple (i.e., not consistent) temporary equilibrium. The former concept can be seen not as a description of reality but as a criticism of the latter concept. What a theorist treats as a constant in a short-run model is what he thinks adjusts slowly: what he assumes to reach its equilibrium value he supposes to adjust rapidly. If this is correct, then temporary equilibrium theory is based on the assumption that expected prices adjust slowly even in the face of evidence of disequilibrium, while present prices respond rapidly to equate supplies and demands.

An assessment of this case will best await the presentation of the formal model.

A temporary equilibrium model

For the sake of simplicity of presentation I shall assume two periods, the 'present' and the 'future'. This is too simple for certain applications, notably the assessment of the effects of speculation on interest rate movements and of the manner in which previous debt influences present equilibrium, but these are not concerns of this paper. A subscript '0' represents the present, a subscript '1', the future. Hence, in particular, p_0 is the vector of goods prices in the present in terms of unit of account. Future goods prices are conjectural values concerning which agents have different opinions. However, one good is assumed to have a futures market to allow for lending and borrowing. One could think of this good as 'money', but it is only money in its role as unit for expressing deferred payments, so not very much significance should be attached to the term. Each agent is presented by present markets with the same price vector:

$$\begin{bmatrix} p_0 \\ \pi \end{bmatrix} \tag{1}$$

where π is the present price of future money. The ith agent ($i = 1, \ldots, m$) expects money prices in the future to be p_1^i, so for him prices (of present and future goods) are

$$\begin{bmatrix} p_0 \\ \pi p_1^i \end{bmatrix} \tag{2}$$

In the light of these prices, all of which he treats as definite values, the ith agent chooses his action as a couple of net excess demand vectors

$$\begin{bmatrix} x_0^i \\ x_1^i \end{bmatrix} \qquad (3)$$

If i is a household; or excess supply vectors

$$\begin{bmatrix} y_0^i \\ y_1^i \end{bmatrix} \qquad (4)$$

if i is a firm. Naturally the action partly exists only in the agent's mind. The vectors x_0^i or y_0^i represent market transactions in present markets, but the same is not true for x_1^i or y_1^i. However, these are represented indirectly by demands or supplies of future money.

We can now generate demand functions on lines similar to those of static competitive general equilibrium theory. The only complication concerns the distribution of profits by firms – obviously, since how much profit a particular firm will make is a matter for conjecture. For simplicity I assume that firms distribute profit to their owners in period 1, the future. However, households conjecture what those distributions will be. If a firm makes a profit in the present in excess of its investment requirements, then it lends this surplus on the bond market for later distribution. This way of treating profits, which is not essential to the argument, has the advantage that there is no profit distribution in the present. If a household expects to receive dividends in the future it can borrow money in anticipation to finance present expenditure should it so choose. The assumption of course implies that households have a disincentive to save because they see firms as saving for them; on the other hand, firms are less inclined to borrow because they are re-investing profits in real assets or in bonds. This is not an unrealistic way of viewing the matter.

If the ith agent is a household, he conjectures that he will receive $D(p_0, \pi)$ in the future from firms in which he enjoys an interest. D is a continuous function of p_0 and π, defined for all non-negative values of (p_0, π), non-negative and bounded above. The household's choice problem can now be expressed as a basically orthodox budget-constrained utility maximization problem:

$$\max U^i(x_0^i, x_1^i)$$

subject to

$$p_0 x_0^i + \pi p_1^i x_1^i \leqslant \pi D(p_0, \pi) \qquad (5)$$

The solution to (5) will be assumed unique for each value of (p_0, π) and standard assumptions of quasi-concavity of U^i and boundedness will make the solution a continuous function of (p_0, π). Having decided on (x_0^i, x_1^i), the household will then transact in present markets, demanding x_0^i of present goods. The demand for future money is

$$p_1^i x_1^i - D(p_0, \pi) \tag{6}$$

which is the excess of future net expenditure over anticipated dividend income. The budget constraint in (5) requires that the present value of this money must be matched by underspending in the present. Hence, designating the demand for future money by m^i, the budget constraint is

$$p_0 x_0^i + \pi m^i \leqslant 0. \tag{7}$$

A household for which $m^i > 0$ is saving; one for which $m^i < 0$ is borrowing. The budget constraint will be satisfied with equality as the household will not waste an opportunity to consume. Thus

(x_0^i, m^i) is a continuous function of (p_0, π),

$$\text{satisfying } p_0 x_0^i + \pi m^i = 0 \tag{8}$$

We denote firms by superscripts j. The jth firm has a set of possible plans S^j of which a typical element is

$$(y_0^j, y_1^j). \tag{9}$$

The firm maximizes the present value of profit according to its own price expectations. That is, it solves

$$\max p_0 y_0^j + \pi p_1^j y_1^j \tag{10}$$

subject to

$$(y_0^j, y_1^j) \in S^j.$$

Assuming S^j strictly convex and bounded above, the firm's choice, given p_1^j, depends upon (p_0, π) continuously. The firm buys forward money m^j to satisfy

$$p_0 y_0^j - \pi m^j = 0. \tag{11}$$

Thus, if $p_0 y_0^j > 0$, so that the firm generates present profit in excess of its investment requirements, it lends in the bond market. If, on the other hand, $p_0 y_0^j < 0$, the firm requires funds to invest and it borrows (sells forward money). Thus we have:

(y_0^j, m^j) is a continuous function of (p_0, π)

$$\text{satisfying } p_0 \cdot y_0^j - \pi m^j = 0. \tag{12}$$

Existence of a temporary equilibrium now follows from a standard fixed-point theorem argument. The economy global excess demands for present goods and future money are:

$$\left(\sum_i x_0^i - \sum_j y_0^j, \quad \sum_i m_i + \sum_j m_j \right) \tag{13}$$

denoted (X_0, M). (X_0, M) is a continuous bounded function of (p_0, π), homogeneous of degree 1 in these prices and satisfying

$$p_0 X_0 + \pi M = 0. \tag{14}$$

These properties suffice (see Arrow and Hahn, 1971, ch. 5) for there to exist non-negative (p_0, π) values such that

$$X_0 \leqq 0$$

and

$$M \leqslant 0 \tag{15}$$

which is temporary equilibrium. Where a present good, or conceivably future money, is in excess supply it will have a zero price, as otherwise (14) and (15) could not be simultaneously satisfied.

Evidently (15) carries no implication concerning the balance of supplies and demands that would emerge were agents to attempt to put their future plans into effect.

Constrained temporary equilibrium

The temporary equilibrium model of the preceding section assumes a 'perfect' capital market in which agents can lend or borrow as much as they wish anonymously. In the Arrow–Debreu model such an assumption is a more-or-less natural extension of static competitive theory. As I have argued elsewhere (Bliss, 1975a, b), it does not make sense for temporary equilibrium. The problem is to reconcile allowing agents to hold different price expectations and to behave as they choose, given those expectations, with the assumption that the obligations that they then undertake to pay money in the future are perfect substitutes for each other.

An obvious step in the direction of easing this problem is to constrain agents somewhat. This will be achieved by assuming that there exists a set of *reference prices*, $\bar{p}_1$, for future money which will be used to check the feasibility of any agent who has supplied future money (borrowed) discharging his obligation.

For a consumer this will mean that, for some feasible x_1^i (the feasibility of which may depend on his choice of x_0^i), he can satisfy

$$\bar{p}_1 x_1^i \leqslant m^i + D(\bar{p}_1) \tag{15}$$

where $D(\bar{p}_1)$ is an estimate of his dividend income based on reference prices. If one assumes that there is a feasible x for each $\bar{p}_1$ such that

$$\bar{p}_1 x \leqslant D(\bar{p}_1) \tag{16}$$

(i.e., that the consumer does not need money for the future), then (15) has effect only if $m^i < 0$ (i.e., the consumer borrows).

For a producer the implication is

$$p_1 y_1^j \geqslant -m^j \tag{17}$$

that is, the future profit at reference prices must be sufficient to pay any money to the repayment of which the firm has committed itself. If, for all y, $(y, 0)$ is feasible (i.e., the firm does not have to be active in the future), then (17) is automatically satisfied if $m^j \geqslant 0$ (i.e., the firm has not borrowed).

The consequence of constraining borrowing agents to solvency at reference prices is to confine their choices to constraint sets. If firms have convex production sets and households convex consumption sets, then (15) and (17) give rise to convex constraint sets. Naturally demand and supply functions are affected by this addition of constraints, but as the sets are convex their continuity is not upset and we retain (8) and (12).

Hence, formally, imposing constraints on borrowing through the vehicle of reference prices does not upset the existence of temporary equilibrium. Therefore it offers the possibility of a more reasonable equilibrium in which, at least, agents with absurdly optimistic expectations concerning future prices are constrained not to make their optimism the basis for borrowing that the market would regard as unsound.

This analysis leaves several loose ends untied and badly requires extension. An obvious question is: where does the reference price vector $\bar{\mathbf{p}}_1$ come from? As it plays the role of a set of prices that the market regards as reasonable ones on which to count in borrowing money, one would naturally think of it as some kind of average. Formally, all that is needed is that $\bar{\mathbf{p}}_1$ should be assigned a value, and this could depend on all the price expectations of agents, and moreover on $\mathbf{p}_0$ and π. Further elaborations suggest themselves: $\bar{\mathbf{p}}_1$ need not even take the same value for each agent. The market could apply a different test to farmers borrowing capital for agricultural purposes from that which it applies to manufacturers.

Such elaborations of the model are however tangential to the main issue, which is that it is somewhat artificial to assume a market view concerning prices, which suggests accord, when in fact the assumption on which the theory is founded is that agents disagree concerning prices.

In closing this section I shall sketch a different approach which has interesting implications for macroeconomic theory. When we treat only of the capital market as a single entity we are aggregating extremely. Assume instead that the capital market is an agency for placing bonds. If a borrower comes to the market to sell future money, the market attempts to place his bond with a lending agent according to whose price expectations the borrower will be able to repay. This approach gives rise to a rationing equilibrium in which an agent is faced not with an additional test but rather with a variable borrowing limit according to his choice of action.

I shall assume that the capital market is efficient. This means that the allocation that results from the placing of bonds is such that no re-allocation could improve the *ex ante* welfare of one agent without lowering that of another. The fact that households' expectations concerning dividends are variables makes the analysis complicated, and I shall ignore this aspect by treating those values as constants. The *ex ante* 'welfare' of agent i (here either a firm or a household) is a function of $\mathbf{p}_0$, π and β^i- or β^i+ where β^i+ is the maximum amount agent i is able to lend and β^i- is the maximum he is allowed to borrow. We treat firms as individuals whose 'welfare' is the profit they expect to make. The capital market might be seen as maximizing

$$\sum_i \alpha^i V^i(\mathbf{p}_0, \pi, \beta^i+, \beta^i-) \tag{18}$$

where α^i is an arbitrary weight, $\mathbf{p}_0$ and π are treated as constants and V^i is the indirect welfare function of agent i. It does this by choosing numbers b^{ik}, being the amount of i's lending that is placed with k

subject to the condition that b^{ik} shall be zero if i expects k not to be able to repay all his borrowings, and also to the balance conditions

$$\sum_i b^{ik} = m^i(\mathbf{p_0}, \pi, \beta^i+, \beta^i-)$$

$$\sum_k b^{ik} = -m^k(\mathbf{p_0}, \pi, \beta^i+, \beta^i-)$$

(19)

where m^j is the jth agent's demand for future money. A solution to this problem will exist as (18) is bounded above (by the unconstrained outcome when β is set to values that allow each agent to borrow and lend as much as he pleases) and the feasible set is closed.

However, the solution to this problem is not a temporary equilibrium of any kind. The agents are assumed, since present goods are represented in the indirect welfare function only by their prices, to be able to trade unconstrained in those goods. There is no means of guaranteeing that an unconstrained equilibrium (with no rationing) can be obtained in present goods markets while we treat the capital market in the present manner. This is the only valid example I have been able to find of disequilibrium spreading from one market to another in which the price is flexible and is therefore potentially important.

Consistent temporary equilibrium

To return to the main theme, so long as we suppose that the capital market rations borrowers only through a reference price vector $\bar{\mathbf{p}}_1$, a constrained temporary equilibrium has been shown to exist. The market however has obtained a lot of information in vetting the plans of borrowers. This is the fact that will be exploited in the extension of the analysis to consistent temporary equilibrium.

The market does not obtain information concerning the projected plans of lenders, since it would be absurd to suppose that they have to submit themselves to a test. It will be assumed that all borrowers are firms and all lenders are households, and in fact that all households are identical (in other words, we are thinking of a 'representative' household). For each $(\mathbf{p_0}, \bar{\mathbf{p}}_1)$ value the market knows the planned net supplies of firms in the future

$$\sum_j y_1^j.$$

(20)

From this information it can calculate the dividend payments that will go to households if future prices are indeed $\bar{p}_1$; and if it knows the tastes of representative household (and it already knows how much that household has saved), it knows how much money the household will dispose of in the future. This makes it possible to calculate the excess demands of households in the future, denoted X. Notice that household price expectations determine how much they will save but play no further role in this calculation as the market assumes that prices will be $\bar{p}_1$, not whatever various households may expect.

We have reached the point in the argument that was outlined in the introduction. If the market assumes any $\bar{p}_1$ a constrained temporary equilibrium exists. But the value of future net excess demands can be calculated as

$$X - \sum_j y_1^j \tag{21}$$

and if this vector is not zero, for goods with positive prices, the assumption of $\bar{p}_1$ is inconsistent.

However, excess demands for present goods, future money and calculated demands for future goods in (4) all depend continuously on $(p_0, \pi\bar{p}_1)$. Moreover, they satisfy

$$p_0 \left(\sum_i x_0^i - \sum_j y_0^j \right) + \pi\bar{p}_1 \left(X - \sum_j y_1^j \right) = 0. \tag{22}$$

The market ensures this budget constraint rule when it imputes to households' future dividend incomes its own estimate of firms' *ex post* profits. We are back in familiar territory; a standard fixed-point theorem argument will ensure that a consistent temporary equilibrium exists.

The result is obvious in certain regards, as can be seen from the manner in which it was obtained. However, it implies a surprising conclusion. The capital market, by applying a suitable reference price test, can enforce equilibrium, in the sense of consistency of plans, regardless of agents' price expectations, and even though it can only deter borrowing not enforce it. Imagine, to take an extreme case, that all firms think a certain good will have no value in the future, and thus will not (voluntarily) plan to produce it, while consumers will demand it. The reference price of this good can be set very high, and firms will react to the signal that planning to produce it enables them to get borrowing plans past the market. So they produce it simply to enable them to do the other things that they want to do, and production is generated of a good that the producers expect to be valueless. This is an extreme case, but it serves well to illustrate how different consistent temporary equilibrium is from Arrow–Debreu equilibrium.

Conclusion

The analysis is exceedingly exploratory, and nothing emerges that looks like a convincing model even at the level of formal theory. However, this is not the result of the author's perverse pleasure in complicating good simple models. Rather, it seems that complications are inescapable once one takes seriously the need to treat the capital market as more than an exchange of anonymous bonds. The analysis is concerned with problems that arise out of Keynes's way of looking at the world and, in that limited sense, is 'Keynesian'. But the particular issues are not ones to which Keynes gave a prominent position in his writings, and the conclusions of the main model are not 'Keynesian' in character. As a temporary equilibrium of one kind or another usually exists, it follows that, if prices could and did move to suitable values, present markets could be cleared without constraining agents (see Bliss, 1975b). I find this unremarkable, since it has always seemed obvious to me that some kind of price 'stickiness' would have to be invoked to rule out even the possibility of temporary equilibrium and because Keynes, despite Leijonhufvud's (1969) attempt to establish the opposite conclusion, seems to have been concerned with this case.

References

Arrow, K. J. and Hahn, F. H. (1971) *General Competitive Analysis*, Holden Day.
Bliss, C. J. (1975a) *Capital Theory and the Distribution of Income*, North-Holland.
Bliss, C. J. (1975b) 'The reappraisal of Keynesian economics: an appraisal', in M. Parkin and A. R. Nobay (eds), *Current Economic Problems*, Cambridge University Press.
Bliss, C. J. (1976) 'Capital theory in the short run', in M. Brown, K. Sato and P. Zarembka (eds), *Essays in Modern Capital Theory*, North-Holland.
Hicks, J. R. (1939) *Value and Capital*, Oxford University Press.
Leijonhufvud, A. (1969) *On Keynesian Economics and the Economics of Keynes*, Oxford University Press.
Malinvaud, E. (1977) *The Theory of Unemployment Reconsidered*, Basil Blackwell.

7

Economic Fluctuations with an Imperfectly Competitive Labour Market

OLIVER D. HART

Introduction

In the last few years, a considerable amount of work has been done showing that various Keynesian phenomena can be captured in a model in which prices are fixed and demands and supplies are equilibrated by the adjustment of quantities (see, e.g., Grandmont, 1977). A weakness of this approach is that it provides no explanation of how prices are determined and, more particularly, of why an agent who is 'rationed' in a market does not attempt to change his buying or selling price. In a previous paper (Hart, 1982), I considered an alternative approach to modelling Keynesian phenomena. I showed that a number of Keynesian features can be captured in a model where agents are imperfect competitors and where prices are set optimally by agents, given the (downward-sloping) demand curves facing them. In such a model, 'rationing' is voluntary and occurs because the change in price necessary to remove a rationing constraint is too large to be profitable for an agent. The model considered in Hart (1982) was timeless. The purpose of the present paper is to generalize the imperfectly competitive model of Hart (1982) to include time. An example is given to show that an imperfectly competitive economy may experience employment fluctuations, owing to variations in demand, that a perfectly competitive economy would not experience.

The model

We consider a standard Samuelsonian overlapping generations model. Each generation lives for two periods and works only when young.

153

The per capita endowment of labour of the young is T hours. We will assume that the total population is constant over time and is given by N young people and N old people.

The labour of the young is used by firms to produce current consumption. Each firm is assumed to have a constant returns to scale technology given by $Y = kL$, where L is labour input and Y is output. Without loss of generality, we assume $k = 1$. In order to simplify matters, we will assume that firms are perfect competitors in their product markets, and will restrict our attention to the implications of imperfect competition in the labour market. The assumptions of constant returns and perfect competition for firms imply that profits will be zero in equilibrium.

The young will be assumed to save by holding money (they have no initial endowment of money). It will be assumed that there is no other means of transferring wealth from period to period, such as a forward market or stock market. The old spend the money they have accumulated from their youth on second-period consumption. It will be assumed that there is no disutility of work so that in a competitive labour market the young would supply their labour inelastically.

We will assume that there are two types of young people: a fraction λ will be assumed to have a von Neumann–Morgenstern utility function $U(x_1, x_2)$, where $x_1 \geqslant 0$ is consumption when young and $x_2 \geqslant 0$ is consumption when old; while the remaining fraction $(1 - \lambda)$ will be assumed to derive utility only from consumption when they are old. We assume:

(A1) $U(x_1, x_2)$ can be written as $\phi[\hat{U}(x_1, x_2)]$ where $\hat{U}$ is homogeneous of degree one and ϕ is either the log function or a power function; i.e., $\phi(y) = \log y$ or y^c; U is non-decreasing in x_1, x_2, and is increasing in x_1, x_2 when $x_1, x_2 > 0$; U is continuous, concave, and strictly quasi-concave; U has continuous partial derivative when x_1 or $x_2 > 0$; and

$$\frac{(\partial U/\partial x_2)\,(x_1, 0)}{(\partial U/\partial x_1)\,(x_1, 0)} = \infty \qquad \text{for all } x_1 > 0.$$

The first part of (A1) guarantees that a young person's preferences are homothetic with respect to lotteries of (x_1, x_2) pairs. Note that the restriction on the form of ϕ ensures that ϕ exhibits constant relative risk aversion.

In order to study economic fluctuations, we introduce a stochastic component into the model. In particular, we will assume that for each generation λ is a random variable, denoted $\tilde{\lambda}$ where

$$\tilde{\lambda} = \begin{cases} \lambda_1 \text{ with probability } \pi \\ \\ \lambda_2 = 1 \text{ with probability } (1 - \pi) \end{cases} \tag{1}$$

where $0 \leqslant \pi \leqslant 1$ and $\lambda_1 < \lambda_2 = 1$. A high value of λ in a generation corresponds to a high level of demand for current consumption. In what follows, we will often refer to situations in which $\tilde{\lambda} = \lambda_2$ as 'booms' and to situations in which $\tilde{\lambda} = \lambda_1$ as 'slumps'.

We assume that the realization of $\tilde{\lambda}$ is public information, that is, that everybody knows that the economy is in a slump or a boom, and that the $\tilde{\lambda}$ of different generations are independently distributed.

We are interested mainly in describing equilibrium for the case where the labour market is imperfectly competitive. It is useful first, however, to consider the case where the labour market is perfectly competitive.

Case 1   Equilibrium when the labour market is perfectly competitive

We will confine our attention to stationary-state, rational expectations equilibria. Let p_i be the equilibrium price of current consumption when $\lambda = \lambda_i$, $i = 1, 2$. Then a young person who carries £m of money over to the second period of his life will have second-period consumption equal to (m/p_1) if $\lambda = \lambda_1$ for the next generation and consumption equal to (m/p_2) if $\lambda = \lambda_2$ for the next generation. Given price p for the first-period consumption, a 'regular' young person, by which we mean one with utility function $U(x_1, x_2)$, will solve

$$\max \left[\pi U \left(x_1, \frac{m}{p_1} \right) + (1 - \pi) U \left(x_1, \frac{m}{p_2} \right) \right] \quad \text{s.t. } px_1 + m \leqslant i \tag{2}$$

where i is income from work. Since preferences are homothetic by (A1), we can write the solution to this problem as

$$x_1 = H(p, p_1, p_2) i$$

$$m = [1 - pH(p, p_1, p_2)] i. \tag{3}$$

Note that $0 \leqslant pH(p, p_1, p_2) \leqslant 1$ for all p.

In the case where the labour market is perfectly competitive, equilibrium will involve full employment since there is no disutility of work. Furthermore, since firms are perfectly competitive and face constant returns to scale, the wage rate equals the current price of output: p_1 when $\lambda = \lambda_1$, p_2 when $\lambda = \lambda_2$. Therefore total income equals $w_1 T$ when $\lambda = \lambda_1$, $w_2 T$ when $\lambda = \lambda_2$. It follows that the total demand for current consumption is given by

$$H(p_1, p_1, p_2)\, \lambda_1 p_1 TN + \frac{M}{p_1} \qquad \text{when } \lambda = \lambda_1$$

(4)

$$H(p_2, p_1, p_2)\, \lambda_2 p_2 TN + \frac{M}{p_2} \qquad \text{when } \lambda = \lambda_2.$$

This is because the total income of the 'regular' young is $\lambda_i p_i TN$ and the remaining demand comes from the old, who hold the total money balances, given by M.

Equilibrium

A stationary-state, rational expectations competitive equilibrium consists of two prices p_1, p_2 satisfying

$$H(p_1, p_1, p_2)\, \lambda_1 p_1 TN + \frac{M}{p_1} = TN = H(p_2, p_1, p_2)\, \lambda_2 p_2 TN + \frac{M}{p_2}.$$

(5)

Proposition 1 Under (A1), a stationary-state rational expectations competitive equilibrium exists. Furthermore, in every equilibrium, $p_1 < p_2$.

Proof (5) implies that

$$p_1 TN\,[1 - \lambda_1 p_1 H(p_1, p_1, p_2)] = p_2 TN\,[1 - \lambda_2 p_2 H(p_2, p_1, p_2)].$$

Letting $\alpha = p_1/p_2$ and using the fact that $H(p, p_1, p_2)i$ is homogeneous of degree zero in prices and income, we may rewrite this as

$$\alpha\,[1 - \lambda_1 \alpha H(\alpha, \alpha, 1)] = 1 - \lambda_2 H(1, \alpha, 1) = 1 - H(1, \alpha, 1).$$

When $\alpha = 1$, the left-hand side (LHS) of this equation is greater than the right-hand side (RHS). When α is close to zero, the RHS is greater than the LHS; for if not, $\lim_{\alpha \to 0} H(1, \alpha, 1) = 1$ and $[1 - H(1, \alpha, 1)]/\alpha$ is bounded as $\alpha \to 0$, which, by the last part of (A1), is not consistent with $H(1, \alpha, 1)$ satisfying the first-order conditions of problem (2) when $p = 1$, $p_1 = \alpha$, $p_2 = 1$. By continuity of demand, it follows that

$$\alpha\,[1 - \lambda_1 \alpha H(\alpha, \alpha, 1)] = 1 - \lambda_2 H(1, \alpha, 1)$$

has a solution $0 < \hat{\alpha} < 1$.

Note that $\lambda_1 < 1$ and $\hat{\alpha}H(\hat{\alpha}, \hat{\alpha}, 1) \leq 1$ imply that $1 - \lambda_2 H(1, \hat{\alpha}, 1) > 0$. Now define

$$\hat{p}_2 = \frac{M}{TN[1 - \lambda_2 H(1, \hat{\alpha}, 1)]}, \qquad \hat{p}_1 = \hat{\alpha}\hat{p}_2.$$

Then $(\hat{p}_1, \hat{p}_2)$ satisfies (5) and so is a competitive equilibrium.

In order to establish $p_1 < p_2$ for every competitive equilibrium, note that

$$M = p_1 TN[1 - \lambda_1 p_1 H(p_1, p_1, p_2)] = p_2 TN[1 - \lambda_2 p_2 H(p_2, p_1, p_2)]$$

so that, dividing both sides of (5) by M, we get

$$\frac{H(p_1, p_1, p_2)\,\lambda_1}{\lambda_1[1 - p_1 H(p_1, p_1, p_2)] + (1 - \lambda_1)} + \frac{1}{p_1}$$

$$= \frac{TN}{M} = \frac{H(p_2, p_1, p_2)\,\lambda_2}{\lambda_2[1 - p_2 H(p_2, p_1, p_2)] + (1 - \lambda_2)} + \frac{1}{p_2}. \qquad (6)$$

However, by homotheticity of the derived preferences for x_1 and m,

$$\frac{H(p, p_1, p_2)}{1 - pH(p, p_1, p_2)} = \frac{x_1}{m}$$

is decreasing in p. Since $\lambda H/[\lambda(1 - pH) + (1 - \lambda)]$ is increasing in λ, it follows that (6) cannot hold if $p_1 \geq p_2$.   Q.E.D.

In general, it appears that without further conditions there is no guarantee that the competitive equilibrium is unique.

To summarize case 1, competitive equilibrium is characterized by full employment in both states. In order to bring this about, the price of output has to fall in slumps relative to booms in order to reduce the desire of the young to save and in order to increase the old's command over current consumption through the real balance effect.

Case 2   Equilibrium when the labour market is imperfectly competitive

We consider now how the characteristics of equilibrium change if we replace the assumption that the labour market is perfectly competitive by the assumption that it is imperfectly competitive. As in Hart (1982), the type of imperfect competition that we wish to capture is rather special. We wish to capture the idea that workers – through the formation of unions or syndicates – have some monopoly power in the labour market, but that no syndicate is significant relative to the economy as a whole; in particular, no syndicate has any appreciable influence on the overall level of economic activity. In order to do this we assume that, for trading purposes, the economy is divided up into a large number of different but identical labour and output markets. Each market will be assumed to be a small version of the aggregate economy in the sense that the ratio of firms to consumers and of regular young to irregular young consumers is as in the aggregate economy (in order to make the division into sub-markets feasible, we take $2N$, the total population, to be very large). It will be assumed that agents are assigned to the various markets and cannot move between them. In addition, there is no trading across markets. (For further details, see Hart, 1982.)

We will make the following additional assumptions:

(A2)   Any two firms in the same product market are also in the same labour market.[1]

(A3)   The consumers from any given labour market are distributed uniformly across the different product markets. The old consumers are also distributed uniformly across the different product markets.

We continue to assume that each firm is negligible relative to its product market, so that firms are perfect competitors in the product market. Individual firms are also assumed to be negligible relative to their labour markets, and so are perfect competitors there too. In contrast, we assume that the workers in each labour market form a single syndicate which acts as a monopolistic seller of labour. In this paper we will not deal with the more general case, where labour markets are oligopolized rather than monopolized – on this, see Hart (1982).

Consider a typical labour market. By (A2), the firms in this labour market come from an integral number of product markets – r, say – as illustrated in figure 1. Let I be the total (money) income of young consumers in these r product markets, and let $\hat{M}$ be the money holdings of the old consumers in these r product markets. Then the demand curve for output in the corresponding labour market when $\lambda = \lambda_i$ is given by

$$H(p, p_1, p_2) \lambda_i I + \frac{\hat{M}}{p} \tag{7}$$

where p is the price of current consumption. But, given that firms face constant returns to scale and are perfect competitors, $p = w$, which equals the wage rate set by the syndicate in this labour market.

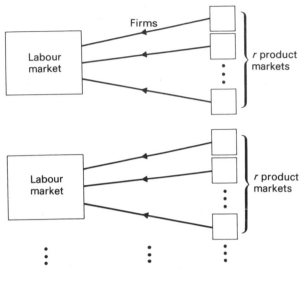

FIGURE 1

Therefore the demand curve for labour facing the syndicate in a typical labour market when $\lambda = \lambda_i$ is

$$H(p, p_1, p_2) \lambda_i I + \frac{\hat{M}}{p} \tag{8}$$

where p is the wage rate.

The choice for each syndicate is between choosing high wage rates and high employment levels. We assume that each syndicate selects p to maximize the syndicate's total wage receipts:

$$\max_p \left\{ p \left[H(p, p_1, p_2) \lambda_i I + \frac{\hat{M}}{p} \right] \right\} \quad \text{s.t. } H(p, p_1, p_2) \lambda_i I + \frac{\hat{M}}{p} \leqslant nT \tag{9}$$

where n is the number of workers in each labour market. This is a reasonable objective function for the syndicate if we assume that any unemployment is shared equally between all workers, so that each worker works $(1/n) [H(p, p_1, p_2) \lambda_i I + \hat{M}/p]$ hours. Then maximizing the total wage receipts is equivalent to maximizing the wage receipts per worker. This objective will receive almost unanimous support from syndicate members since, by (A3), for almost all workers, the wage rate selected in a particular labour market has no effect on the price of current (or future) consumption faced by a worker in that labour market.

Note also that (A3) implies that no syndicate can by itself have any appreciable influence on I, since almost all the income of consumers in the product markets that the syndicate's firms find themselves in is earned in labour markets over which this syndicate has no control. Similarly, no syndicate can influence $\hat{M}$. Therefore each syndicate solves (9) taking I and $\hat{M}$ as given.

(9) can be simplified. Note first that the fact that the total number of workers equals the total number of young consumers implies that n equals the number of workers in each labour market which equals the number of young consumers in each group of r product markets. Since the number of young people equals the number of old people, there are also n old people in each group of r product markets. Therefore, dividing the objective function in (9) by n and noting that $\hat{M}$ is exogenous, we may rewrite (9) as

$$\max_p \; p \left[H(p, p_1, p_2) \lambda_i j + \frac{m}{p} \right] \quad \text{s.t.} \; H(p, p_1, p_2) \lambda_i j + \frac{m}{p} \leqslant T \tag{10}$$

where j = income of each young person and $m = M/N$ are the money balances of each old person. Finally, if we regard per capita supply of labour, L, as the syndicate's control variable rather than p, we may rewrite (10) as

$$\max p(L) L \tag{11}$$

where $p(L)$ is the solution to

$$H[p(L), p_1, p_2] \lambda_i j + \frac{m}{p(L)} = L \leqslant T. \tag{12}$$

Note that H is decreasing in p since all goods are normal under homothetic preferences. Furthermore,

$$\lim_{p \to 0} H(p, p_1, p_2) = \infty; \qquad \lim_{p \to \infty} H(p, p_1, p_2) = 0.$$

Hence, for each $L > 0$, (12) can be solved uniquely for $p(L)$. It is also easy to see that $p(L)$ is continuous in L since H is continuous. Therefore (11) has a solution, although it may not be unique. We denote by $\mathcal{L}(p_1, p_2, \lambda_i, j)$ the set of solutions to (11).

We are now in a position to define a symmetric imperfectly competitive equilibrium – where the word 'symmetric' indicates that prices, incomes, etc., are the same in all labour and product markets.

Definition A stationary-state, rational expectations, symmetric, imperfectly competitive equilibrium consists of a vector $(p_1, p_2, L_1, L_2, j_1, j_2)$, where p_i is the price of current consumption (and the wage rate) when $\lambda = \lambda_i$, L_i is the supply of labour of each young person when $\lambda = \lambda_i$, and j_i is the income of each young person when $\lambda = \lambda_i$, and

$$j_i = p_i L_i, \qquad\qquad\qquad i = 1, 2 \qquad\qquad (13)$$

$$L_i \in \mathcal{L}(p_1, p_2, \lambda_i, j_i), \qquad\qquad i = 1, 2 \qquad\qquad (14)$$

$$H(p_i, p_1, p_2) \lambda_i j_i + \frac{m}{p_i} = L_i \leqslant T, \qquad i = 1, 2. \qquad (15)$$

Here (13) defines income, (14) says that the labour supply decision L_i is optimal when $\lambda = \lambda_i$, and (15) says that, given the labour supply decisions L_1, L_2, the resulting prices for current consumption are p_1, p_2. Note that, if we set $L_i = T$ in (15), we get back to the definition of a competitive equilibrium given previously.

Our analysis of imperfectly competitive equilibrium is made considerably simpler by the following observation. The system we are studying is a homogeneous one since, by assumption, firms face constant returns to scale and consumer preferences are homothetic. This suggests that, if we start off with an (imperfectly competitive) equilibrium where $L_1 < T$, $L_2 < T$, then if we raise L_1, L_2 by $100k$ per cent, and maintain $L_1, L_2 \leqslant T$, we will still be in equilibrium. To see that this is indeed the case, consider a $100k$ per cent rise in L_1, L_2 accompanied by a $100k$ per cent fall in p_1, p_2. This keeps j_1, j_2 constant. Since homothetic preferences imply that H is homogenous of degree -1 in (p, p_1, p_2), the new relationship between p and L in (12) is given by

$$\hat{p}[L(1 + k)] = \frac{p(L)}{1 + k}.$$

Setting $L' = L(1 + k)$, we may rewrite

$$\max \hat{p}(L') L' \qquad \text{s.t. } L' \leqslant T$$

as

$$\max p(L) L \qquad \text{s.t. } L \leqslant \frac{T}{1 + k}.$$

Since the constraint $L \leqslant T/(1 + k)$ is more stringent when $k > 0$ than when $k = 0$, it follows that, if $\tilde{L} < T$ maximizes $p(L)L$ subject to $L \leqslant T$, then $\tilde{L}' = \tilde{L}(1 + k)$ maximizes $\hat{p}(L')L'$ subject to $L' \leqslant T$ as long as $\tilde{L}(1 + k) \leqslant T$; i.e., $L_i(1 + k)$ satisfies (14). In addition (15) clearly holds. Since we can continue these $100k$ per cent increases until full employment is reached in one state, we have proved proposition 2.

Proposition 2   Assume (A1)–(A3). If an imperfectly competitive equilibrium exists, then an imperfectly competitive equilibrium exists with $L_i = T$ for $i = 1$ or $i = 2$, that is with full employment in at least one of the states $\lambda = \lambda_1, \lambda = \lambda_2$.

What the proposition tells us is that, in the homogeneous world we are studying, unemployment is not an inevitable consequence of imperfect competition *in the absence of stochastic elements*. For if λ is not a random variable, if an imperfectly competitive equilibrium exists, then one exists with full employment (unemployment equilibria may also exist, however).[2] It should be emphasized that this result depends crucially on homogeneity and is not true, for example, in the non-homogeneous system studied in Hart (1982).

The likelihood of unemployment equilibria

The remainder of this section is devoted to showing that, when demand is stochastic, imperfect competition in the labour market may well prevent full employment in both booms and slumps, although, as the above proposition tells us, full employment in one of these states is possible.

    To simplify matters, we will from now on restrict our attention to the case where π is close to zero, that is, to the case where slumps are rare. This is not because our results do not generalize to other circumstances, but simply because the analysis is more straight-forward in this case.

    As π tends to zero, the consumers' maximization problem (2) becomes in the limit:

$$\max U\left(x_1, \frac{m}{p_2}\right) \qquad \text{s.t. } px_1 + m \leqslant i. \tag{16}$$

We may rewrite this as:

$$\max U(x_1, x_2) \qquad \text{s.t. } px_1 + p_2 x_2 \leqslant i. \tag{17}$$

Since U is homothetic, the solution to (17) can be written as

$$x_1 = h\left(\frac{p}{p_2}\right)\frac{i}{p_2}. \tag{18}$$

Comparing (18) to (3), we see that

$$h(p/p_2) = p_2 H_\pi(p, p_1, p_2) = H_\pi\left(\frac{p}{p_2}, \frac{p_1}{p_2}, 1\right) \quad \text{when } \pi = 0,$$

where we use the subscript π to show that H depends on π.

The function $h(x)$ tells us the demand for current consumption when the price of current consumption is x, the price of future consumption is one with certainty, and income is one. Since current consumption is a normal good under homothetic preferences, we know that h is non-increasing in x. Let $\bar{x} = \inf(x > 0 \mid h(x) = 0)$, where we set $\bar{x} = \infty$ if $h(x) > 0$ for all $x > 0$. In other words, $\bar{x}$ is the lowest price at which demand for current consumption becomes zero. We will make a number of assumptions about h:

(A4) h is twice differentiable for $0 < x < \bar{x}$, differentiable to the left at $x = \bar{x}$ if $\bar{x} < \infty$, and $h' < 0$ for all $0 < x < \bar{x}$.

(A5) $|\eta(x)| \equiv |h'(x)x/h(x)|$, the absolute value of the price elasticity of demand, is strictly increasing in x for $0 < x < \bar{x}$.

(A6) $\bar{x} > 1$, $|\eta(1)| > 1$ and $|\eta(x)| < 1$ for x small enough.

(A7) For π small enough and $0 < p/p_2 < \bar{x}$, $\partial H_\pi/\partial p(p, p_1, p_2)$ exists, and is continuous in p, and

$$\lim_{\pi \to 0} \frac{\partial H_\pi}{\partial p}(p, p_1, p_2) = \frac{1}{p_2^2} h'\left(\frac{p}{p_2}\right).$$

(A4) and (A7) are regularity assumptions. It is easy to show by standard continuity arguments that

$$H_\pi(p, p_1, p_2) \to \frac{1}{p_2} h(p/p_2) \quad \text{as } \pi \to 0.$$

(A7) says that the derivatives of the two functions also converge. Presumably, (A7) can be derived from primitive assumptions on the utility function U.

The strong assumptions are (A5) and (A6). These say that (a) the absolute value of demand elasticity is increasing in own price, and (b) demand is elastic when the price of current consumption is equal to the price of future consumption and inelastic when the price of current consumption is small enough relative to the price of future consumption. Neither (a) nor (b) is implied by maximizing behaviour. However, (a) is often regarded as the 'normal' case for demand functions, while the first part of (b) turns out – perhaps surprisingly – to be essential for establishing the existence of equilibrium. Note that it can be shown that[3]

$$\lim_{x \to 0} \inf |\eta(x)| \leqslant 1$$

(otherwise the budget constraint is violated for small x), so that the second part of (b) is actually quite weak. (Note that (b) rules out the Cobb–Douglas case.)

By virtue of (A5) and (A6), there exists a unique x^*, $0 < x^* < 1$, satisfying $|\eta(x^*)| = 1$. We are now ready to state our main theorem.

Theorem Assume (A1)–(A7). Then there exist numbers $\lambda_1^* > 0$, $0 < \pi^* < 1$ such that: (1) if $\pi < \pi^*$, there exists a (stationary state, rational expectations, symmetric) imperfectly competitive equilibrium, and every such equilibrium exhibits full employment in booms, i.e. $L_2 = T$. (2) If $\pi < \pi^*$ *and* $\lambda_1 < \lambda_1^*$, and if $x^* > 1 - h(1)$, then every imperfectly competitive equilibrium exhibits unemployment in slumps, i.e. $L_1 < T$.

Proof We prove (2) first. Suppose (2) is false. Then, however small λ_1 is, we can choose a sequence of imperfectly competitive equilibria as $\pi \to 0$ such that there is full employment when $\lambda = \lambda_1$. From (15), this means that

$$H_\pi(p_1, p_1, p_2) \lambda_1 p_1 L_1 + \frac{m}{p_1} = L_1 = T \geqslant L_2 = H_\pi(p_2, p_1, p_2) \lambda_2 p_2 L_2 + \frac{m}{p_2} \tag{19}$$

Take limits as $\pi \to 0$. Without loss of generality, we may assume that

$$p_1 \to \bar{p}_1, p_2 \to \bar{p}_2, L_2 \to \bar{L}_2, L_1 \to \bar{L}_1 = T,$$

where some of these numbers may be infinite. Hence (19) becomes

$$\bar{\alpha} h(\bar{\alpha}) \lambda_1 \bar{L}_1 + \frac{m}{\bar{p}_1} = \bar{L}_1 \geqslant \bar{L}_2 = \lambda_2 h(1) \bar{L}_2 + \frac{m}{\bar{p}_2} \tag{20}$$

where $\bar{\alpha} = (\bar{p}_1/\bar{p}_2)$. (20) implies that

$$m = \bar{p}_1 \bar{L}_1 - \bar{\alpha} h(\bar{\alpha}) \lambda_1 \bar{p}_1 \bar{L}_1 = \bar{p}_2 \bar{L}_2 - h(1) \lambda_2 \bar{p}_2 \bar{L}_2.$$

Repeating the argument of the proof of Proposition 1, we can write (20) as

$$\frac{\bar{\alpha} h(\bar{\alpha}) \lambda_1 \bar{L}_1 + m/\bar{p}_1}{\bar{p}_1 \bar{L}_1 - \bar{\alpha} h(\bar{\alpha}) \lambda_1 \bar{p}_1 \bar{L}_1} = \frac{\bar{L}_1}{m} \geqslant \frac{\bar{L}_2}{m} = \frac{\lambda_2 h(1) L_2 + m/\bar{p}_2}{\bar{p}_2 \bar{L}_2 - h(1) \lambda_2 \bar{p}_2 \bar{L}_2}, \tag{21}$$

that is,

$$\frac{\lambda_1 h(\bar{\alpha})}{(1-\lambda_1)+\lambda_1[1-\bar{\alpha}h(\bar{\alpha})]} + \frac{1}{\bar{\alpha}} \frac{\bar{L}_1 \bar{p}_2}{\bar{m}} \geqslant \frac{\lambda_2 h(1)}{1-\lambda_2+\lambda_2[1-h(1)]} + 1. \quad (22)$$

(22), and the facts that $\lambda_1 < \lambda_2$ and that $h(x)/1 - xh(x)$ is decreasing in x, imply that $\bar{\alpha} < 1$. Furthermore, as $\lambda_1 \to 0$, $\lim \sup \bar{\alpha} \leqslant 1 - h(1)$ (recall that $\lambda_2 = 1$).

In addition, we know from (14) that p_i solves (10). Hence we have the two first-order conditions

$$p_1 \frac{\partial H_\pi}{\partial p}(p, p_1, p_2)\bigg|_{p=p_1} + H_\pi(p_1, p_1, p_2) \leqslant 0 \quad (23)$$

$$p_2 \frac{\partial H_\pi}{\partial p}(p, p_1, p_2)\bigg|_{p=p_2} + H_\pi(p_2, p_1, p_2) \leqslant 0. \quad (24)$$

Taking limits of (23) as $\pi \to 0$, we get, using (A7),

$$\bar{\alpha}h'(\bar{\alpha}) + h(\bar{\alpha}) \leqslant 0 \quad (25)$$

that is, $|\eta(\bar{\alpha})| \geqslant 1$. Combining this with the fact that

$$\lim_{\lambda_1 \to 0} \sup \bar{\alpha} \leqslant 1 - h(1)$$

we obtain a contradiction of $x^* > 1 - h(1)$. This proves that there is unemployment in slumps when λ_1 is small enough.

We now turn to the existence question. Consider the solution to the following equations:

$$H_\pi(p_2, \alpha p_2, p_2) \lambda_2 p_2 T + \frac{m}{p_2} = T \quad (26)$$

$$\alpha p_2 \frac{\partial H_\pi}{\partial p}(p, \alpha p_2, p_2)\bigg|_{p=\alpha p_2} + H_\pi(\alpha p_2, \alpha p_2, p_2) = 0 \quad (27)$$

where $\alpha = p_1/p_2$. The first condition says that there should be full employment in a boom, and the second condition says that syndicates satisfy their first-order conditions in a slump. Using the fact that H_π is homogeneous of degree -1, we may rewrite (27) as

$$\alpha \frac{\partial}{\partial p} H_\pi(p, \alpha, 1)\bigg|_{p=\alpha} + H_\pi(\alpha, \alpha, 1) = 0 \quad (28)$$

that is, the elasticity of demand in the slump must equal -1. Now, in the limit $\pi = 0$, (28) becomes

$$\alpha h'(\alpha) + h(\alpha) = 0. \quad (29)$$

By (A5) and (A6), we can find $\alpha < \hat{\alpha} < 1$ such that the LHS of (29) is negative when $\alpha = \underline{\alpha}$ and positive when $\alpha = \hat{\alpha}$. By (A7), the LHS of (28) is negative when $\alpha = \underline{\alpha}$ and positive when $\alpha = \hat{\alpha}$ for π small enough. Hence by continuity we can solve (28) for π small enough.

Having found α to satisfy (28), we may now find p_2 to solve (26). For the LHS of (26) $\to \infty$ as $p_2 \to 0$, and $H_\pi(p_2, \alpha p_2, p_2) \lambda_2 p_2$ is bounded above by unity as $p_2 \to \infty$ by the argument of the proof of proposition 1.

We now show that the p_1, p_2 obtained in this way, together with

$$L_1 = \frac{m/p_1}{1 - \lambda_1 p_1 H_\pi(p_1, p_1, p_2)}, \qquad L_2 = T, j_1 = p_1 L_1, j_2 = p_2 L_2$$

characterize an imperfectly competitive equilibrium as long as

$$\frac{m/p_1}{1 - \lambda_1 p_1 H_\pi(p_1, p_1, p_2)} \leqslant T.$$

All that remains to be shown is that (14) holds, that is, that (10) is solved. However, by (A5), $|\eta(x)|$ is increasing in x. Hence, by (A7),

$$\left| \frac{p \dfrac{\partial}{\partial p} H_\pi(p, \alpha, 1)}{H_\pi(p, \alpha, 1)} \right| \tag{30}$$

is increasing in p for π close to zero. Therefore the absolute value of the elasticity of demand for labour facing a syndicate when $\lambda = \lambda_1$ exceeds 1 for $p > p_1$ and is less than 1 for $p < p_1$. It follows immediately from this that p_1 solves (10). A similar argument shows that p_2 solves (10) since, given that $\alpha < 1$, the absolute value of elasticity of demand exceeds unity if π is small when $\lambda = \lambda_2$, $p = p_2$ by (A6), and is also greater than unity when $p > p_2$.

On the other hand, if

$$\frac{m/p_1}{1 - \lambda_1 p_1 H_\pi(p_1, p_1, p_2)} > T \tag{31}$$

then the competitive equilibrium $p_1 = \hat{p}_1$, $p_2 = \hat{p}_2$, $L_1 = T$, $L_2 = T$, $j_1 = \hat{p}_1 T$, $j_2 = \hat{p}_2 T$ is an imperfectly competitive equilibrium. To see this, denote the p_1, p_2 that solve (26) and (28) by $\tilde{p}_1, \tilde{p}_2$. Then (26) and (31) imply that (19) holds with strict inequality at $(\tilde{p}_1, \tilde{p}_2)$. Arguing as in (19)–(22), we see that $\tilde{\alpha}$ satisfies (22) with strict inequality. On the other hand, $\hat{\alpha} = (\hat{p}_1/\hat{p}_2)$ satisfies (22) with equality. Since the LHS of (22) is decreasing in α, we may deduce that $\tilde{\alpha} < \hat{\alpha}$. Hence, by (28) and (A5), (A7), labour demand is elastic at $p_1 = \hat{p}_1$, and so $p_1 = \hat{p}_1$ solves (10) by the argument given above. Since $\hat{\alpha} < 1$ by proposition 1, the argument given above also establishes that $p_2 = \hat{p}_2$ solves (10). Hence the competitive equilibrium is an imperfectly competitive equilibrium when (31) holds.

We have established the existence of an imperfectly competitive equilibrium when π is small, with full employment in booms and with either full employment or unemployment in slumps. The final step is to note that, when π is small, every imperfectly competitive equilibrium has full employment in booms. For if not, (24) holds with equality. Taking limits as $\pi \to 0$, we get $h'(1) + h(1) = 0$, which contradicts (A6).   Q.E.D.

The intuition behind part (2) of the theorem is quite straightforward. If λ_1 is small, then in order to sustain full employment in a slump, the price of current consumption p_1 must fall a great deal. But if $x^* > 1 - h(1)$, this fall is such as to make the demand for current consumption and for labour inelastic at p_1. As a result, syndicates can increase the wages of their members by raising p_1, and they will choose to do this, thus causing unemployment.

To put it another way, starting at the equilibrium unemployment level in a slump, the reduction in wages that would be necessary to guarantee full employment for a syndicate's members is, as a result of the inelasticity of demand, too large to be worthwhile for any syndicate.

As we have noted above, utility-maximizing behaviour implies that demand for consumption becomes inelastic at sufficiently low prices – more precisely,

$$\lim_{x \to 0} \inf |\eta(x)| \leqslant 1$$

since otherwise the budget constraint is violated at low prices. Of course, the condition $x^* > 1 - h(1)$ is considerably stronger than this. It is worth noting that it will be satisfied if one takes a Cobb–Douglas utility function and perturbs it appropriately.

Note that the theorem applies to the case where π is small. Thus it provides a theory of infrequent slumps with unemployment. Two points should be borne in mind. First, even though the slumps are infrequent, they will be serious for those generations affected. Second, the limiting case $\pi = 0$ was studied only for simplicity. In general, one would expect similar theorems to be true for the case of large π.

The role of government policy

It is interesting to ask whether there is any role for a government stabilization policy in the economy that we have studied. Since the model is so rudimentary, only very simple policies can be considered.

One thing that the government might try to do is to increase demand when $\lambda = \lambda_1$ through a balanced budget fiscal policy. Suppose, to simplify matters, that the government can identify the 'irregular' young – those who do not desire current consumption. Let the government tax this group and spend the proceeds in the same way as the 'regular' young, according to the demand function $H_\pi(p_1, p_2, p_2)i$. Suppose, further, that the government distributes the goods and money it purchases in this way to the population. The effect of this policy is to raise λ_1. When π is small, this will increase employment in slumps, while maintaining full employment in booms.

To see that employment will increase in slumps, note that, arguing as in (20)–(22), but for the case $L_1 \leqslant L_2 = T$, yields

$$\frac{\bar{L}_1}{T} = \frac{\bar{L}_1}{\bar{L}_2}$$

$$= \left(\frac{\lambda_1 h(\bar{\alpha})}{(1-\lambda_1) + \lambda_1[1 - \bar{\alpha}h(\bar{\alpha})]} + \frac{1}{\bar{\alpha}}\right) / \left(\frac{\lambda_2 h(1)}{1 - \lambda_2 + \lambda_2[1 - h(1)]} + 1\right)$$

(32)

where $\bar{\alpha}$ is the unique solution of (29). It is immediate from (32), however, that $\bar{L}_1$ is increasing in λ_1, which proves the result.

Thus the government can stabilize activity levels by an appropriate balanced budget fiscal policy. In fact, if the government taxes all of the income of the irregular young, then λ_1 will become equal to one and no real fluctuations will occur at all: complete stabilization will result. Note that we have shown that stabilization is possible: whether complete or incomplete stabilization is desirable from a welfare point of view is another matter, which we will not deal with here.

We may ask whether monetary policy is also useful for stabilization purposes. Suppose that the government implements the following monetary policy: increase each old consumer's money balances by $100k_1$ per cent when $\lambda = \lambda_1$ and by $100k_2$ per cent when $\lambda = \lambda_2$. Represent an imperfectly competitive equilibrium now by mappings $p_1, p_2, L_1, L_2, j_1, j_2$ from R_+ to R_+, with the interpretation that $p_1(m)$ is the price of current consumption when $\lambda = \lambda_1$, given that m is the per capita money holding of each old person after injections by the government; $L_1(m)$ is employment of each young person when $\lambda = \lambda_1$, given that m is the per capita money holding of each old person; etc. It is easy to show that, if $(\hat{p}_1, \hat{p}_2, \hat{L}_1, \hat{L}_2, \hat{j}_1, \hat{j}_2)$ is an imperfectly competitive equilibrium for the economy of the preceding section with $m = 1$, then there is an imperfectly competitive equilibrium for the economy with the above monetary policy, given by $p_1(m) = \hat{p}_1 m$, $p_2(m) = \hat{p}_2 m$, $L_1(m) = \hat{L}_1$, $L_2(m) = \hat{L}_2$, $j_1(m) = \hat{j}_1 m$, $j_2(m) = \hat{j}_2 m$. (There may be other equilibria, however.) In this equilibrium, employment and output are just as they would be if the government did not pursue an active monetary policy, that is, if $k_1 = k_2 = 1$ – the only effect of the monetary policy is on prices. In this sense, a monetary policy of the type described above is neutral.

We see then that monetary policy, in contrast to fiscal policy, would not seem to be useful for stabilizing fluctuations. There are two reasons for this. First, as in Lucas-type models (see Lucas, 1972), agents have rational expectations. Second, workers set the wage rate to maximize per capita wages, and the solution to this maximization problem is homogeneous of degree one in prices, incomes and money balances (see expression (10)). Note that the neutrality of money result is in sharp contrast to what is found in fixprice models (see Grandmont, 1977). There, monetary policy may be useful for stabilization since, given that prices are fixed, changes in the money supply will affect real variables.

Note that, as in Lucas-type models, more complicated monetary policies, such as stochastic policies or policies that affect the rate of return on holding money, will generally have real effects. Whether such policies are useful for stabilization purposes is another matter.

Summary

In this paper, we have developed a model of an economy with an imperfectly competitive labour market. We have shown that fluctuations in demand which, under perfect competition, result in price fluctuations but not output fluctuations may, under imperfect competition, lead to output and employment fluctuations as well as price fluctuations. We have also shown that a balanced budget fiscal policy can be used to stabilize such fluctuations but that a simple monetary policy cannot.

The model that we have considered is very rudimentary. Among the more extreme assumptions that we have made are that there is only one good each period; that every labour market is unionized and that there is no competitive 'fringe'; that there is no disutility of labour; and that money is the only store of value. Given these very restrictive assumptions, none of our results can be taken that seriously. The purpose of this paper was not, however, to obtain general results but rather to show that Keynesian-type phenomena can be modelled in a framework in which prices are set optimally by agents instead of being fixed exogenously. Only further work can show whether the insights suggested by our approach are robust.

Notes

1 This implies in particular that there are at least as many product markets as labour markets.

2 It may seem from the argument before proposition 2 that the converse of proposition 2 should also hold; i.e., that if there is an equilibrium with full employment in one state, then there are also equilibria with unemployment in both states. This is not true, however. For if $\tilde{L}$ maximizes $p(L)L$ subject to $L \leqslant T$, it does *not* follow that $\tilde{L}(1 + k)$ maximizes

$$\hat{p}(L')L' = p\left(\frac{L'}{1 + k}\right)\left(\frac{L'}{1 + k}\right)$$

subject to $L' \leqslant T$, when $k < 0$. The point is that, when $k < 0$, the constraint $L = L'/(1 + k) \leqslant T/(1 + k)$ is *less* stringent than the constraint $L \leqslant T$. See also part (1) of the theorem below, where sufficient conditions for every equilibrium to exhibit full employment in at least one state are given.

3 See, for example, the appendix of Hart (1982).

References

Grandmont, J.-M. (1977) 'Temporal general equilibrium theory', *Econometrica*, vol. 45, pp. 535–72.

Hart, O. (1982) 'A model of imperfect competition with Keynesian features', *Quarterly Journal of Economics*, vol. 97, pp. 109–38.

Lucas, R. E. (1972) 'Expectations and the neutrality of money', *Journal of Economic Theory*, vol. 4, pp. 103–24.

PART IV

Rational Expectations and Macroeconomic Fluctuations

8

Monetary Information and Macroeconomic Fluctuations

JOHN BOSCHEN and HERSCHEL GROSSMAN

Current research in macroeconomics focuses considerable attention on models that appeal to incomplete information about monetary disturbances in an attempt to reconcile assumptions of rational expectations and market clearing with a relation between money and macroeconomic fluctuations. Evaluation of these so-called 'equilibrium models' requires understanding of the precise content in this context of the three key ideas. (1) 'Rational expectations' means that private agents gather and use information efficiently and, more specifically, that they behave as if they understand the economy's essential stochastic structural relations, including the pattern governing the determination of the stock of money. (2) 'Market clearing' means that transactions in individual markets realize all perceived gains from trade. This assumption has taken two alternative forms. Specifically, Lucas (1972, 1973) and Barro (1976) assume that prices and quantities equate spot demands and supplies, whereas Azariadis (1978) assumes that quantities are set contractually to satisfy perceived productive-efficiency conditions, which are similar to spot market-clearing conditions, but that certain prices are set contractually to satisfy risk-sharing-efficiency conditions, which mean that wages are not equated to perceived marginal products. For present purposes, these two forms of market clearing have the same implications. (3) Incomplete information means that only local information about prices is contemporaneously available and that a part of the behaviour of monetary aggregates is neither anticipated nor contemporaneously perceived. Specifically, equili-

The National Science Foundation and the John Simon Guggenheim Memorial Foundation have supported this research. We have received useful comments from Mark Edwards, Oliver Hart, Robert King, Axel Leijonhufvud and Edmond Malinvaud.

173

brium models assume that monetary policy is partly stochastic, and, with the exception of the recent work of King (1981), existing equilibrium models also assume that no data on the current money stock are available. These models, however, assume that accurate data about past values of the money stock are currently available.

The most striking implication of equilibrium models, derived explicitly by Barro (1976), is a neutrality proposition that says that macroeconomic fluctuations – specifically, the time pattern of differences between actual and natural levels of real variables such as aggregate output and employment – evolve independently of those monetary actions that reflect systematic responses to macroeconomic fluctuations. Because private agents correctly anticipate systematic monetary policy and understand how monetary policy affects the market-clearing conditions, which govern the determination of real variables, their behavioural responses to systematic monetary policy have an impact on market-clearing prices but do not affect the difference between actual and natural levels of real variables. As a complement to this neutrality proposition, existing equilibrium models also imply that the pattern of macroeconomic fluctuations depends in a significant way on the subset of monetary actions that is non-systematic. Because of incomplete information, private agents are unable to distinguish random monetary disturbances from relative disturbances. Consequently, their behavioural responses to random monetary disturbances, in contrast to their behavioural responses to systematic monetary policy, produce changes in real variables.

One troublesome feature of existing equilibrium models is their cavalier and unrealistic assumptions about the availability of monetary data. The Federal Reserve Board currently issues preliminary monetary data with only an eight-day lag and then revises these data over a period of months or years. These revisions result from such factors as computational corrections, benchmark changes reflecting fuller reporting, and conceptual changes reflecting financial innovations. Existing equilibrium models, however, abstract from both the existence of contemporaneous preliminary monetary data and the process of gradual accumulation of revised monetary data. The neglect of contemporaneous data implies that private agents act as if they ignore readily available and apparently relevant information, an implication that seems inconsistent with the idea of rational expectations. In contrast, the neglect of the process of data correction implies that private agents act as if they have an unrealistically large amount of information.

In his recent paper, King (1981) makes a start at rectifying this problem by introducing contemporaneously available monetary data into an equilibrium model. In King's model, these data take the form of an estimate of the current money stock, subject to a random error that is fully corrected in the next period. The important new implication derived from King's analysis is that real variables such as aggregate output and employment are uncorrelated with these contemporaneously available monetary data.

The model developed in the present paper expands on King's analysis by taking explicit account of the gradual process of accumulation of revised monetary data. Our model, like King's model, includes a contemporaneous estimate of the money stock, but instead of King's assumption that this estimate is corrected in the next period, we assume that developing the finally reported value of the current money stock involves more than one revision and takes more than one period. Our model also allows explicitly for systematic monetary policy in the form of a target monetary growth rate that responds to the past behaviour of aggregate output.

The main result from the analysis that follows is that, despite the more complete specification of the accumulation of monetary data, systematic monetary policy and their interaction, the present model turns out to have implications similar to those derived by Barro and King. Specifically, our analysis implies that aggregate output and employment are independent of systematic monetary policy and are uncorrelated with the contemporaneous measure of money growth implied by the difference between the currently available estimates of current and past money stocks.

This latter implication would seem to be a readily testable hypothesis, and an obvious conjecture would be that it is not consistent with the relevant data. In fact, econometric results reported by Barro and Hercowitz (1980), as well as more extensive econometric analyses reported in Boschen and Grossman (1982), confirm this conjecture. These results provide apparently strong evidence against the equilibrium approach to modelling the relation between monetary disturbances and macroeconomic fluctuations.

Setup of the model

In the existing literature, the development of the incomplete-information paradigm has focused on various, but mutually consistent, stories about information. The following setup is based on the story told by Friedman (1968), in which the representative worker infrequently purchases many of the items that he consumes and, hence, infrequently observes their prices. The representative worker, consequently, does not know precisely the extent to which a change in the nominal value of his product involves a change in his terms of trade between leisure and consumption. His subjective belief about consumption prices, and hence about the relevant real value of his productive services, is the critical expectational variable in the model. The incorporation of rational expectations in the model means that this subjective belief is equal to a true mathematical expectation conditional on available information. The structural equations of the model describe the supply and demand for a representative good, the maket-clearing condition that determines the output and price of this good, the behavioural pattern of the monetary authority, the nature of available monetary data and the formation of rational expectations about average prices.

The current supply of representative good z depends on the subjective belief of the representative producer of this good about the relation between the current price of this good and average prices. Specifically, we assume the log-linear form

$$y_t^s(z) = \alpha [p_t(z) - E_t(z) p_t] + n(z) \tag{1}$$

where

$y_t^s(z)$	is the log of the current supply of good z;
$p_t(z)$	is the log of the current money price of good z;
$E_t(z) p_t$	is the current subjective belief of the representative producer of good z about the average of the logs of money prices;
α	is the positive and constant elasticity of supply with respect to the difference, $p_t(z) - E_t(z) p_t$; and
$n(z)$	is the log of the 'natural' level of output of good z.

The current demand for good z depends on the value of aggregate money balances deflated by $p_t(z)$ and on random disturbances to aggregate demand and to the relative demands for the various goods. Specifically, we assume the log-linear form

$$y_t^d(z) = M_t - p_t(z) + v_t + \epsilon_t(z) \tag{2}$$

where

$y_t^d(z)$	is the log of the current demand for good z;
M_t	is the log of the finally reported value of the current money stock;

v_t is a random variable distributed according to $v_t \sim N(0, \sigma_v^2)$, uncorrelated serially and uncorrelated with the other random variables in the model; and

$\epsilon_t(z)$ is a random variable distributed according to $\epsilon_t(z) \sim N(0, \sigma_\epsilon^2)$, uncorrelated serially, uncorrelated with the other random variables in the model, and summing to zero across all goods; i.e., $\Sigma_t \, \epsilon_t(z) = 0$.

A more general formulation of the supply and demand functions would include the terms $p_t(z) - E_t(z) \, p_t$ and $M_t - p_t(z)$ in both of the functions, and also would allow for random disturbances to supply and to aggregate demand. These and other possible generalizations would complicate the algebraic analysis of the model without changing the main conclusions regarding the role of monetary information.

Note that we are careful *not* to define M_t to be the log of the true value of the current money stock. This implied distinction between true values and finally reported values is necessary to make the setup of the model strictly consistent with the rational expectations assumption that private agents behave as if they know the structure of the economy. Presumably, individuals can acquire this knowledge only from observational experience, a process that implies, as regards the relations between aggregate variables, that, because producers of good z would not directly experience aggregate variables, these variables as contained in the specified structural equations can represent only the most accurate available measurements as reported in revised and corrected published data. The construction of these data implies that individuals, like statisticians and econometricians, cannot know the remaining inaccuracies in the data, and hence cannot learn from observational experience the structural relations between the true values of these quantities.

The market-clearing condition for good z is that $p_t(z)$ adjusts to satisfy the equality

$$y_t(z) = y_t^s(z) = y_t^d(z) \tag{3}$$

where $y_t(z)$ is the log of the actual current output of good z. This part of our model is the same as King's model. The rest of the model involves specification of available information, of the determination of M_t, and of the formation of $E_t(z) \, p_t$.

Currently available monetary data include a preliminary estimate of the finally reported value of the current money stock and reported values of the money stocks of previous periods. These reported values include some estimates that have already been revised but, like the estimate of last period's money stock, have not yet been finalized. For the current money stock, we assume a log-linear estimating relation, which is identical to King's formulation,

$$\hat{M}_t = M_t + \delta_t \tag{4}$$

where

$\hat{M}_t$ is the log of the latest published estimate of the money stock; and

δ_t is a random variable distributed according to $\delta_t \sim N(0, \sigma_\delta^2)$, uncorrelated serially, and uncorrelated with the other random variables in the model.

Monetary policy involves a target monetary growth rate, which incorporates both a constant term and a systematic response to past differences between actual and natural levels of aggregate output, and a random factor. Specifically, we assume a log-linear relation of the form

$$M_t = \hat{M}_{t-1} + \phi_t + g_t \tag{5}$$

where

$\phi_t = \phi_0 + \phi_1(y_{t-1} - n)$; and

$\hat{M}_{t-1}$ is the log of the current estimate of last period's money stock;

y_{t-1} is the aggregate across all goods of the logs of output last period; i.e., $y_{t-1} = \Sigma_z y_{t-1}(z)$;

n is the aggregate across all goods of the logs of the natural levels of output; i.e., $n = \Sigma_z n(z)$;

ϕ_0 is the constant element in systematic monetary policy;

ϕ_1 is the elasticity of the variable element in systematic monetary policy; and

g_t is a random variable distributed according to $g_t \sim N(0, \sigma_g^2)$, uncorrelated serially, and uncorrelated with the other random variables in the model.

Within the context of equation (5), the random variable, g_t, has at least two possible interpretations, corresponding to different monetary policy processes. One possible process is that M_t results from adding ϕ_t and a random variable, x_t, directly to $\hat{M}_{t-1}$ – that is,

$$M_t = \hat{M}_{t-1} + \phi_t + x_t.$$

In this case, g_t is equivalent to x_t. A second possible process is that M_t results from adding ϕ_t and x_t to M_{t-1} – that is,

$$M_t = M_{t-1} + \phi_t + x_t.$$

This equation is identical to King's formulation of monetary policy except for the inclusion of ϕ_t. Given a log-linear estimating relation for M_{t-1} in the form

$$\hat{M}_{t-1} = M_{t-1} + \eta_t$$

where η_t is a random variable, we can express the second monetary policy process as

$$M_t = \hat{M}_{t-1} + \phi_t + x_t - \eta_t.$$

In this case, g_t is equivalent to the difference, $x_t - \eta_t$. In general, these two processes imply different values for σ_g^2 and for g_t and hence have different quantitative implications for the behaviour of y_t. These two processes, however, have the same implication for the relation between y_t and $\hat{M}_t - \hat{M}_{t-1}$.

The assumed rationality of expectations prescribes that the subjective belief, $E_t(z)\,p_t$, is equal to the true mathematical expectation of p_t conditional on the information currently known to producers of good z. Specifically,

$$E_t(z)\,p_t = E\,[P_t \mid I_t(z)] \qquad (6)$$

where $I_t(z)$ is the assumed information set. This set contains useful knowledge about the structure of the economy that includes the form of the structural equations (1)–(6), the values of the parameters, α, ϕ_0 and ϕ_1, the natural levels of output of good z and of aggregate output, $n(z)$ and n, and the form of the stochastic disturbances, v_t, $\epsilon_t(z)$, g_t and δ_t. The information set also contains useful data that include the current price of good z, $p_t(z)$, the past level of aggregate output, y_{t-1} and the monetary data, $\hat{M}_t$ and $\hat{M}_{t-1}$. Note that, by implication, the information set includes the current value of systematic monetary policy, ϕ_t. The potentially useful information that is not in $I_t(z)$ includes the current average of prices, p_t, the current level of aggregate output, y_t, the finally reported values of the current and last period's money stock, M_t and M_{t-1} and the realizations of the stochastic disturbances, v_t, $\epsilon_t(z)$, g_t and δ_t.

Solution of the model

Theoretical analysis of the model specified by equations (1)–(6) involves finding a solution for the current output of representative good z and, hence, for aggregate output that satisfies the market-clearing condition, given by equation (3), subject to expectations being formed rationally, as specified by equation (6). The method of undetermined coefficients, applied in similar contexts by Lucas (1972) and Barro (1976), provides a solution procedure. The first step is to substitute equations (1) and (2) into the market-clearing condition, given by equation (3), to obtain an equation that relates $p_t(z)$ to M_t, $E_t(z) p_t$ and other variables:

$$p_t(z) = (\alpha + 1)^{-1} [\alpha E_t(z) p_t + M_t + v_t + \epsilon_t(z) - n(z)]. \tag{7}$$

The second step is to use equations (4) and (5) separately to eliminate M_t from equation (7). Combining equations (4) and (7) gives

$$p_t(z) = (\alpha + 1)^{-1} [\alpha E_t(z) p_t + \hat{M}_t - \delta_t + v_t + \epsilon_t(z) - n(z)]. \tag{8a}$$

Combining equations (5) and (7) gives

$$p_t(z) = (\alpha + 1)^{-1} [\alpha E_t(z) p_t + \hat{M}_{t-1} + \phi_t + g_t + v_t + \epsilon_t(z) - n(z)]. \tag{8b}$$

The third step is to conjecture a solution for $p_t(z)$ that is a linear combination of a constant term, which allows for known variables, and each of the stochastic disturbances:

$$p_t(z) = \Pi_0 + \Pi_1 g_t + \Pi_2 \delta_t + \Pi_3 v_t + \Pi_4 \epsilon_t(z). \tag{9}$$

Aggregating equation (9) across all goods yields a solution for average prices in the form

$$p_t = \Pi_0 + \Pi_1 g_t + \Pi_2 \delta_t + \Pi_3 v_t. \tag{10}$$

The assumed rationality of expectations means that the subjective belief, $E_t(z) p_t$, is equal to the true mathematical expectation of equation (10) conditional on $I_t(z)$. This expectation is given by

$$E_t(z) p_t = \Pi_0 + \Pi_1 E_t(z) g_t + \Pi_2 E_t(z) \delta_t + \Pi_3 E_t(z) v_t, \tag{11}$$

where $E_t(z) g_t$, $E_t(z) \delta_t$ and $E_t(z) v_t$ are true mathematical expectations conditional on $I_t(z)$.

The fourth step is to calculate $E_t(z) g_t$, $E_t(z) \delta_t$ and $E_t(z) v_t$. In forming these expectations, producers of good z can combine the known structural equations describing market clearing, monetary policy and monetary information, as in equations (8a) and (8b), to obtain the following two equations between linear combinations of stochastic variables and linear combinations of known variables. Rearranging equation (8a) gives

$$-\delta_t + v_t + \epsilon_t(z) = (\alpha + 1)\, p_t(z) - \alpha E_t(z)\, p_t - \hat{M}_t + n(z). \tag{12}$$

Rearranging equation (8b) gives

$$g_t + v_t + \epsilon_t(z) = (\alpha + 1)\, p_t(z) - \alpha E_t(z)\, p_t - (\hat{M}_{t-1} + \phi_t) + n(z). \tag{13}$$

Equations (12) and (13) enable the producers of good z to infer the values of the sums: $-\delta_t + v_t + \epsilon_t(z)$ and $g_t + v_t + \epsilon_t(z)$.

Given the linear normal structure of the model, the relations between the conditional expectations and the known linear combinations of stochastic variables have the form of regression equations:

$$\begin{bmatrix} E_t(z)\, g_t \\ E_t(z)\, \delta_t \\ E_t(z)\, v_t \end{bmatrix} = [R] \begin{bmatrix} -\delta_t + v_t + \epsilon_t(z) \\ g_t + v_t + \epsilon_t(z) \end{bmatrix}, \tag{14}$$

where $[R]$ is a matrix of regression coefficients given by

$$[R] = \begin{bmatrix} 0 & \sigma_g^2 \\ -\sigma_\delta^2 & 0 \\ \sigma_v^2 & \sigma_v^2 \end{bmatrix} \begin{bmatrix} \sigma_\delta^2 + \sigma_v^2 + \sigma_\epsilon^2 & \sigma_v^2 + \sigma_\epsilon^2 \\ \sigma_v^2 + \sigma_\epsilon^2 & \sigma_g^2 + \sigma_v^2 + \sigma_\epsilon^2 \end{bmatrix}^{-1}$$

$$= \Delta^{-1} \begin{bmatrix} -\sigma_g^2(\sigma_v^2 + \sigma_\epsilon^2) & \sigma_g^2(\sigma_\delta^2 + \sigma_v^2 + \sigma_\epsilon^2) \\ -\sigma_\delta^2(\sigma_g^2 + \sigma_v^2 + \sigma_\epsilon^2) & \sigma_\delta^2(\sigma_v^2 + \sigma_\epsilon^2) \\ \sigma_g^2\sigma_v^2 & \sigma_\delta^2\sigma_v^2 \end{bmatrix}$$

and

$$\Delta = \sigma_\delta^2\sigma_g^2 + \sigma_\delta^2\sigma_\epsilon^2 + \sigma_g^2\sigma_\epsilon^2 + \sigma_v^2\sigma_g^2 + \sigma_v^2\sigma_\delta^2.$$

The fifth step is to determine the coefficients, $\Pi_0, \ldots, \Pi_3$. The procedure is to substitute into equation (11) the values of $E_t(z)\, g_t$, $E_t(z)\, \delta_t$ and $E_t(z)\, v_t$ given by equation (14), and then to substitute into either equations (8a) or (8b) the resulting value of $E_t(z)\, p_t$ given by equation (11). Equation (8a) or (8b) then gives an expression for $p_t(z)$ that is a linear combination of the predetermined and exogenous variables, where the weights involve the undetermined coefficients,

$\Pi_0, \ldots, \Pi_4$, and the variances of the stochastic variables. Equating each of these weights to the corresponding coefficient in the trial solution given by equation (9) yields a system of five simultaneous equations that we can solve for $\Pi_0, \ldots, \Pi_4$. Using equation (8b), these equations are

$$\Pi_0 = (\alpha + 1)^{-1}[\alpha\Pi_0 + \hat{M}_{t-1} + \phi_t - n(z)],$$

$$\Pi_1 = (\alpha + 1)^{-1}\{\alpha\Delta^{-1}[\Pi_1\sigma_g^2(\sigma_\delta^2 + \sigma_v^2 + \sigma_\epsilon^2) + \Pi_2\sigma_v^2(\sigma_v^2 + \sigma_\epsilon^2)$$
$$+ \Pi_3\sigma_\delta^2\sigma_v^2] + 1\},$$

$$\Pi_2 = (\alpha + 1)^{-1}\alpha\Delta^{-1}[\Pi_1\sigma_g^2(\sigma_v^2 + \sigma_\epsilon^2) + \Pi_2\sigma_\delta^2(\sigma_g^2 + \sigma_v^2 + \sigma_\epsilon^2)$$
$$- \Pi_3\sigma_g^2\sigma_v^2],$$

$$\Pi_3 = (\alpha + 1)^{-1}\{\alpha\Delta^{-1}[(\Pi_1 - \Pi_2)\,\sigma_g^2\sigma_\delta^2 + \Pi_3\sigma_v^2(\sigma_g^2 + \sigma_\delta^2)] + 1\},$$

and

$$\Pi_4 = (\alpha + 1)^{-1}\{\alpha\Delta^{-1}[(\Pi_1 - \Pi_2)\,\sigma_g^2\sigma_\delta^2 + \Pi_3\sigma_\delta^2(\sigma_g^2 + \sigma_\delta^2)] + 1\}.$$

The solutions to these equations are

$$\Pi_0 = \hat{M}_{t-1} + \phi_t - n(z),$$

$$\Pi_1 = (1 + \alpha\sigma_g^2\sigma_\epsilon^2\Delta^{-1})[1 + \alpha(\sigma_g^2\sigma_\epsilon^2 + \sigma_\delta^2\sigma_\epsilon^2)\,\Delta^{-1}]^{-1},$$

$$\Pi_2 = \alpha\sigma_g^2\sigma_\epsilon^2\Delta^{-1}[1 + \alpha(\sigma_g^2\sigma_\epsilon^2 + \sigma_\delta^2\sigma_\epsilon^2)\,\Delta^{-1}]^{-1}, \text{ and}$$

$$\Pi_3 = \Pi_4 = [1 + \alpha(\sigma_g^2\sigma_\epsilon^2 + \sigma_\delta^2\sigma_\epsilon^2)\,\Delta^{-1}]^{-1}.$$

The final step is to use these expressions for $\Pi_0, \ldots, \Pi_4$ together with the market-clearing conditions and either the supply function or the demand function to obtain a solution for current aggregate output in terms of the predetermined and exogenous variables. Substituting equation (2) into equation (3) implies

$$y_t(z) = M_t - p_t(z) + v_t + \epsilon_t(z). \tag{15}$$

Aggregating equation (15) across all goods gives

$$y_t = M_t - p_t + v_t. \tag{16}$$

Using equation (5) to replace M_t with $\hat{M}_{t-1} + \phi_t + g_t$ and using equation (10) and the solutions for Π_0, Π_1, and Π_2 to eliminate p_t yields the expression for current aggregate output:

$$y_t = n + (1 - \Pi_1)\,g_t - \Pi_2\delta_t + (1 - \Pi_3)\,v_t. \tag{17}$$

Straightforward algebraic manipulation reveals that the values of $1 - \Pi_1$, of Π_2, and of $1 - \Pi_3$ are all positive but less than unity.

Implications of the solution

Equation (17) indicates that current aggregate output, y_t, equals the natural level of aggregate output, n, plus a linear combination of the realizations of the exogenous random variables that represent the unanticipated part of current monetary policy, g_t, the currently unperceived part of current monetary policy, δ_t, and the unperceived disturbance to aggregate demand, v_t. The coefficients of this linear combination are, as indicated by the expressions for Π_1, Π_2, and Π_3, themselves functions of the variances of these random variables, σ_g^2, σ_δ^2, and σ_v^2, and the variance of the random disturbance to relative demands, σ_ϵ^2. The calculated values for Π_1 and Π_3 imply that y_t is positively related to g_t and to v_t. This result obtains because producers of good z mistake some of the increase in the money price of good z that results from positive values of g_t or v_t to be an increase in the relative price of good z. The calculated value of Π_2 implies that y_t is negatively related to δ_t. This result obtains because, as King points out, a high preliminary estimate of the money stock causes the expectations of producers of good z about average prices to be too high and their expectations about the relative price of good z to be correspondingly too low.

The correspondence between the solution for y_t given by equation (17) and the solution that King obtains for his model depends on which of the interpretations of g_t discussed above is relevant. For the case of g_t equivalent to x_t, equation (17) is identical to King's solution. For the case of g_t equivalent to $x_t - \eta_t$, equation (17) differs from King's solution to the extent that η_t and σ_η^2 differ from zero.

King shows that in his model the covariance between y_t and his contemporaneous measure of money growth, $\hat{M}_t - M_{t-1}$, is equal to zero. Now, let us calculate the covariance between y_t and the contemporaneous measure of money growth, $\hat{M}_t - \hat{M}_{t-1}$, that applies in the present model. Observe that combining equations (4) and (5) implies

$$\hat{M}_t - \hat{M}_{t-1} = g_t + \delta_t + \phi_t. \tag{18}$$

Thus we have from equations (17) and (18),

$$\mathrm{cov}\,(y_t, \hat{M}_t - \hat{M}_{t-1}) = \mathrm{cov}\,[n + (1 - \Pi_1)\,g_t - \Pi_2\,\delta_t + (1 - \Pi_3)\,v_t,$$

$$g_t + \delta_t + \phi_t] = (1 - \Pi_1)\,\sigma_g^2 - \Pi_2\,\sigma_\delta^2. \tag{19}$$

Substituting the calculated values of Π_1 and Π_2 into equation (19), we obtain

$$\operatorname{cov}(y_t, \hat{M}_t - \hat{M}_{t-1}) = 0. \tag{20}$$

Equation (20) provides the basis for the econometric tests reported in Boschen and Grossman (1982). These tests imply rejection of the hypothesis, represented by equation (20), that current aggregate output is independent of the contemporaneous measure of money growth. Because this hypothesis seems to be an inescapable implication of the equilibrium approach to macroeconomic modelling, these empirical results also imply rejection of this approach.

References

Azariadis, C. (1978) 'Escalator clauses and the allocation of cyclical risks', *Journal of Economic Theory*, vol. 18, June, pp. 119–55.

Barro, R. J. (1976) 'Rational expectations and the role of monetary policy', *Journal of Monetary Economics*, vol. 2, January, pp. 1–32.

Barro, R. J. and Hercowitz, Z. (1980) 'Money stock revisions and unanticipated money growth', *Journal of Monetary Economics*, vol. 6, April, pp. 257–67.

Boschen, J. and Grossman, H. I. (1982) 'Tests of equilibrium macroeconomics using contemporaneous monetary data', *Journal of Monetary Economics*, vol. 10, November, pp. 309–33.

Friedman, M. (1968) 'The role of monetary policy', *American Economic Review*, vol. 58, March, pp. 1–17.

King, R. (1981) 'Monetary information and monetary neutrality', *Journal of Monetary Economics*, vol. 7, March, pp. 195–206.

Lucas, R. E. Jr (1972) 'Expectations and the neutrality of money', *Journal of Economic Theory*, vol. 4, April, pp. 103–24.

Lucas, R. E. Jr (1973) 'Some international evidence on output–inflation trade-offs', *American Economic Review*, vol. 63, June, pp. 326–34.

9

Foundations of a Likelihood Theory of Employment and Inflation

EZIO TARANTELLI

Introduction

The aim of this paper is to put forward a probability theory of the Phillips curve and its implications for the productivity–price–labour force nexus in the post-Keynesian model of the labour market. By way of introduction, I summarize the reasons that render both the so-called 'Holt's law' on the near constancy of turnover rates (Modigliani and Tarantelli, 1979) and job search theory invalid. On the basis of this result and some of its implications, I discuss and formalize the view of the labour market in terms of expected probability theory which I am putting forward here. These paragraphs discuss, moreover, the implications of such a change for the instability of the Phillips curve, and for the interactions of the model proposed here with fiscal and monetary policy. One of the central characteristics of the model, is that it endogenously generates the reasons for the rigidity downwards (and, under certain conditions, also upwards) of money wages in a world of rational expectations. This model can generate the anti-cyclical loops initially observed by Lipsey, as an effect of the cyclical and structural variations on the flow of hirings. The final section contains the conclusion and some implications.

This work is part of a research project carried out for the econometric model of the Bank of Italy (M2 B.I.) with Franco Modigliani. My first debt is to Franco Modigliani, for having continually suggested relevant and interesting problems, for his ideas, and for many useful suggestions and comments. I would also like to thank S. Fischer, G. P. Galli, J. Hicks, M. Piore and R. Solow. Responsibility for errors is mine alone.

185

The invalidity of 'Holt's law' on the rate of turnover, and the fallacy of job search theory

The rate of turnover (the flow of hirings and the flow of separations) is not a 'stochastic parameter' (cf. Holt in Phelps *et al.*, 1970), as it would be according to what R. Hall has called 'Holt's law' (which might more correctly be called 'Holt's conjecture' – see Modigliani and Tarantelli, 1979). On the contrary, the rate of turnover is a variable, the changes in which reflect precise market laws and institutional determinants. It has in particular been shown (Modigliani and Tarantelli, 1979) that the two major components of the rate of turnover – the flow of hirings, f_a, and the flow of separations, f_s – increase as an effect of higher levels of demand, that is, for lower levels of the unemployment rate, u.

This is the result of the structural effect of the introduction into the productive process, corresponding to higher levels of aggregate demand, of less 'employable' groups of labour, known to be characterized by higher turnover rates (Hall, 1972). In particular, a higher unemployment rate implies a lower proportion of the less employable groups of labour, that is, a higher share of more employable workers in the total employed. These workers are characterized by better career possibilities and seniority rights, and hence also by lower quitting rates. This labour group is, moreover, the first to be hired and the last to be fired (with changes in demand for labour). It is therefore structurally characterized by lower rates of turnover (flow of both hirings and separations).

The empirical tests of Modigliani and Tarantelli suggest, furthermore, that the flow of hirings (and of separations) tends to vary in the presence of changes in the level of aggregate demand as a cyclical effect of two determinants. First, as regards the flow of hirings, an increase in the supply of jobs increases the probability of being hired. This is due to the fact that an increase in the number of vacancies can lead to a reduction in the number of unemployed only with a certain delay (during which the flow of hirings increases). Second, when demand for labour increases, the probability that a worker will agree to fill a vacant post (for a given offered wage) increases as a result of the lower level of information on the improvement of market conditions that workers normally have by comparison with firms.[1]

It is well known that Holt's version of the Phillips curve is based on an inverse relation between the money wage rate demanded by an unemployed worker and the time, T_u, for which the worker has been unemployed in search of a job; or

$$\dot{w} = w^d (T_u); \quad w^{d'} < 0. \tag{a}$$

In equilibrium, with f_a and f_s taken as stochastic parameters,

$$f_a = P_u u = \frac{u}{Tu} \tag{b}$$

where P_u, the probability of a hiring, is identically equal to the reciprocal of the duration of unemployment. Obviously, to the extent that f_a may be taken as constant, at least to a first approximation, it is possible to derive from the foregoing money wage function in terms of P_u an equation in terms of u (given f_a): namely, the familiar job search Phillips curve:

$$\dot{w} = \hat{w}^d (u; f_a); \quad \hat{w}^{d'} < 0. \tag{c}$$

This way of solving the problem has recently been criticized on the basis of two major considerations.

1   A substantial proportion of those seeking employment do not spend any time, T_u, on the labour market, but go directly from one job to another. The reason is that the advantage of being unemployed (in terms of greater information) for a worker seeking a job is normally less than the wage cost of spending a period unemployed (instead of, for instance, using the telephone – even the telephone of the company where the worker is employed!) to seek a better offer.

2   Even independently of (1), Holt's model is able to explain the rate of change in money wages of, at most, a very small proportion of the labour force: that of the frictional unemployed. Holt's model cannot, on the other hand, explain that rate of change of money wages of the great majority of the labour force comprising the employed, or the rate of money wages offered to the involuntarily unemployed.

Towards a likelihood theory of finding an alternative job

The above considerations (i.e. regarding the structural and cyclical changes in the flow of hirings) suggest that it is highly misleading to base the Phillips curve on the time spent searching for a job, T_u, instead of on the probability that a worker has of finding a job, P_u.

For example, it can be shown that, if the flow of hirings, f_a, is variable (as in *disequilibrium*), it is no longer true that P_u and T_u are reciprocals (as in equation (b) above) but that, on the contrary, they can diverge substantially. In this case, equation (c) above would not be derivable from equation (a), the latter assuming a wage behaviour of the (frictional) unemployed that depends only on the time spent looking for a job. Let us see why in greater detail.

In disequilibrium, the probability of finding a job can no longer be expressed as the reciprocal of the average period of unemployment. The average period of unemployment is a weighted average (where the weights are the various groups of unemployed) of the periods *spent* unemployed; whereas the present (and expected) probability of being hired can be expressed through the (empirically observable) relationship, $P_u = f_a/u$:

$$P_u = f_a/u \neq 1/T_u. \tag{b'}$$

That is, the present (and expected) value of P_u may diverge, even very substantially, from $1/T_u$ inherited from the *past*. At the start of a period of economic recovery following a recession, for instance, P_u and T_u may both be very high. The opposite may be the case in the initial stages of a recession following a period of high employment. The average T_u today is the weighted average of the times spent unemployed, while P_u is a value depending on the present conditions of labour demand and supply. Past and present cannot coincide in disequilibrium.

A similar conclusion is, of course, true for the average time taken to fill a vacancy, T_v, which in disequilibrium does not coincide with the probability of filling a vacancy, P_v:

$$P_v = f_a/v \neq 1/T_v \tag{b''}$$

where v is the vacancy rate. In the initial stages of a recession following a period of high employment, it is clear that P_v and T_v may both be high. The probability of filling a vacancy is, in fact, high as a result of the new unemployed who begin to become available on the labour market at the start of a recession. But the average time to fill a vacancy is also high in such conditions, since until the start of the recession there had been a labour shortage. Again, past and present cannot coincide in disequilibrium.

The probability of a hiring, $P_u = f_a/u$ (or of the filling of a vacant post, $P_v = f_a/v$), depends instead on the flow of hirings (which is identically equal to the flow of fillings of vacancies) and on the level of the unemployment rate (or the vacancy rate, v) and may be independent of the *past* determinants of the average period of unemployment (filling of a vacant post). In addition, the *expected* value of P_u, $P_u^e = (f_a/u)^e$, may be substantially different from $1/T_u$, which refers to a weighted average of the values of past unemployment.

For present purposes, the expected value of P_u would be more relevant than its actual present value. The reason is that wage bargaining (whether between worker and firm or between trade union and firm) determines the level of money wages for the entire future periods of validity of the contract, and (with a few exceptions only) not only for the 'day' when the contract is concluded. For this reason, it seems plausible to assume that both demanded and offered wages depend, respectively, on the expected probabilities of a hiring for the workers and of filling a vacancy for the firm for the average period of expected validity of the wage contract. The firm will tend to offer a higher money wage the lower is the expected probability of filling a vacancy. A money wage rate lower than that implied by the expectations regarding these variables means, in fact, higher costs (and risks) of renewed bargaining for the firm and/or a higher expected flow of quits (with the associated costs in terms of training, lower productivity, work disorganization, etc.). Symmetrical considerations apply to workers.

Since, moreover, the relationship $P_u^e = (f_a/u)^e$ refers to the expected probability of finding work (the probability of finding work at any given instant being clearly close to zero) and not to a length of employment, it is clearly relevant not only for the frictional unemployed but also for workers who go from one job to another directly, without spending a period unemployed. This same relationship may also determine the wages demanded by employed workers remaining in the job, who constitute the great majority of the labour force.

For this last group of workers in particular, it may be assumed that the increase in money wages demanded is an increasing function of the expected probability of finding an *alternative* (better) job after a threat of quitting. The key point of connection between this last group of workers (including those in the 'internal' labour market) and workers seeking a job in the labour market is constituted by the so-called ports of entry and exit (quitting and dismissal) from the external labour market to the internal one.

Two implications of this approach seem noteworthy. (1) The proportion of potential quits by employed workers is an increasing function of the expected value of P_u, or P_u^e. (2) The wage increase that a firm is forced to accept for all workers is an increasing function of the wage differential from the *alternative* wages potentially available to those workers who might threaten to quit.

On the basis of the above analysis, it may be postulated that the rate of change of the money wages demanded by the employed and unemployed, $\dot{w}^d$, is an increasing function of the expected probability of finding, respectively, an alternative (better) job or of coming out of the state of unemployment:

$$\dot{w}^d = \psi(P_u^e) = \psi(f_a/u)^e; \qquad \psi' > 0. \tag{1}$$

It may similarly be postulated that the rate of change of the money wages offered by the firm, $\dot{w}^0$, is a decreasing function of the expected probability of filling a vacant post:

$$\dot{w}^0 = \phi(P_v^e) = \phi(f_a/v)^e; \qquad \phi' > 0 \tag{2}$$

where v is the vacancy rate.

The expected value of the vacancy rate may obviously be expressed identically in the form (adding and subtracting expected $U + L = LF$)

$$v^e = \left(\frac{V}{LF}\right)^e = \left(\frac{U}{LF}\right)^e + \left(\frac{V+L}{LF}\right)^e - \left(\frac{LF}{LF}\right)^e = u^e + j^e - 1 \tag{3}$$

where V, LF and U denote, respectively, the number of vacancies, the labour force and the number of unemployed, while $j^e = (J/LF)^e$ is the expected ratio of the total jobs offered (total employed, L, plus vacancies, V) to the total labour force.

We rewrite the above system of equations by taking account also of an expected rate of change in the price level, $\dot{p}^e$:

$$\dot{w}^d = \hat{\psi}(u^e, f_a^e) + \dot{p}^e \tag{1'}$$

$$\dot{w}^0 = \hat{\phi}(u^e, f_a^e; j^e) + \dot{p}^e \tag{2'}$$

$$\dot{w}^d = \dot{w}^0. \tag{4}$$

Equation (4) is, of course, always true for employed workers. For the by far smaller group of the unemployed (which at this stage of discussion will not be given a breakdown), equation (4) is, instead, an equilibrium equation adopted solely to keep the model simple (which has been relaxed elsewhere; see Tarantelli forthcoming). Clearly, the above system of three equations determines the three unknowns, $\dot{w}^d$, $\dot{w}^0$ and u^e, for any given value of f_a^e (for f_a^e variable, see the next section), $\dot{p}^e$ and j^e. This last may be interpreted as the Keynesian parameter of aggregate demand ($j^e = F(Y)^e$) which determines the equilibrium solution of the system and, as we shall see, the 'cyclical' and 'structural' variations of f_a discussed earlier.

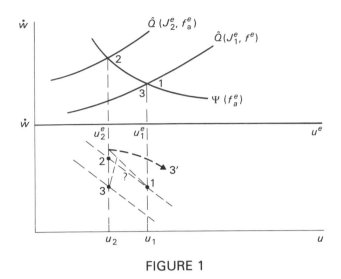

FIGURE 1

Let us now suppose that the economic system is in equilibrium in figure 1, with $\dot{w} = \dot{\pi}$, the rate of growth of labour productivity, and $\dot{p} = \dot{p}^e = 0$ and $u_1^e = u_1$ (point 1 in the diagram). If, as the result of an increase in aggregate demand, j_1^e increases to j_2^e, for $j_2^e > j_1^e$, the rate of change of wages goes from 1 to 2 in both the upper and lower portions of the diagram. This implies an increase in prices, which in a world of rational expectations would be entirely transferred to money wages.

Implications for Keynesian monetary and fiscal policy

In the last two or three decades, since the implementation of the new 'Keynesian economics', the effects of an increase in the rate of inflation on the expected unemployment rate have tended to depend heavily on the so-called reaction function of the Keynesian state. The demand management role of the Keynesian state suggests that this reaction function boils down to a positive co-variance (at least, beyond a certain threshold rate) between the wage and price inflation rate and the expected unemployment rate. The higher the inflation rate, the tighter is the monetary and/or fiscal squeeze that workers and firms have come to expect from the Keynesian state, and hence the higher is the expected rate of unemployment.

Thus, if the effective unemployment rate falls below, and/or the wage price inflation rate exceeds, certain levels considered 'normal' on the basis of the past functioning of economic policy, then workers and firms will expect a more restrictive monetary and/or fiscal policy, and vice versa. In this sense, the reaction function of the Keynesian state may imply an expected negative co-variance between the present inflation rate and the expected probability of finding a job.

These expectations of the Keynesian state's reaction function cannot be reflected in the traditional Phillips curve, but are reflected in the functioning of the above model. The reason for this difference is that the above model is specified in terms of the expected instead of the actual unemployment rate. This implies an interaction between the rate of change of money wages and the expected unemployment rate in the upper part of figure 1, an interaction that in turn depends on the reaction function of the Keynesian state. In this sense, the fundamental difference between the expected reaction function of the pre-Keynesian state lies in the role of stabilizing the inflation rate and aggregate demand that the Keynesian state has taken on over the last 20 or 30 years.

This implies, going back to the example of figure 1, that the increase in wages, and in the inflation rate that follows an initial increase in aggregate demand from j_1^e to j_2^e will then react on j^e (*after* this increase in the inflation rate), through the reaction function that workers and firms attribute to the Keynesian state. If, in particular, on the basis of the entire past functioning of monetary and fiscal policy – of 'Keynesian economics' – the expected co-variance between the present rate of increase of prices and the expected probability of finding a job, $p_u^e = (f_a/u)^e$, is negative, the example discussed in figure 1 now implies an increase in u^e for any given level of f_a^e.

These expectations of a monetary and/or fiscal squeeze will be systematically reflected also in the behaviour of firms, which will now expect a lower j, for instance j_1^e. This in turn, implies a change in the wage rate from, say, 2 to 3^2 in the upper portion of the figure, and hence a smaller $\dot{w}$ than that found in 2 (for any given rate of change in expected prices).

It should be noticed that the expectations of a lower probability of finding a job, and hence of a lower j^e, may not have repercussions on the actual unemployment rate (as opposed to the expected rate) in the lower part of figure 1. The reason is that the lower probability

of finding a job depends on the reaction function to the higher inflation rate that workers and firms attribute to the post-Keynesian state,
while the actual unemployment rate depends on the economic policy
actually followed, which may not coincide with the expected one.

It follows that, in the lower part of the figure, the change from 2
to 3, or say to 3', will depend on the growth of actual unemployment
by comparison with that of expected unemployment, which, in disequilibrium, may obviously diverge, even substantially. This divergence depends on the economic policy actually followed in the short
run, relative to the economic policy that the market, on the basis of
the expected reaction function, attributes to the post-Keynesian
state. This in turn implies that the traditional Phillips curve, in terms
of $\dot{w}$ and u, by contrast with what happens for the Phillips curve in
terms of $\dot{w}$ and u^e proposed here, is fundamentally indeterminate
(question mark in lower section of the diagram), with both clockwise
and anti-clockwise loops as shown in the diagram.

It might also be observed that there is an asymmetry between the
shift from 1 to 2 and the shift from 2 to 3 in the upper portion of
the figure. In the shift from 1 to 2 there is, along with the increase
in j^e and the decrease in u^e, a corresponding decrease in the actual
value of u; while in the shift from 2 to 3 the actual value of u does
not necessarily follow the reduction in j^e and the increase in u^e. The
reason for this asymmetry is to be sought in the fact that, in my
example, the initial increase in j^e derives from an increase in the level
of aggregate demand, Y (as an effect of, for instance, an unexpected
increase in the money supply), which in turn influences expected
demand, Y^e, and hence j^e. This initial increase in aggregate demand
implies a reduction in the actual value of u as well as the expected u.

In the shift from 2 to 3, on the other hand, the initial cause of
the decrease in j^e is *not* a reduction in effective demand Y (which
would imply an increase in the value of u), but is derived from the
fact that, as soon as the rate of price increase exceeds certain levels,
the 'co-variance effect' that I stressed above (and that might be
called 'rational pessimism') implies a decrease in Y^e and hence in
j^e for any given level of u. The actual value of u may thus be entirely
independent of these changes. On the other hand, there is no reason
whatever to suppose in general that there is any great correlation
between u and u^e in the shift from 1 to 2, as I have implicitly assumed
for ease of explanation. This makes the instability of the traditional
Phillips curve in terms of $\dot{w}$ and u, with respect to the 'non-orthodox'
Phillips curve proposed here in terms of $\dot{w}$, f_a^e and u^e, still greater.

The 'reaction function' of the Keynesian state

This effect of 'rational pessimism' obviously depends on the form of the co-variance between $\dot{p}$ and j^e, for which I suggest as a first approximation the following expected (by workers and firms) reaction function (RF) of the Keynesian state. In the latter, the point of inflection in RF, $\dot{p}_n$, may be taken as indicating the 'normal' rate of change of prices to which, say, the economy has become accustomed (and similarly for the rate of change expected of j, j_n^e – equal, say, to the natural rate of growth). This in turn implies that, at the start of an expansion in demand, as long as the rate of change in prices does not go above a certain level, the government reaction function in figure 2 does not imply an appreciable reduction in j^e. In this way, the expansion in demand may presumably last until $\dot{p}$ reaches the level beyond which any increase will make more probable a reduction in j^e. The system then shifts from 2 to 3 in figure 1, along the lines discussed above.

The dot-dashed line in figure 2 represents the locus of the $\dot{w}^d = \dot{w}^0$ points of the system of equations (1)–(4) for different levels of j^e. It should be noted that, if j and j^e both initially increase, as in the experiment in figure 1, the system shifts from 1 to 2 in figure 2. In general, the approach to the new (which in the example coincides

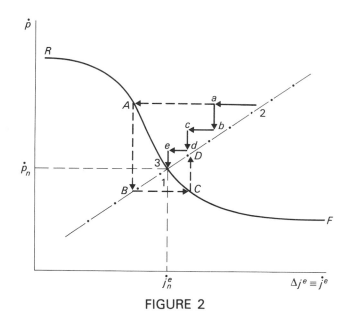

FIGURE 2

with the old) equilibrium, 3, depends on the rapidity of adjustment by firms in equation $(2')$ to the expected reduction in j^e. If this reduction in j^e by firms takes the expected RF function *à la lettre*, this approach may be cyclical, along the 'cob-web' A–B–C–D, etc., back to 3. Otherwise, the 'web' is more direct, as shown in figure 2, along the path a–b–c–d–e back to 3.

In the latter case, the expected RF function may be taken to indicate the 'direction' on which monetary and fiscal policy is presumed to embark following the movement from 1 to 2, if the inflation rate remained at the new higher level corresponding to 2, rather than an immediate policy target. This means that, as soon as j^e goes down from the level corresponding to 2 to a in the figure, and the inflation rate goes down to b, the new 'signal' for the direction of fiscal and monetary policy is no longer a but becomes c; and so on, along the 'ladder' in the figure, towards j_n^e. The approach to j_n^e is, instead, cyclical if the expected reaction function implies a more rapid adjustment of fiscal and monetary policy in terms of j^e from 2 to A, which is followed by a lower inflation rate B and another very fast adjustment, this time in the direction of an increase in j^e, with economic policy going to C, etc., along the 'cobweb' in the diagram.

Of these two interpretations of the expected reaction function, the first (direct approach) is perhaps the more realistic. But the second (cyclical approach) cannot be excluded, especially in periods when economic policy needs a 'touch of the brake' or a deceleration in the rate of growth of demand directly from 2 to A, such as happens, for instance, in times of currency crisis or other cases of overshooting.

The position and the form of the expected RF depend on the general conditions in which economic policy is operating. This implies that it is not necessarily the case, for instance, that in the previous experiment the direct or cyclical convergence will be towards the point 'of departure', 1. If, in this process, the central bank's objective of $\dot{p}_n$, for instance, increases, as may be the case in a period of transition to a regime of variable change rates, in the presence of higher foreign reserves, etc., the approach to the new *dis*equilibrium will correspond to $j_*^e > j_n^e$ (and vice versa). In a world of rational expectations there is, clearly, only one possible long-run, sustainable level of j^e, which corresponds in my model to a 'natural' p_u^e.

In disequilibrium, however, the system may, as in the above examples, move away from this level even for very considerable periods, in accordance with the change in the inflation rate and/or the policy reaction function.

The above model is clearly compatible both with a single natural unemployment rate with a perfectly vertical long-run Phillips curve (for example, the rational expectations hypothesis) and with a negatively sloped curve, depending on the assumed coefficient of rate of change of expected prices, $\dot{p}^e$, in equations (1') and (2'). If, for instance, a coefficient of less than 1 is assumed (rather than the hypothesis of rational expectations), the model generates not a single long-term value of $u = u^e$ and of j^e, but several equilibrium levels (a long-run Phillips curve with a negative slope). In the latter case, the position of the RF function may not be constant; for example, a non-unique vector of 'natural' values of j^e, $u^e = u$ and $f^e_a = f_a$ even in the long run.

As I have said, the position of the RF curve depends in the short run on firms' and workers' evaluation of government policy on exchange rates, the state of the reserves, etc. Expectations of a devaluation, higher levels of the reserves, etc., shift the RF curve upwards (e.g., the European Monetary System presumably shifted it downwards). This implies various possible combinations of $\dot{p}$ and j^e in figure 2, and various approaches to the 'new' equilibrium once the system has, as in the experiment of figure 1, moved away from it.[3] This does not, on the other hand, affect the stability of the locus of equilibrium points in the upper section of figure 1, but only the stability of the Phillips curve in the lower section of that figure.

On the ($\dot{w}$, u^e) plane the 'non-orthodox' Phillips curve proposed here in terms of $(f_a/u)^e$ is perfectly determined, independently of the shifts in RF in figure 2. Only the traditional Phillips curve in the lower part of figure 1 is indeterminate. It is, in fact, the more indeterminate the less u is correlated with u^e (and hence, the more the system is in disequilibrium). This, in turn, suggests interesting reflections on the reasons why the 'record' of the Phillips curve has, up to the second half of the 1960s, been clearly better than that for the subsequent period, following the May 1968 Western industrial unrest and the September 1973 oil crisis.

The above model strongly suggests that the desired variable in the wage equation is a measure of $(f_a/u)^e$. As is known, however, even the available estimates of f_a (not to speak of f^e_a) are not very credible. In particular, to the extent that (as in some countries, such as Italy) these refer to firms that employ more than a certain number of workers, the 'Hall effect' suggests a systematic underestimate of changes in f_a (in these cases one might perhaps argue in favour of a proxy such as $(f_a/u)^\alpha$, $\alpha > 1$). The empirical estimate of $p^e_u = (f_a/u)^e$ clearly implies even tougher empirical problems. It is, on the other hand, presumable that to the extent that variables like u^e, f_a^e and v^e are recognized as relevant, they may be more accurately estimated, as has recently happened for $\dot{p}^e$ (by direct questionnaires and perhaps using techniques of distributed lags and/or Arima models).

Some preliminary results, both for the United States and Italy, strongly support the superiority of the 'probability Phillips curve' proposed here over the traditional version of the Phillips curve. In these tests, which will be presented in a forthcoming paper, u^e was estimated by taking the (rational expectations) central bank 'official' forecast for the next year. The value of f_a^e was, in turn, estimated by inserting the value of u^e expected in each period into an equation of the type estimated for f_a by Modigliani and Tarantelli (1979) and discussed above.

The reason for the downward rigidity of money wages

Suppose now that the system is in conditions of stochastic equilibrium, around the natural unemployment rate, with $\dot{p}^e = \dot{p} = \dot{p}_n = 0$. If aggregate demand falls (because, for instance, of an unexpected reduction in the rate of change of the money supply), so that the unemployment rate increases above its natural level, p_u^e and $\dot{p}^e$ will also fall (see figure 3).

But, as for figure 1, as long as the expected co-variance between the rate of inflation and the expected probability of finding a job is negative, the reduction in the inflation rate will induce monetary and/or fiscal reflationary expectations, so that j^e will increase accordingly, along the lines of the above 'reaction function' in figure 2. The economic system will thus move from 1 to 2 and back towards 3 (see note 2) in the upper portion of figure 3. As before, the initial fall in aggregate demand may imply a movement from 1 to 2 also in the lower section of figure 3, so that the effective unemployment rate goes up.

But when the fall in $\dot{p}$ causes reflationary expectations, and hence higher demanded and offered money wages, this does not imply a correspondingly lower unemployment rate. In fact, the actual unemployment rate may, even for a considerable time, remain above its previous (natural) level. This is due to the well-known fact that, as all experience of monetary and fiscal policy since the General Theory has shown, 'you can pull a string, but you can't push it.' This implies that, in the lower section of the figure, the system will shift from 1 to 2 to 3. If the agents' belief in the capacity of economic

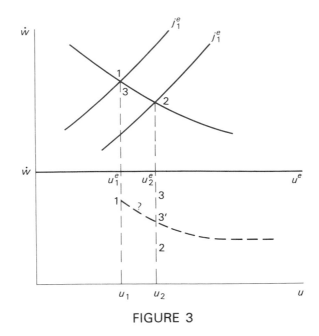

FIGURE 3

policy to come out of a recession is less strong than that of its bringing about a recession, then the movement may be closer to 3' rather than 3.

These expectations on the state's reaction may imply, further, a result that I would regard as important, namely the fact that in this model such expectations are capable of explaining the downward rigidity of the rate of change in money wages (and the rate of inflation). This 'endogenous rigidity', which is shown by the broken line in the lower section of figure 3, is due as in the foregoing case to an effect of expectations of reflationary policy (which we might perhaps call 'rational optimism'), in case, say, the actual rate of unemployment increases above u_2. This does not trigger a lower $\dot{w}$ as long as people expect j^e_{-1} to increase towards j^e_1 or, at least, not to fall. As before, the reflationary policy may take some time to show its effects. But the simple expectation of this policy is enough to generate the downward rigidity of money wages and of prices just discussed. The system may, thus, experiment a $\dot{w}$ corresponding to u^e_2 in the upper section of figure 3 and yet experiment at the same time with an actual level of u higher than u_2 in its lower section – for example a downward rigidity of money wages.

This downward rigidity of the Phillips curve is strictly symmetrical and complementary with respect to the upward rigidity of the rate of change in money wages that is implied in the experiment discussed for figure 1. On the other hand, a moment's reflection will show that, on the basis of plausible hypotheses on the 'reaction function' of the government in figure 2, the downward rigidity of money wages that this model implies is, in general, rather greater than its upward rigidity.

The reason is essentially the fact that it is often less difficult for economic policy to accept the cost of, say, a devaluation in the exchange rate (which is, as I have said, one of the expected parameters that define the position of RF, in figure 2) than to accept the social and political costs of an unemployment rate that is considered excessive. In this sense, it will be noted, the non-linearity of the traditional Phillips curve (that is, its hyperbolic form in econometric estimates) may be explained within this model. The 'non-orthodox' Phillips curve in terms of u^e may well be steeper than the traditional one in terms of u to the right of the natural rate, and, indeed, the 'non-orthodox' curve proposed here in terms of p_u^e may well even have a negative portion; but 'rational optimism' expectations make that portion unlikely to be relevant in a world of Keynesian expectations.

If, on the other hand, the exchange rate is devalued, the reaction function shown in figure 2 shifts upward. The expectations of entrepreneurs and workers will be more likely to include the possibility of devaluation the more the system is in a floating rate system (and/or the more precarious is the external monetary equilibrium). Exchange rate policy (and the variables that determine it), in other words, interacts endogenously, in the viewpoint of this model, with the process of determination of money wages. This makes plausible, on the basis of the entire experience of post-Keynesian economic policy, an upward rigidity of money wages that is less than their rigidity downwards.

Anti-cyclical loops and the non-orthodox Phillips curve

In the second part of the last section, for ease of exposition, I assumed that the flow of hirings, f_a, is a given parameter. It is easy to show that all the properties of the above model are still valid once f_a is allowed to vary, as it must, in accordance with the basic approach and the lines described in the second section.

The variability of f_a, moreover, allows anti-clockwise loops to be generated in Lipsey's fashion around our 'non-orthodox' Phillips curve, in terms of p_u^e or of u^e and f_a^e (for any given $\dot{p}^e$).

This reformulation of the model is illustrated in figure 4, where it is assumed that, for a given level of $\dot{p}^e$, j^e increases from j_1^e to j_2^e. The corresponding increase in f_a^e implies, for given values of the other variables, an increase in p_u^e and in p_v^e. These increases in turn imply, on the hypothesis of the model, a shift upwards and to the right of the money wage demand curve towards the corresponding broken curve and a downward right shift of the offered money wage curve towards the other broken curve.

In figure 4, this means a shift from A to B rather than from A to C, as would be the case if f_a^e did not vary. To the extent that j_2^e

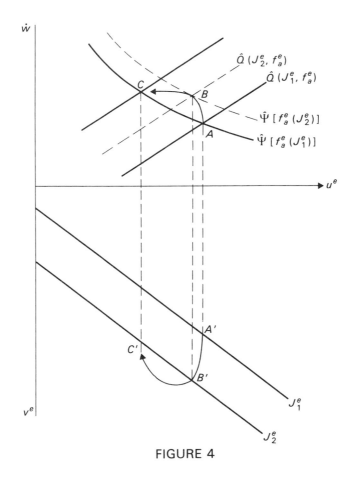

FIGURE 4

remains at its new higher level, the cyclical (transitory) effect of the increase in f_a^e will tend to vanish. But that can obviously not be said of the structural effect of the change in f_a^e induced by the new level of j^e (a higher share of the less 'employable' (i.e., marginal workers) in total employment, as argued above). This also implies that, in equilibrium, B will tend towards C, though without ever reaching it. This implies an anti-clockwise loop around the non-orthodox Phillips curve in the upper portion of figure 4.

Both these effects may clearly cause anti-clockwise loops also on the observed Phillips curve, and hence may strengthen its basic indeterminacy, as discussed above.

It should also be noted that, when f_a^e is taken to be variable (rather than a parameter, as in job search theory), the short-run 'equilibrium' non-orthodox Phillips curve proposed here does not coincide with the curve of demanded wages. On the contrary, the equilibrium curve is the locus of the equilibrium points of the model at which the rates of change of demanded and offered wages are equal for differing levels of j^e and for corresponding differing levels of f_a^e. As the experiment discussed for figure 4, for instance, implies, the non-orthodox Phillips curve will lie between points B and C but not *on* C, because of the structural effect on f_a^e of an increase in j^e as discussed above. This in turn implies, as I have shown rigorously elsewhere (Tarantelli, 1974), a short-run equilibrium non-orthodox curve with a greater slope than the $\dot{w}^d$ curve.

In the lower portion of the figure it is also easy to verify, finally, that for differing levels of f_a^e, the model generates anti-clockwise loops around the 'expected' 'Beveridge curve', in terms of u^e and v^e, which correspond to those obtained in the upper portion of the same figure.

Conclusions

I have put forward a model to explain not only the variations in money wages of the unemployed, but also, and especially, the wage behaviour of the employed. The central hypothesis is that the wage behaviour of the employed depends on the probability an employed person has of finding an alternative ('better') job. For the smaller group of the unemployed, this hypothesis becomes the probability of finding a job at all. In this model the unemployed are a residual group whose number is determined by the number of jobs offered. The unemployed are unemployed not because of the existence of conditions of imperfect information (with the exception of the frictionally unemployed), but because of the non-existence of a greater number of offered jobs and as a result of the downward (even more than upward) rigidity of prices and money wages in a world of Keynesian expectations on j^e.

The above model may also allude to some interesting lines of discussion as to the reason why, while Keynes was writing the *General Theory* based on the assumption of downward rigidity of money wages, money wages paradoxically fell (as they had several times in history before the Keynesian revolution). Before the Keynesian revolution there could be no expectations that, once the system was on the right-hand side of the natural unemployment rate, there would be a monetary or fiscal policy of demand reflation. Keynes was literally inventing this policy of reflation at that very time. In this sense, it may be said that Keynesian economics not merely has assumed money wages to be rigid downwards, but also has supplied an important economic reason[4] for that rigidity, with reference to the behaviour of the unemployed: the expectation that the Great Depression cannot be repeated.

The reaction function through which individuals consider that the government responds to changes in the inflation rate in figure 2, moreover, is not based on the existence of conditions of imperfect information. The function simply implies that the regressive expectations (originated by Keynesian policies) are rational.

Finally, the above model no longer assumes (schizophrenically) the existence of 'rational' expectations solely with reference to $\dot{p}^e$, but also with reference to u^e (rather than u). This type of confusion between u and u^e is similar to the current confusion of those who, until recently, confused $\dot{p}$ with $\dot{p}^e$ as the relevant variable in the Phillips curve. For this, the model suggests that the traditional Phillips curve is badly specified and more unstable (with both clockwise and anti-clockwise loops) than the non-orthodox one proposed here (with anti-clockwise loops) in terms of u^e and f_a^e.

The present model thus suggests that the greater instability of the traditional Phillips curve with respect to the 'true' one proposed here can be characterized as a case of:

(1) an *error* in the variable used: u instead of u^e, and
(2) the *omission* of the variable f_a^e. This error and omission at the same time highlight
(3) the *schizophrenia* of the traditional approach, which specifies the Phillips curve, besides an *expected* variable (the rate of increase

in expected prices), a *current* variable (the rate of unemployment), rather than the expected unemployment rate and expected flow of hirings.

Notes

1 As regards the flow of separations, it can incidentally be noticed that this variable may also tend to increase in the presence of a rise in the unemployment rate, since the increase in dismissals tends to exceed the fall in the flow of quits (and vice versa). The net effect of these two changes is, on the other hand, *a priori* uncertain.

2 Naturally, point 3 will not in general, at least not in the short run, coincide with the initial position 1 (as I have presumed to simplify the drawing of the diagram) but will lie, say, somewhere between 2 and 1.

3 Modigliani and Papademos (1977) have recently proposed a model that specifies the costs and benefits of an optimum policy, referring to the trade-off between present and/or expected unemployment and inflation. In the present model the effective course of monetary and fiscal policy is, instead, exogenous. The possibility of fusing together these two aspects of the problem (in particular by studying the effects of fiscal and monetary policy packages with specific examples within the model put forward here) suggests interesting themes for analysis, but does not fall within the scope of this paper.

4 In this paper, of course, I do not consider non-economic reasons for the downward rigidity of money wages, such as, for instance, the behaviour of the trade unions or the effect of 'maintenance of differentials' between one group of workers and another (Tarantelli, forthcoming) which Keynes discusses (along with the possible effects of imperfect information and of the trade unions) in the *General Theory* (1936, pp. 13–14).

References

Hall, R. E. (1972) 'Turnover in the labor force', *Brookings Papers on Economic Activity*, no. 3.

Keynes, J. M. (1936) *The General Theory of Employment, Interest and Money*, Harcourt Brace, New York.

Malinvaud, E. (1977) *The Theory of Unemployment Reconsidered*, Basil Blackwell.

Modigliani, F. and Papademos, S. (1977) 'Optimal demand policies against stagflation', paper presented to the conference on 'The Economic Crisis of the 1970s: Lessons for Stabilization Policies', September 1977, Baden, Austria.

Modigliani, F. and Tarantelli, E. (1979) 'Structural and transitory determinants of labor mobility, Holt's conjecture and the Italian experience', *Banca Nazionale del Lavoro*. (For the unfortunately missing graphs in this translation, see the original version in Italian in *Moneta e Credito*, June 1979.)

Phelps, E. *et al.* (1970) *Microeconomic Foundations of Employment and Inflation Theory*, W. W. Norton.

Tarantelli, E. (1974) *Studi di Economia del Lavoro*, Giuffre.

Tarantelli, E. (forthcoming) *The Economics of Neo-Corporatism*, chapter XIII.

Index

205